Experimenting

Experimenting

ESSAYS WITH SAMUEL WEBER

Edited by

SIMON MORGAN WORTHAM AND GARY HALL

FORDHAM UNIVERSITY PRESS

New York 2007

Copyright © 2007 Fordham University Press

Library of Congress Cataloging-in-Publication Data

Experimenting : essays with Samuel Weber / edited by
Simon Morgan Wortham and Gary Hall—1st ed.
p.   cm.
Includes bibliographical references and index.
ISBN-13: 978-0-8232-2814-0 (cloth : alk. paper)
ISBN-13: 978-0-8232-2815-7 (pbk. : alk. paper)
1. Criticism—History—20th century.   2. Psychoanalysis
and literature.   3. Deconstruction.   4. Weber, Samuel,
1940-   —Criticism and interpretation.   I. Morgan
Wortham, Simon.   II. Hall, Gary, 1962–
PN94.E97   2007
801′.950904—dc22
2007040880

Printed in the United States of America
09 08 07   5 4 3 2 1
First Edition

CONTENTS

ACKNOWLEDGMENTS

Some parts of this book have been published previously. Susan Bernstein's essay "It Walks: The Ambulatory Uncanny" was originally published in *MLN* 118.5 (2003): 1111–39. © The Johns Hopkins University Press, reprinted with the permission of The Johns Hopkins University Press. An earlier version of the essay included here by Andrew McNamara was published as "Apprehension? Performativity and Medium-Specificity in Modern Art," *The South Atlantic Quarterly* 101.3 (2002): 479–99. Simon Morgan Wortham's chapter draws on his book *Samuel Weber: Acts of Reading* (Aldershot: Ashgate, 2003). Permissions to republish are gratefully acknowledged.

The editors would like to thank Samuel Weber for his astute interventions and immense generosity in assisting with all aspects of this book, and would also like to thank the contributors to this volume for all their patience and hard work in bringing it to completion. A debt of gratitude is also owed to Helen Tartar, for her much-valued commitment and support.

EXPERIMENTING

Experimenting

Simon Morgan Wortham and Gary Hall

For several decades, the work of Samuel Weber has influenced writers and thinkers across a range of subjects and disciplines in the arts and humanities—including literary, critical and cultural theory, cultural, media and communication studies, new media and technology, psychoanalysis, and continental philosophy. Within such fields, Weber's "remarkable" and "inaugural" texts have been especially important to the deconstructive tradition, as Jacques Derrida once confirmed.[1] That Weber has proved so influential to so many for so long—longer than almost any other figure of comparable stature currently at work within this tradition—owes partly to the singular position he holds in relation to the domains of literary theory and Continental philosophy. Paul de Man wrote of Weber that he was "probably the only person in his generation" who was "equally at home with and directly informed about contemporary literary theory and its antecedents in Germany, France and the US."[2] Taught by Adorno, Szondi, and de Man, Weber played an important role in the process of translation and publication that saw deconstruction come to prominence in the United States—he translated Derrida's "Signature Event Context" (1977) and *Limited Inc.* (1988), for instance—while moving deftly between French, German, and Anglo-American literary and philosophical traditions and languages in order to pursue a practice of reading in which the

very question of translation frequently takes center stage. But the continuing interest and significance of Weber's work is no doubt also due in large
part to his ability to *reactivate* and *transform* the legacy of literary and philosophical enquiry bequeathed to us by figures such as Kant, Nietzsche,
Benjamin, Heidegger, de Man, and Derrida, not least by exposing the deconstructive tradition to contemporary questions in the arenas of media,
technology, politics, and culture. In fact, it is hard to think of anyone who,
by articulating a "deconstructive practice" in this way, has been able to
elucidate the dramatic and profound relevance of deconstruction to these
particular fields quite so precisely. And yet, rather like Derrida, Weber
always seeks to develop rather than simply follow or apply those whom he
reads and studies, his penetrating analyses thus serving to transform and
at times dislocate the intellectual project, program, or disposition of the
text in question, whether it be that of Kant, Marx, Kierkegaard, Freud,
Lacan, Heidegger, Benjamin, Tocqueville, Agamben (as in the case of the
two new essays by Weber published here for the first time), or, indeed,
Derrida himself.

In this sense, Weber's work is always *experimental*. Writing of Bache-
lard's notion of the new scientific spirit as a very specific kind of experimentation in his introduction to *Institution and Interpretation* (1987/2001),
Weber defines "modern" experimentalism as a situation in which "cognitive objects are . . . to be identified not by reference to an intrinsic quality,
their *form*, but rather by their capacity to be *deformed* and *transformed*."[3]
Thus, the deformative and transformative force of the "object" of "cognition" arises, for Weber, not simply from the object itself, but from a
curious and complicated encounter which is not reducible to the conventional structure of subject and object: an event that, for him, cannot be
thought in simple terms of presence, identity, representation, or self-
containment. What this means, as far as arriving at an understanding of
Weber's own work is concerned, is that, like the Kierkegaardian "experiment" of which he has written on a number of occasions,[4] it is not possible to stabilize or systematize Weber's experimental encounters with a
series of critical "objects" by reference to a general conceptual framework—psychoanalysis, perhaps, in the case of *Return to Freud* (1978) and
The Legend of Freud (1982/2000), or deconstruction in that of *Institution
and Interpretation* and *Mass Mediauras* (1996)—of the kind that maintains
a purely static recognizability from a fixed perspective over time. Instead,
very much like the Kierkegaardian experiment or, indeed, the "modern,"
"scientific" spirit of experimentation, Weber's writing is always—and already—*on the move*.

In Weber's own readings of a number of seminal texts ranging across several centuries (and taking in the writing of, among others, Sterne, Balzac, Baudelaire, Hoffman, Kafka, Saussure, Artaud, Jameson, and Fish), the deformative transformations that occur alongside the process of cognition constitute an abiding interest, beginning with the problems he finds in Kant's philosophy, notably in regard to issues of critical and aesthetic judgment. And since, as Weber insistently demonstrates, something else, something *other*, always intervenes and participates in the identification and delimitation of an object of enquiry, questions of ethics and of critical responsibility are always implicitly bound up with the way he reads. Yet this is less a matter of taking up an ethical or responsible *position* than of assuming a kind of movement that seeks to do justice in its response. To this end, Weber complements his interest in the canonical texts of philosophy and literature, and in unraveling the very assumptions and premises that enable them to be written, with a number of studies that appear to move off in other directions. Examples of the latter are evident throughout his career, as many of the chapters in this volume make clear: from his early 1973 essay on the uncanny, "The Sideshow, or: Remarks on a Canny Moment," through those in *Institution and Interpretation* on the ambivalence of the humanities and the limits of professionalism, and on to the volumes edited with Hent de Vries, *Violence, Identity, and Self-Determination* (1997) and *Religion and Media* (2001). Nowhere is this movement in Weber's writing perhaps more apparent, however, than in his two recent books on theatricality and targeting.

Above and beyond any innate connection with a specific genre, theatricality is the name Weber gives to a certain kind of experience or event— both in the literary field and outside it—which remains irreducible to classical narrative closure, dialectical resolution or conceptual self-containment. What Weber demonstrates with this notion of theatricality, most recently in *Theatricality As Medium* (2005), is how the desire to bring the text to a point of closure and completion implies a wish for mastery and detachment, a desire that is itself little more than a compromise formation, an always provisional and unsustainable suppression and separation of the "other" in and from "oneself." In short, it is an impossible wish-fulfillment that must remain riddled with tension and conflict. This inevitably inconclusive struggle thus constitutes an ambivalent dynamics of interpretation and institution in which the momentary stabilization—or arrestation—of a situation otherwise menaced by unplaceable uncertainty and anxiety comes at the price of *effects of reading* that only cause the repressed to return.

Significantly, when Weber talks of theatricality in such ways, he rarely limits himself merely to the playhouse or the text—although by redefining the meaning of such terms, neither does he depart from them entirely. In *Targets of Opportunity: On the Militarization of Thinking* (2005), for example, Weber focuses on the opportunistic targeting of perceived threats on the part of Western and pro-Western powers today, particularly the United States. Weber presents this as just such an attempt to arrest anxiety by giving it a face, a name, a form. However, the contemporary "targets" of Western intelligence and military action are actually *identified* as a function of a concept and logic of "opportunity," he maintains, and they pop up only on condition of "windows of opportunity" (one thinks of the attempt to assassinate Saddam Hussein on the eve of the Iraq war). Indeed, in a way that is integral to the logic of this militaristic thinking, *the target itself moves*, shifting from Bin Laden to Saddam, Afghanistan to Iraq, North Korea to Iran, thus powerfully reproducing and sustaining—but at the same time also ultimately destabilizing and undermining—the very rationale of "opportunity" being played out. Since this same opportunity is always contingent upon continually shifting spatiotemporal factors—a picture of fast-paced change—the object or target of opportunity must be conceived of, less as a self-identical or self-contained entity (the "cause" or "origin" of the problem, for example), than as a particular fixing point. As a consequence, this "targeting" not only serves to bring anxiety under control by releasing it on a locatable target, but also works to downplay or exclude from consideration other, more difficult aspects of the problem: not least, the complex array of forces and network of conditions that actually define contemporary "global" geopolitical realities. The logic of targeting thus involves a dangerous paradox: to *hit* the mark is always simultaneously, and unavoidably, to *miss* it, and thereby to expose oneself to the unforeseen, which itself then assumes a much more destructive power.

It is quite possible, therefore, to detect in Weber's writings a number of connections between the inherent instability of the object, the impossible desire for narrative (or disciplinary or institutional) closure, the conflict-ridden wish for (professional) interpretative mastery and the vastly destructive and always "deconstructible" project of ideological and political domination today. Nor should one overlook some of the other integrative possibilities for reading Weber's work: for instance, the idea that what books such as *Unwrapping Balzac* (1979), *The Return to Freud*, *The Legend of Freud*, *Institution and Interpretation*, *Mass Mediauras*, and *Religion and Media* have in common is a "deconstructive" concern with the analysis of institutions—of literature, psychoanalysis, the university, the mass media, religion, and so forth. Yet, on the basis of the perspective we are developing here, one should clearly think twice before attempting to produce a collection of essays with the aim of introducing or summarizing Weber's work according to what might be, in effect, a unifying narrative, or otherwise presenting his writing as a more or less consistent and homogenous body of theory, or a self-contained expression of an originating intention. Not only would doing so actually run counter to many of the insights his work produces concerning the extent to which an identity, an object, a form or text includes an irreducible relationship to alterity (the manner in which, ultimately, it *comes from the other*); but it would also risk reactivating the very logic and practice of "targeting" that Weber warns us has become so dangerous today. Indeed, to devise and present a collection on Weber in such a fashion would, in effect, be to try to arrest and stabilize in a single fixing point—a point of "critical" recognition, or of theoretical, conceptual, or thematic foundation—precisely the uncertainty and anxiety (and ambivalence and apprehension, for that matter, as we shall see) that Weber's various experimentations occasion, experimentations in which the very meaning of the "literary" or the "political" become transformed in highly productive yet undoubtedly unsettling ways.

All of which explains why this collection—from its introduction through to the various essays it contains—is necessarily marked by a double gesture. On the one hand, it is of course impossible (and far from desirable) to simply drive Weber's writing to a point at which it might find its purity or essence in a complete lack of coherence, identity, form, or focus. As Weber himself tells us, his work constantly registers and reenacts the Derridean motif of iterability, so that it always bears signs of a linguistic and discursive "grammaticality" that renders it repeatable, reproducible, and recognizable—something that is obviously necessary if Weber's writing (or that of anyone else, for that matter) is to achieve its critical and strategic ambition: if it is to be *read*. Yet, on the other hand, iterability also includes difference and transformation in repetition, of a kind that remains unavoidable and yet unpredictable. (One can never know *how* the "work" will be read.) Just as the effects of iterability cannot be fixed, stabilized, anticipated, or exhausted for Weber by contextualizing them within a comprehensive explanatory framework, so his own writings cannot in all responsibility be reduced to a mere "target" (the goal and pretext of an "opportunistic" exposition or, indeed, collection).

In *Experimenting: Essays with Samuel Weber*, this dislocating difference gives rise to a series of chapters that are marked by a variety of styles, approaches, and emphases. Aware not just of the strategic importance but also of the fundamental necessity of a certain degree of recognizability in Weber's work, some of the contributors to this volume seek to explicate certain of the key aspects or motifs to be found in his writing —ambivalence, indebtedness, theatricality, dreaming, the uncanny, virtuality, self-referentiality, iterability, performativity—with a view to suggesting the dislocating movements that take place at the "heart" of the Weberian text, precisely at the moment a semblance of cohesive thematicity appears to emerge. The essays by Simon Morgan Wortham and Peter Fenves on Weberian theatricality, iterability, and technics can be characterized in this way. In these chapters, what appears as seemingly traditional explication and exposition frequently turns out to involve a more stealthy (counter-)movement that, while recognizing the impossibility of dispensing with narrative, refuses to be reduced to mere narrativization.

Simon Morgan Wortham's "Of Debts, Dreams, and Jokes: or, Weberian Theatricality" begins with the question of indebtedness as itself a highly significant one for writers such as Weber, whose relationship to figures like Derrida—and those whom Derrida himself inherits—acquires a complexity that borders on the inestimable. Such indebtedness faces us all, and demands to be reckoned with, although it can never be resolved (or, consequently, be fully repaid). This chapter proceeds to link the complicated and incalculable (though always uncancellable) nature of the debt, such as it is treated by Weber, to the (psychoanalytic) experience of the joke. In an entirely unavoidable way, the joke thus provides the setting for academic or intellectual inheritance, legacy, and gift giving, and establishes the very scene in which the question arises: how may the debt— irredeemable and unremitting as it is—be assumed otherwise? If the force of debt, bordering on a joke, pervades Weber's critical practice, this chapter reads Weber in order to introduce a further term, that of the dream— the dream of psychoanalysis—which itself helps to define the dislocating (and theatrical) movement of Weber's writings, beyond simple adherence to or departure from the object that one comprehends or inherits, and beyond simple following or leave-taking in relation to a tradition or scene of reading. It is here, then, that the very countermovement of Weber's critical experimentation is traced.

In "*Technica Speciosa:* Some Notes on the Ambivalence of Technics in Kant and Weber," Peter Fenves addresses one of the book's main interests, that of technics, declaring Weber's voice to be perhaps the most significant since that of Walter Benjamin when it comes to combining questions of art and aesthetics with those of the medium and technicity.

Fenves's chapter begins by positioning Kant's fundamentally ambivalent relation to technics as constitutive of his entire philosophical project, before proceeding to explore the possible reasons for Kant's decision to discard technics as a key organizing principle or operating term for the vast critical program set out in the *Critique of Judgment*. In contrast to some of the other contributions in this collection, Fenves's essay thereby seems to locate the significance of Weber's writing in a more "properly" philosophical tradition. And yet it is the "proper" itself—of the "technical," and of technical "authorship" in and of the aesthetic realm—that remains insistently at issue here as perhaps the very question of ambivalence. Throughout his reading of Kant, Fenves seeks to do justice to some of Weber's abiding concerns in texts such as "Ambivalence: The Humanities and the Study of Literature" (in *Institution and Interpretation*) and *Mass Mediauras*, by scanning the possible connections between aesthetics, technics, interpretation and institutions. But as Fenves's chapter develops, the impression given is one of the Weberian project becoming exposed to an always shifting interpretation of Kantian "ambivalence," an ambivalence that reorders (and, indeed, disorders) the correspondences between the "technical," the "aesthetic," "the medial," and the "institutional" at each time of asking. The ambivalence of these various relationships among such ostensibly distinct yet interconnected fields is therefore one that each and every inheritor of the tradition must necessarily assume and enact in singularly different ways, and it is in this sense that Fenves experiments with Weber here.

If it is the various implications and effects, in and for Weber's writings, of the ambivalent and the theatrical that are explored by these two essays, other chapters included in this collection look to evaluate the significance of Weber's writings more for a range of current debates—for example, about art, technology, visual culture, the mass media, and the institution of the university. In "Surfing Technics: Direction and Dispersion in the Age of Information," Randy Rutsky shows how the movement in Weber's writings has an important bearing on contemporary issues related to media and technology. Weber has written extensively on both of the latter, his work continually moving around and through a rhetoric in which place, movement, and direction are "brought-to-the-fore." Indeed, his texts on the subject are strewn with terms and concepts such as emplacement and displacement, setting-in-place and unsettling, bringing-forth and going-on, destination and dispersion. At the same time, these concepts are themselves unsettled in Weber's work and cast into ambiguous and shifting relations. Taking his cue from the chapters on Heidegger, Benjamin, and television in *Mass Mediauras*—"Upsetting the Setup: Remarks on Heideg-ger's 'Questing After Technics'," "Mass Mediaurus, or: Art, Aura and Media in the Work of Walter Benjamin," and "Television: Set and Screen"—Rutsky illustrates how our notions of media and information technologies continue to be defined by the figures of direction and becom-ing lost, navigation and drift, concentration and dispersion. Perhaps even more importantly, Rutsky is able to suggest how we might figure our rela-tion to the world of information differently: not simply in terms of our ability to navigate it, to place ourselves in relation to it, but also in terms of a movement that, like information itself, is more complex, more ambiv-alent, and more fluid, and that he describes as "surfing" (of television channels, the Web, and of information culture more generally.)

Gary Hall's chapter, "IT, Again: How to Build an Ethical Virtual Insti-tution," continues with this focus on contemporary debates in general, and on technology and the media in particular, speculating on the forms that an ethico-political "deconstructive" institution specifically designed to exploit the unique properties of the World Wide Web might take. In doing so, Hall engages substantially and rigorously with the work of Sam-uel Weber: not just with what are in this context his most obviously rele-vant texts, *Institution and Interpretation* and *Mass Mediauras*, nor even Weber's recent accounts of the institution in an era of increasing virtuali-zation—"The Future Campus: Destiny in a Virtual World" (1999) and "The Future of the Humanities: Experimenting" (2000); but also with a much earlier essay from 1978 called "It," in which Weber discusses an-other form of IT, iterability. This detailed engagement with Weber en-ables Hall to show how the development of an online, virtual "counter institution" provides an opportunity for the humanities in general, but cultural studies in particular, to take on, rather than merely act out, the effects of the institutional ambivalence Weber describes in *Institution and Interpretation*. Hall thus demonstrates that it is indeed possible to envisage at least one alternative form of institutionalization of the kind Weber looks toward at the end of (the first edition of) that book, when he writes about conceiving "institutionalized practices of a 'discipline' that would assume the ambivalent demarcations that make it, and them, possible."[5]

Without doubt some of the contributors to the collection have deliber-ately allowed themselves to become seduced or distracted by other writers and by different texts and contexts, including ones never mentioned by Weber and that remain foreign and heterogeneous to Weber's own explic-itly stated range of interests and concerns. Yet, by so doing, they are able to open up and expose Weber to what is unfamiliar both *to* and *in* him:

thus experimenting *with* Weber. Hall's engagement with Weber's work on the institution of the university from the direction of open access and the "academic gift economy" could be taken as a case in point. Two further examples are provided by Marc Redfield and Andrew McNamara with their chapters on gender and ambivalence and art and self-reflection respectively. Redfield, like Fenves and Hall, draws attention to the fundamental role played in Weber's work by the concept of "ambivalence," denoting as it does the tension and instability of an aporia or double bind, and constituting Weber's version of Derridean "difference." For instance, in his 1997 essay "Wartime," in *Violence, Identity, and Self-Determination*, Weber writes that "ambivalence marks the ineffaceable intrusion of the foreign, the alien, the other into the constitution of the self and same" and "names the constitutive violence against which the constitution of the subject and the self retains the status of a persona, in the etymological sense of a mask."[6] Weber goes on to argue that this "constitutive ambivalence" characterizes "the medium 'television' no less than the Freudian drives,"[7] and that powerfully synthetic move is typical of Weber's criticism, which mimes as it interrogates the excessive syntheses of ambivalence. In his chapter "Ambivalence: Media, Technics, Gender," Redfield thus reveals how Weber has moved easily—yet always carefully and rigorously—back and forth between questions of interpretation and questions of institution. Yet there is one respect in which Weber's work has been curiously disinterested or disinvested in ambivalence, according to Redfield: Weber rarely, if ever, examines the role of gender in the texts he reads. Even his pathbreaking early books on Lacan and Freud, *Return to Freud* and *The Legend of Freud*, display relatively little interest in the question of sexual difference that endlessly haunts psychoanalysis. Weber's reading of Baudelaire's "A une passante" in "Mass Mediaurus, or: Art, Aura and Media in the Work of Walter Benjamin" likewise ignores the crucial role played by gender in the passages or scenes under analysis. However, Redfield's concern in drawing attention to this seeming disinterest on Weber's part is not to find the latter's work in some way lacking. It is rather to suggest that a subterranean figure for ambivalence in his writing is the fetish—the figure that simultaneously (that is, ambivalently) forecloses and commemorates sexual difference. In this way, Redfield argues for the ineffaceable role—and ambiguity—of gender within the interrelated questions concerning technics, aesthetics, and politics that Weber's work has so brilliantly explored. Like other essays in the collection, Andrew McNamara's chapter "Modernism and the Medium: On Greenberg

and Weber" is also concerned with ambivalence, though McNamara examines it chiefly in terms of what he calls aesthetic apprehension. Where
Redfield concentrates primarily on the importance of the concept of ambivalence to Weber, McNamara draws upon a trilogy of essays concerning
Kant: "Ambivalence" (in *Institution and Interpretation*), "The Foundering
of Aesthetics" (1998), and "The Unraveling of Form" (*Mass Mediauras*,
1996). In conjunction with these Kant commentaries, McNamara highlights Weber's scrutiny of self-referentiality, identification, representation,
and the issue of the medium (or media in general)—primarily through
discussions in "The Future of the University: The Cutting Edge" (1996),
Mass Mediauras, and "Theory on TV" (in *Religion and Media*). McNamara
shows how the very same considerations are pivotal to modernism in the
visual arts. While he explains that Weber's work "does not emerge from
an art history or visual arts background," he asserts that Weber's analyses
of these issues has much to offer modernist studies. Weber's work confirms the critical insights of Clement Greenberg, Thierry de Duve, and
Rosalind Krauss in focusing upon issues of the medium, representation,
and self-reference, but it also serves as a challenge to them. For McNamara, that challenge occurs where one confronts the apprehensive features
of aesthetic inquiry. Thus, McNamara stages a dramatic confrontation
with traditional understandings of modernism by highlighting Weber's
claim that modernist self-referentiality is, as McNamara puts it, "the predominant way of grasping knowledge and of understanding our orientation to the world." Self-referentiality should not therefore be viewed as a
"recent development" or as an experimental, "avant-garde innovation,"
but as an ongoing process of much broader provenance. Fittingly, McNamara's essay proceeds to adopt a somewhat ambivalent position with regard to the arguments about "self-referentiality" it locates in Weber's
work. On the one hand, he welcomes its challenge to more familiar understandings of modernism. On the other, McNamara asserts that Weber's
critical analyses may prove capable of counteracting his conclusion that
modernist art practices remain part and parcel of the modernist urge to
"self-referentiality." McNamara thus experiments with Weber by means
of a detailed examination of the ways in which modern art is not simply
dominated by "self-referentiality," but struggles "to evade this form of
referencing." For McNamara, this ambivalence opens up ways of evaluating the legacy of modernism—not least in terms of the resistance it might
pose to "distinctively modern" forms of domination.

Susan Bernstein's "It Walks: The Ambulatory Uncanny," meanwhile,
looks at the uncanny in relation to Weber, starting with his seminal work

on this subject from the early 1970s: the essay "The Sideshow, or: Remarks on a Canny Moment," reprinted in the republished and expanded edition of *The Legend of Freud* (2000). Of particular interest to Bernstein is the manner in which the theme of the "unheimlich" inhabits and haunts Weber's work. But her essay also suggests a mode of thinking about his mobility and multipositionality with respect to a series of critical problems having to do with vision, textuality, the body, and the uncanny itself.

It should be evident by now that all the chapters in this volume are written in a spirit of experimentation—a spirit that frequently follows Weber precisely by not following him, by departing as a way of returning, by remaining on the move in a way that keeps open the sense of direction. It is very much in this spirit that some contributors to *Experimenting* have taken the decision to pay their respects to Weber without regularly invoking his name. Instead, they have demonstrated their indebtedness more obliquely, by reinhabiting certain texts—in particular, certain psychoanalytic texts—that it would be difficult to imagine thinking or reading without Weber. The chapter by Avital Ronell, another important inheritor of Derrida, "On Risk-Taking in the Psychoanalytic Text," is exemplary in this regard, and it calls to be read in just this fashion. Taking its cue from the idea, implicit in Weber, of the psychoanalytic experiment as inducing "professional phobias" on the basis of its "risk-taking" and "epistemological uncertainty"—an "experimental cast" it in fact shares with modern science—Ronell's chapter reenacts such experimentation in part by means of the shocking disregard she seems to pay to professional debt. (Here, indeed, one thinks of a number of essays in which Derrida adopts a similar protocol of "reading," not simply to downplay his debts but to seek to do justice "otherwise" to their deep radicality.) This move, then, opens up the question of the very grounds of testing—and of reality-testing, notably in psychoanalysis—by means of which truth or value is posited or ascertained: frequently, through a process of comparison which, at a more radical level, often includes an "irremissible warp or omission" of perhaps just the kind found in Ronell's own essay. Thus, in one sense, Ronell repays her debts to the Weberian experiment precisely by refusing to register the traditional measure of indebtedness, and her dazzling interrogation of psychoanalysis and testing therefore both establishes and destabilizes the grounds by which Ronell's chapter might be itself be "tested," not least as an accompaniment to Weber: experimenting *with* Weber. In this light, the collection as a whole seeks to move productively between (counter) exposition and (radical) experimentation.

At one level, then, the reader will find here a wide-ranging body of critical studies that powerfully reflect the distinctive transitions which occur in Weber's writings between deconstruction, psychoanalysis, philosophy, art, aesthetics, literature, media, technology, politics, and culture. At the same time, the essays that make up *Experimenting* are also marked by a number of differences, disjunctions, shifts, and breaks (in style, tone and procedure) taking place in relation to Weber's work—albeit very much in the spirit of Weber's own experimentalism. Yet despite the varied spectrum of critical emphases and approaches, each chapter in this volume can nonetheless be seen to be articulating itself in a singular way, so as to be able to respond all the more responsibly to the powerfully singular qualities of Weber's texts. What is more, each does so precisely according to the double bind, the double gesture or double negotiation demanded by the Weberian experiment, whereby fidelity to the text or author in question demands that a certain infidelity be observed and enacted.

Given his own concern with self-referentiality and with the problematic status of framing, it is oddly fitting that the collection should be "framed" by two new essays from Weber himself. Once again, each of these texts demonstrates Weber's long-standing and continuing interest in moving from close "theoretical" readings of the literary and philosophy tradition to analyses of supposedly more practical, political, "real world" issues such as globalization, the events of 9/11, the attack on Iraq, and the "war on terror." The essay that opens the volume, provocatively titled "God Bless America!" is, appropriately enough, concerned with inauguration or founding. It explores various connections between the legal and constitutional foundation of the United States as revealed in its inaugural texts, focusing on the direction currently being taken by America's "global" cultural politics—not least, via its very relationship to the future. Meanwhile, the essay from Weber that closes *Experimenting* provides a rigorous analysis of *State of Exception* (2005), an important and influential book by Giorgio Agamben dealing with law, violence, language, mediality, and the state. Here, Weber is able to reintroduce a number of critical figures into the scene of reading—among them Benjamin and Kafka—in a way that somewhat defamiliarizes (reenacts otherwise) Agamben's project, powerfully theatricalizing in the text a sense of opening to the possibility of an "other." In their openness to what is still unpredictable and thus futural, both of these chapters imply a call beyond programmatic readings or answers. It is a call to which the essays in *Experimenting*, all in their different ways, seek to respond.

CHAPTER I

"God Bless America!"

Samuel Weber

"We the People..."

In the almost two centuries since Tocqueville published the first volume of *De la démocratie en Amérique* (*Democracy in America*)[1] so much has changed that it is both astonishing and sobering to discover, again and again, how suggestive and incisive many of the analyses of this book still are. Nowhere is this more striking than where Tocqueville discusses the distinctive political significance of the American judicial system, *Du pouvoir judiciaire aux États-Unis et de son action sur la société politique* (On the judicial power in the United States and its action on political society). In this chapter, Tocqueville argues that although the American judiciary conserves the traditional traits of European legal systems, it nevertheless has a political power that is unknown in Europe and distinctively characteristic of American society. What strikes the foreign observer first and foremost is how

> il n'y a pour ainsi dire pas d'événement politique dans lequel il n'entend pas invoquer l'autorité du juge; et il en conclut naturellement qu'aux États-Unis le juge est une des premières puissances politiques. (I, 167)

there is so to speak no political event in which the authority of the judge is not invoked; and from this he concludes, naturally enough, that in the United States the judge is one of the primary political powers.

What is remarkable, however, is how this politicization of the judiciary, through its judges, turns out in fact to entail rather a "judicialization" of the political, since the American legal system preserves the three characteristics that traditionally distinguish judicial systems elsewhere. The first of these traits is that of serving as an "arbiter" of disputes:

> Pour qu'il y ait lieu à action de la part des tribunaux, il faut qu'il y ait contestation. Pour qu'il y ait juge, il faut qu'il y ait procès.

> In order for the courts to become active, there must be a dispute. For there to be a judge, there must be a trial.

The second trait consists in the fact that the judiciary must always address "particular cases" and not with general principles—not at least directly. It can confirm or undermine the power of these principles through its verdicts, but it can never "attack the general principle directly." The third defining trait of the judiciary is that it can never act spontaneously, but only in response: "only when called." Thus, were it to act directly as as "censeur des lois," ("judge of the laws") (169) it would overstep its defining limits.

Having recalled these three traits of the judiciary, Tocqueville notes that all three are respected by the American legal system, and nevertheless, its judges have a political power that is unheard of in Europe. This power is based on the fact that unlike their European counterparts, judges in the United States interpret and apply not merely the laws of the land, but also and above all, the one, single, basic law that founds the republic, the Constitution:

> Les Américains ont reconnu aux juges le droit de fonder leurs arrêts sur la constitution plutôt que sur les lois. En d'autres termes, ils leur ont permis de ne point appliquer les lois qui leur paraîtraient inconstitutionnelles. (169)

> Lorsqu'on invoque, devant les tribunaux des États-Unis, une loi que le juge estime contraire à la constitution, il peut donc refuser de l'appliquer. Ce pouvoir est le seul qui soit particulier au magistrat américain, mais une grande influence politique en découle. (171)

> The Americans have accorded judges the right to base their verdicts on the Constitution rather than on the laws. In other words, they have permitted them to not apply laws that they deem unconstitutional.

When a law that the judge deems contrary to the Constitution is invoked, he can therefore refuse to apply it. This power is the sole that is distinctive to the American judge, but it has enormous political implications.

Thus, the "application" of a law, through the judicial system, entails a double judgment: not just that of deciding whether the (general) law applies to the particular "case," but also whether that general law is consistent with the Constitution. The force of individual laws is thus relativized and made dependent upon the Law that "constitutes" the political framework presupposed by those laws and *within which* alone they are functional.

This situation, which as Tocqueville emphasizes, is peculiar to the American judiciary, has enormous implications that go far beyond the immediate sphere of the legal system. It suggests that the application of any law—and one could extend this to any general *concept* or *rule*—to a particular "case" entails a simultaneous process by which the *general rule or law itself is open to question*, in the sense of requiring justification or legitimation by reference to another, higher or more fundamental principle, here embodied in the Constitution. As a result, everything—and this may provide far-reaching insights into everything connected to American democracy—will come to depend on just how this recourse to the founding document is construed by those who interpret it.

Here Tocqueville's account seems to have been reversed by the course of history:

> En France, la constitution est une œuvre immuable ou censée telle. Aucun pouvoir ne saurait y rien changer. . . . Une constitution américaine n'est point censée immuable comme en France; elle ne saurait être modifiée par les pouvoirs ordinaires de la société, comme en Angleterre. Elle forme une œuvre à part, qui, représentant la volonté de tout le peuple, oblige les législateurs comme les simples citoyens, mais qui peut être changée par la volonté du peuple, *suivant des formes qu'on a établies.* (160, my italics)

> In France the constitution is an immutable work or thought to be such. No power is authorized to change it. . . . An American constitution is not considered to be immutable as is the case in France. It could also not be modified by the ordinary powers of society, as in England. It forms a work apart, which, representing the will of an entire people, is binding for legislators as for simple citizens, but which can be changed by the will of the people, *following the forms that have been established.*

Since the 1830s, when Tocqueville wrote, the situation he described has clearly changed, but the terms in which he articulates the situation remain appropriate: they just must be reattributed. First and most obviously, the United States today still retains its original constitution, amended, whereas that of France dates from 1958. Second, while the French Constitution consists of eighty-nine articles, the U.S. Constitution has only added twenty-seven amendments to its original eight articles. The "mutability" of the two documents has thus been reversed since Tocqueville wrote: by comparison with the constitution of the (Fifth) French Republic, that of the United States seems almost "immutable."

This appearance of immutability gives Tocqueville's assertion that the American Constitution "forms a work apart" new meaning: positive laws can come and go, it suggests, but the American Constitution stays the same, impervious to time, at least in its essentials. And since, as Tocqueville observes, the Constitution is "a work apart" insofar as it is held to "represent the will of the entire people," this will also appears as having the characteristic of *staying the same over time.*

This difference between the French and American constitutions emerges with clarity when one compares their respective modalities of transformation. The French Constitution (Article 89) provides that revisions be proposed "concurrently" by the President of the Republic and the Government, and that they be ratified either by popular vote, in a referendum, or by a two-thirds majority of Parliament convoked in special session. The procedure, as prescribed in Article 5 of the U.S. Constitution, is far more difficult:

> The Congress, whenever two thirds of both Houses shall deem it necessary, shall propose Amendments to this Constitution, or, on the Application of the Legislatures of two thirds of the several States, shall call a Convention for proposing Amendments, which, in either Case, shall be valid to all Intents and Purposes, as Part of this Constitution, when ratified by the Legislatures of three fourths of the several States, or by Conventions in three fourths thereof, as the one or the other Mode of Ratification may be proposed by the Congress.

Two-thirds majorities in either of the two houses of Congress, or of all the state legislatures, are required to propose an amendment and three-quarters of either group to ratify it. This difference has significant implications for the way that "the will of all the people" is "represented" in and by the respective constitutions. Compare the two preambles:

> Le peuple français proclame solennellement son attachement aux Droits de l'homme et aux principes de la souveraineté nationale tels qu'ils ont été

définis par la Déclaration de 1789, confirmée et complétée par le préam-
bule de la Constitution de 1946.

The French people solemnly proclaim its attachment to the Rights of Man
and to the principle of national sovereignty such as they have been defined
by the Declaration of 1789, and confirmed and completed by the preamble
to the Constitution of 1946.

We the People of the United States, in Order to form a more perfect
Union, establish Justice, insure domestic Tranquility, provide for the common defence, promote the general Welfare, and secure the Blessings of
Liberty to ourselves and our Posterity, do ordain and establish this Constitution for the United States of America.

The French preamble consists essentially in references to two previous
texts: the *Déclaration des droits de l'homme et du citoyen* (Declaration of the
Rights of Man and of the Citizen) (1789) and the *Preamble* to the Constitution of 1946. It thus defines itself in terms that are both historical and
intertextual. Moreover, by designating "the French people" in the third
person, it thereby acknowledges a certain *distance* to—and from—the subject in whose name it claims to speak (or rather: to write). Democratic
politics is thus still based upon the notion of a sovereign subject, "the
people," but the articulation of that subject is formulated in a manner that
leaves room for, and requires, *interpretation*.

This contrasts sharply with the American Constitution, which purports
to speak not merely *in the name of*, much less as *representatives of*, but rather
directly as the direct expression of the *vox populi*. It is as if the primary goal
or target of the Constitution, that of forming "a more perfect union,"
were *already* prefigured and *virtually* realized in the unmediated identification of the text with the will of the people. The specific textuality of the
Constitution thus recedes before its claim to be a direct expression and
declaration of the sovereign political subject: "We the People of the
United States." In the most rigorous sense of the word, the Constitution
presents itself as a Speech Act actualizing the otherwise only virtual *voice
of the people*.

But for this actualization to remain actual and not subside again into
virtuality, it must be able to resist time. It is here that writing is indispensable. For the "voice" of the people is ephemeral, time-bound in its actual-
izations. Only a written constitution can hope to stay the same over time,
and thus preserve the identity and stability of the collective subject held
to be the source of democratic sovereignty. But the distinctive and primor-
dial authority of the U.S. Constitution as a written document remains

"phonocentric": it is considered to constitute "a work apart," separate and distinct from all other works, including laws, by virtue of its proximity to, indeed identity with, the source of all sovereignty: the popular will. The United States Constitution can thus present itself as the direct, written embodiment of the will of the people. Its aim of achieving "a more perfect union" is thus initially articulated as a univocal identification with that popular will. A people that can speak with one voice *is* already unified, virtually. It need only now perfect the institutions that will allow it, in Hegelian terms, to be not just "in" itself, but *for itself:* which is to say, to realize its substance ("in itself") as *subject* ("for itself").

The necessity for adjudication proceeds from the existence of conflicts, disputes: in other words, either from disunity or from the threat of disunity. The "more perfect union" that constitutes the aim of the American Constitution thus reaffirms and realizes itself through the arbitration and resolution of such conflicts. Insofar, however, as such arbitration implicitly or explicitly appeals to the Constitution as the supreme principle against which all positive law is to be measured, it implies access to an instance that is never simply *present as such*: the undivided will of the people. How access is envisaged is what will determine the hermeneutics upon which American democracy and its institutions depend. Since the 1830s, waves of immigration have made the United States perhaps the most heterogeneous country in the world, at least in demographic terms. And yet, the diversity of its "multicultural" population has never effaced, and indeed surely intensified the project of the American Constitution: that of *forming* "a more perfect union." The U.S. Constitution lays down the law by virtue of its ability to speak in the first person plural. Its "plurality" is thus subordinated to a notion of "firstness" that implies the unity of a constitutive subject, which in turn implies the ability to stay the same over time. It is this durability that distinguishes collective identity from its individual counterpart.

Nothing less is at stake in that "more perfect union" that the Preamble to the U.S. Constitution declares its intention to form. The use of this word by the "founders" may well have been fortuitous. Its significance, however, is not. For the perfecting of the union will necessarily have to operate primarily at the level of form. Form, one of the axiomatic categories of Kant's Third Critique, is defined there, succinctly, as "the agreement of the manifold with a unity (it being undetermined what this ought to be.)"[2] For Kant, the indeterminability of this "unity" is what distinguishes its "formal" character: its substance cannot be defined, but only discerned (as the property of a representation). And yet, whereas Kant insisted on the radical gap that separates the "aesthetic" notion of "form" from all conceptual cognition, the political project of the U.S. Constitution aims to bridge that gap: the union of individuals, and of individual "states," is to be "perfected" through the principles, institutions and laws to which it gives rise. Insofar as the perfection of this union is already prefigured in the speech-actualization of the Constitution itself, the latter has to be considered as being political-theological in essence. Its founders and signers would have doubtless been horrified by such an assertion. Nevertheless, as we will see, it is perhaps the most powerful insight that is developed by Tocqueville, albeit largely implicitly and between the lines of his text. The principle is simple enough:

> Le peuple règne sur le monde politique américain comme Dieu sur l'univers. Il est la cause et la fin de toutes choses: tout en sort et tout s'y absorbe. (I, 119–20).

> The people reigns over the American political world like God over the universe. It is the cause and end of all things: everything proceeds from it and everything is absorbed into it.

The "people" is what informs the Constitution and gives it its form, authority, and power. The Constitution, and the political system it constitutes, can thus be said to be theological, insofar as it presupposes a transcendent subject, "the people," held to be unified and whole, self-identical and self-contained, prior to its manifestation. At the same time it is political, as the full realization of that transcendent subject entails the perfecting of its "union" through the establishment and maintenance of institutions and laws that insure the survival of that "people" over time. Since the identity of the people is conceived on the model of the individual—as essentially indivisible—the problem is to insure its survival above and beyond the mortal term of time granted to empirical individuals.

The supremacy of the Constitution, then, over the actual functioning of the institutions it constitutes, reposes on the priority of a transcendent subject, the "people," over the empirical institutions and individuals through which it is constrained to operate. In political practice this culminates in the way in which the adjudication of legal disputes implies an evaluation of the legitimacy of the law. The law may be given in the present, but its legitimacy depends upon a "perfection" that belongs to the future. But the distance between present and future—and here the difference to Kant emerges most clearly—must never be considered to be entirely heterogeneous, since the temporal axis is oriented and informed by the principle of the (virtually) unified "people." Despite this difference, then, the principle of unity and indivisibility must remain in principle cognizable in order to serve as a criterion upon which the legality of all positive law can be constantly measured and judged.

The dependence of positive law upon a nonpositive, transcendent, but nevertheless accessible notion of a unified people blurs the Kantian distinction between "regulative" and "constitutive": insofar as the notion of the people as its author and object endows the Constitution with its legitimacy, that notion cannot remain entirely regulative, which is to say, inapplicable to particular "cases." Hence, the appeal to "form" as a means of overcoming division and diversity through delimitation. This power of formal unification—a phrase that is strictly redundant, since formalization entails unification—manifests itself as the ability to stay the same over time. Form frames time (and space as well): it "forms a more perfect union."

This is what allows Tocqueville to observe, "The laws do more to maintain the democratic republic in the United States than do physical causes, and customs even more than do the laws" (I:13).[3] For insofar as the laws are ultimately subject to democratic legitimation through the Constitution, they actualize the rule of a subject held capable of governing itself. At the same time, however, the whole process can only function effectively to the extent that each individual positive law can be related to and interpreted in terms of the ultimately transcendent popular will embodied in the Constitution. This reintroduces a moment of instability and potential discord in the application of laws. And it is accentuated insofar as the "people" in its concrete, empirical manifestations can never be simply identified with the "more perfect union" that is its ultimate justification. In between the transcendent unity of the people and the geocultural diversity of its manifestations there appears something that Tocqueville identifies as "*moeurs*," and that, far from resolving the question, often only aggravates it:

> D'où vient, au contraire, qu'à l'ouest les pouvoirs de la société semblent marcher au hasard? Pourquoi y règne-t-il dans le mouvement des affaires quelque chose de désordonné, de passionné, on pourrait presque dire de fébrile, qui n'annonce point un long avenir? (416)

> How, on the contrary, does it happen that in the West the powers of society seem to be driven by chance? Why is business carried on in a disorganized, passionate—one could almost say feverish—manner, one that does not presage a long future?

Here again we come upon one of the relatively rare places where history seems to have proved Tocqueville's judgment erroneous. Far from being short-lived, the *feverishness* of which he writes has become one of the most tenacious "customs" or "mores" of the United States. And yet it is probably the mark of a great thinker to be thought-provoking even (and perhaps especially) when "mistaken." Adorno once observed that misunderstandings allow for the communication of the incommunicable. Tocqueville takes a first step in this direction when, immediately following the question quoted above, he notes:

> Je ne compare plus les Anglo-Américains à des peuples étrangers: j'oppose maintenant les Anglo-Américains *les uns aux autres* et je cherche pourquoi ils ne se ressemblent pas.[4]

> I am not comparing the Anglo-Americans any more to foreign peoples: I am opposing them now to each other and am looking for the reasons why they are not alike.

In other words—and this is surely worth recalling in a context that is concerned with French-American literary-critical relations—behind the ostensible unity of proper nouns, whether individual or collective, there can lurk a disunity that greatly complicates any effort at comparison. Here, Tocqueville distinguishes between the Eastern and Western United States in terms of a greater "feverishness" of the latter in the conduct of "business." To conclude that such feverishness "does not presage a long future" has proved to be somewhat premature. But the jury is still out on just how far such febrility in the conduct of affairs—commercial, domestic, or foreign—can allow for a future that would be anything but a prolongation of the present.[5] Whether as the frenetic tempo of Hollywood "action" films or the "preemptive"/"preventive" strikes currently envisaged and practiced by the U.S. government, the future is never allowed to be "long" but only more of the same.[6] Thus, what Tocqueville considered to be the absence of "*moeurs*" in the nascent society of the Western United States, has in the meanwhile itself become one of the most powerful mores determining the policy of the country at large. The conjunction of the capitalist tendency to monetarize time—chronological time serving as the medium and measure of profitability and profitability—with the promotion of a technology largely devoted to reducing the quantity of "socially necessary labor time" required to constitute the value of commodities, has helped make speed and acceleration the prevailing criteria of social and political power.

But this veneration of speed and power is constantly accompanied by an anxious shadow. In the second volume of *De la Démocratie en Amérique*, which deals more extensively with what Tocqueville refers to as "moeurs," this "febrility" in the conduct of "affairs" reemerges in a chapter that seeks to respond to the question, "Pourquoi les Américains se montrent si inquiets au milieu de leur bien-être":

> C'est une chose étrange de voir avec quelle sorte d'ardeur fébrile les
> Américains poursuivent le bien-être, et comme ils se montrent tourmentés
> sans cesse par une crainte vague de n'avoir pas choisi la route la plus courte
> qui peut y conduire.
>
> L'habitant des États-Unis s'attache aux biens de ce monde, comme s'il
> était assuré de ne point mourir, et il met tant de précipitation à saisir ceux
> qui passent à sa portée, qu'on dirait qu'il craint à chaque instant de cesser
> de vivre avant d'en avoir joui. Il les saisit tous, mais sans les étreindre, et il
> les laisse bientôt échapper de ses mains pour courir après des jouissances
> nouvelles. (II, 171)

> It is strange to see with what sort of feverish ardor the Americans pursue
> their well-being, and how tormented they seem by an incessant but vague
> fear of having not chosen the shortest route that leads there.
>
> The inhabitant of the United States is attached to the goods of this
> world, as though he were certain never to die, and he goes to such extremes
> to seize those that pass within his grasp that one would think him driven
> by the fear of dying at any instant before having had a chance to enjoy
> them.

The Declaration of Independence already had declared "life, liberty and the pursuit of happiness" to constitute the objects of "unalienable rights" that "governments are instituted" to "secure." But the question of just how the "unalienable right" to "life" is to be "secured" by government, or by any other institution, is of course not addressed explicitly in this document or elsewhere.[7] What did not escape Tocqueville's notice, however, was that the conduct of "business" and in particular, the search to acquire the "goods of this world," had emerged as a major attempt to respond to this unelaborated question of how "the right to life" was to be "secured." This connection was perhaps easier for Tocqueville to make in French than it would have been in English, where no one word links well-being (*bien-être*) to goods that can be acquired (*biens*). The right to life, liberty and the pursuit of happiness could thus be subsumed as the right to possess "goods," "life" and "liberty" being a "good" in the sense of a condition of acquiring "goods" and thus acceding to "happiness."

There remains however one unresolved obstacle to the securing of these rights, as the passage quoted makes clear: "L'habitant des États-Unis s'attache aux biens de ce monde, comme s'il était assuré de ne point mourir" ("The inhabitant of the United States is attached to the goods of this world, as though he were certain never to die"). The acquisition of goods seems to function as an attempt to attach oneself to the world as though one would never have to leave it. But all this does is underscore the conundrum and the result is a stubborn sense of trouble ("inquiétude") and a feverish attempt to escape it through speed and acceleration: "Il met tant de précipitation à saisir ceux qui passent à sa portée, qu'on dirait qu'il craint à chaque instant de cesser de vivre avant d'en avoir joui" ("He goes to such extremes to seize those that pass within his grasp that one would think him driven by the fear of dying at any instant before having had a chance to enjoy them").

The right to "life" actualizes itself as the "liberty" to *pursue* a "happiness" that by definition can never be attained. Thus, the "pursuit of happiness," Tocqueville observes, tends to take the form of a race against death:

> Le souvenir de la brièveté de la vie l'aiguillonne sans cesse. Indépendamment des biens qu'il possède, il en imagine à chaque instant mille autres que la mort l'empêchera de goûter, s'il ne se hâte. Cette pensée le remplit de trouble, de craintes et de regrets, et maintient son âme dans une sorte de trépidation incessante qui le porte à changer à tout moment de desseins et de lieu.
>
> La mort survient enfin et elle l'arrête avant qu'il se soit lassé de cette poursuite inutile d'une félicité complète qui fuit toujours. (II, 172)

The memory of the brevity of life torments him incessantly. Independently of the goods he possesses, he imagines at every instant a thousand others that death will prevent him from tasting, if he doesn't hurry up. This thought troubles him and fills him with fears and regrets, maintaining his soul in a sort of incessant trepidation that drives him to change his plans and place all the time.

Death arrives finally and stops him before he has grown bored with this futile pursuit of a complete happiness that is forever fleeing.

The "pursuit of happiness" as the inalienable right to acquire the "biens" ("the goods") held to constitute "bien-être" ("well-being") is interrupted, always more or less prematurely, by an "end" that seems difficult to situate within the horizon of "We, the people."[8] The inevitability of death for individuals thus places a severe limitation on the "unalienable rights" to life, liberty and the pursuit of happiness, especially insofar as these "rights" are construed as the prerogatives of individuals. The individual "pursuit of happiness" is thus subject to constant if virtual pursuit by an "inquietude" that governments can stage as a "spectacle" but hardly "secure."

The spectacle, Tocqueville concedes, is hardly new: "Ce qui est nouveau, c'est de voir tout un peuple qui le donne" (172) ("What is new is to see an entire people involved in its production"). Could it be precisely the *staging of this "spectacle"* that provides the *actual unity* of "We, the People"?

"One Nation, indivisible, under God . . ."

For "We, the People," the "pursuit of happiness" may appear endless, but for the individuals considered to be the essential component and, indeed, the model of a people that founds itself politically by speaking in the first person, that pursuit never can last long enough to reach its goal. For Tocqueville this is a new and distinctive characteristic of modern democracy:

> L'aristocratie avait fait de tous les citoyens une longue chaîne qui remontait du paysan au roi; la démocratie brise la chaîne et met chaque anneau à part. . . . Ainsi, non seulement la démocratie fait oublier à chaque homme ses aïeux, mais elle lui cache ses descendants et le sépare de ses contemporains; elle le ramène sans cesse vers lui seul et menace de le renfermer enfin tout entier dans la solitude de son propre cœur. (II, 126–27)

> The aristocracy had wrought all citizens into a long chain that ascended from the peasant to the king; democracy breaks the chain and isolates each link. . . . Thus, not only does democracy cause each man to forget his predecessors, but it also hides his descendents from him and separates them from his contemporaries. It incessantly throws him back upon himself, alone, and in the end threatens to imprison him entirely in the solitude of his own heart.

Time is always too short for those who are caught up in the isolation of the present moment. It tempts with the narcissistic mirage of self-sufficiency, of "not owing anything to anyone" and "not expecting anything from anyone" (II:127).[9] And although such "individualism"—a word that was still quite new for Tocqueville—appears at first to be much less harmful than the more venerable "egoism" it seems to supplant, it ultimately is reabsorbed by it. Attacking at first only "public virtues," it goes on to undermine "all the others" as well. It does this by undermining all sense of obligation to others through its ideal of self-containment. But this ideal remains haunted by the mortality that is the enabling condition and disabling limit of the *principium individuationis*.

The result is a dilemma that is not so much resolved as evaded through what might be called—although to be sure Tocqueville does not do so—the political theology of democratic individualism.[10] If the tendency to conceive the democratic polity as an indivisible collective is common to most modern nation-states, as the importance accorded to nativity tends to suggest,[11] nowhere is its conflictual character more flagrant than in the American democracy described by Tocqueville. As with the relation of laws to the Constitution, the unity of the "people" must be renewed and actualized over again. It is a task in which the present pledges itself to the future, but to a future understood as the realization of the present. An instance of this can be found in the American "pledge of allegiance," of which Tocqueville could know nothing since it dates from 1892. Initially it consisted in the words, "I pledge allegiance to *my* flag, and to the Republic for which it stands, one nation, indivisible, with liberty and justice to all." In 1923, "my flag" was changed to "*the* flag of the United States of America," against the wishes of its author, Frederic Bellamy, cousin of the famous writer and utopian socialist, Edward Bellamy. The "my" was felt to be too private and proprietary, no doubt, but it reflected the continuing political importance of the first person singular, so very different from the appeal to the plural subject that inaugurates the *Marseillaise*—a collective defined as "*enfants* de la patrie" ("*children* of the fatherland") rather than as its owner. No less significant, however, was the second important change made to "The Pledge of Allegiance," dating from 1954, when following a campaign by the Knights of Columbus, the words "under God" were added to "one nation," which now became "one nation under God." Thus, what was originally an ostensibly secular "patriotic oath" now became a "public prayer."[12]

Tocqueville provides both a prehistory to this development as well as an implicitly problematic interpretation of it. For he emphasizes that the profound political influence of religion in the United States derives from precisely the then distinctive separation of Church and State that characterized American democracy, at least its beginnings. By separating itself from political institutions, religion in America could also distance itself from the latter's abuses and conflicts, and thus place itself above the interminable and petty conflicts of interests that dominate everyday "politics." Religion could in this way situate itself as a supreme arbiter, at a level akin to that of the Constitution itself. Tocqueville's insight is no less applicable today. Where religions have shown themselves to be vulnerable to criticism and attack, it is where they have been most obviously institutionalized: the Catholic Church, for instance, and the traditional Protestant denominations. Where religions have been able to obscure or conceal their institutionalization, as with many of the more recent evangelical "sects," they have largely escaped the kind of public control and opprobrium directed at the older, more exposed religions.

Conversely, the very word "politics" has today become a term of abuse in American political discourse. Debates in Congress about the justification of going to war with Iraq were dismissed as being basely "political," a tactic that the current administration continues to use with considerable effect to blunt all criticism of its policies. The long-standing idiom, "playing politics," is indicative of the low esteem in which "politics" is held in the United States, and probably increasingly in many other parts of the world as well. The growing number of abstentions in national political elections in France in recent years is an unmistakable indication of this tendency. By contrast, it is significant that contemporary French has devised a particular idiom to designate "politicking" in its self-serving form: *la politique politicienne* (the politics of politicians), thereby maintaining, temporarily at least, a relatively neutral connotation for the root-word, *politique* (political).

Thus, by keeping at a certain distance from institutionalized politics, Tocqueville argues, religion in the United States is able to develop a moral authority that is highly political in its effects. For this he cites a variety of factors, many of which are still in force today, although clearly not without modifications. One such is the increasing importance attached to the domestic sphere, to the family as a *locus amoenus*, a refuge and harbor from the fervid and feverish pursuit of "affairs" and fortune that dominates the world outside.

But another factor contributes to the distinctive political power and authority of religion in the United States and it is one that takes us back to our initial discussion of the law:

> Ainsi donc, en même temps que la loi permet au peuple américain de tout faire, la religion l'empêche de tout concevoir et lui défend de tout oser. (I, 398)

> Thus, at the same time the law allows the American people to do everything, religion prevents it from conceiving everything and prohibits it from daring to do all.

The rather surprising assertion that "law permits the American people to do everything" becomes more intelligible when we recall that the legitimacy of law in the United States depends upon its accord with a constitution whose authority, although often considered to be immanent to the text, in fact necessitates recourse to a transcendent instance: the unity of a people existing only in a state of virtuality and never realizable in the actuality of a present moment. Since the temporality of law is that of the present, laws as such are incapable of providing the limitations required to stabilize an otherwise "feverish" pursuit of business and "well-being." Thus, despite the "respect" (I:336) and even "paternal love" (I:337) that Americans feel for the laws of the land, a higher authority is required in order for these laws themselves to function. Ultimately this higher authority is that of the people as a whole which, despite the emphasis on majority rule, cannot be identified with its quantitative manifestation, but rather with the reflexive self-identity that alone makes it capable of self-government:

> Il y a des pays où un pouvoir, en quelque sorte extérieur au corps social, agit sur lui et le force de marcher dans une certaine voie.
> Il y en a d'autres où la force est divisée, étant tout à la fois placée dans la société et hors d'elle. Rien de semblable ne se voit aux États-Unis; la société y agit par elle-même et sur elle-même. Il n'existe de puissance que dans son sein. . . . Le peuple participe à la composition des lois par le choix des législateurs, à leur application par l'élection des agents du pouvoir exécutif; on peut dire qu'il gouverne lui-même. . . . *Le peuple règne sur le monde politique américain comme Dieu sur l'univers.* Il est la cause et la fin de toutes choses; tout en sort et tout s'y absorbe. (I, 119–120, my italics)

> There are countries where a power that is in some way exterior to the social body acts upon it and forces it to move in a certain direction.
> There are others where force is divided, being placed at the same time within society and outside of it. Nothing similar can be seen in the United States. There society acts by itself and on itself. No power exists except what it contains. . . . The people participates in the composition of laws through their choice of legislators, in their application through the election of the agents of the executive branch; it can be said that it governs itself. . . . The people reigns over the American political world like God over the universe. It is the cause and end of all things. Everything proceeds from it and is absorbed into it.

Paradoxically, and indeed one might add, aporetically, this conception of popular sovereignty seeks to collapse transcendence into the perfect immanence of total self-identity, of a "government of the people, by the people and for the people" that "shall not perish from the earth."[13] It should be noted—again a nuance, but not an insignificant one—that Article Two of the French Constitution (1958) cites these words of Lincoln, without quotation marks or attribution, in defining the "principle" of the Republic, but in so doing does not repeat the claim of the people being *imperishable*.[14] It should also be noted that Lincoln's defense of the Union in his Gettysburg Address requires him to affirm not just its endurance but the immortality of its people as a whole, in the face of the death of individual citizen-soldiers on the battlefield; it is their "unfinished work"—unfinished by their death—that "consecrates" the task of defending the Union against the danger of disintegration. It is in this context of asserting the immortality of the people and its union that Lincoln employs the phrase "one nation under God"—the phrase that will later become an integral part of the "pledge of allegiance."

Since the model of national identity is constructed on the model of the individual, held to be indivisible in its isolation, such isolation cannot be considered to be absolute. Rather, it becomes the sign of a privileged position resulting from an alliance with a transcendent creator; like the human individual, the Creator is equally indivisible and reigns alone; but unlike the individual, the "end" of the Creator is at once synonymous with completion and self-fulfillment, and not with interruption and disaggregation.

The relation of the mortal individual to an immortal but equally indivisible self-identity that serves as both its model and its guarantee can only be one of sacrifice: exemplified in the "heroic" deaths of the soldier, for instance, at the battle of Gettysburg, but also in the death of Christ on the Cross. It is this significance of sacrifice that enables the individualist (largely Protestant) political theology of American democracy to identify, as Tocqueville insists, religion above all with Christianity. For it is Christianity that is traditionally associated, at least in the "West," with the claim of bridging the gap between individual mortality and individual salvation through the promise of personal immortality through self-sacrifice. This theological framework, which, as Tocqueville emphasized, had already taken its distance from institutional politics, can equally separate itself from institutional religion and survive in ostensibly secular form as a religiously inspired moral code. Such morality provides the *certitude* so cruelly lacking in the "feverish conduct" of everyday affairs, with which, however, it is perfectly compatible in its complementarity:

> Le christianisme règne donc sans obstacles, de l'aveu de tous ; il en résulte . . . que tout est certain et arrêté dans le monde moral, quoique le monde

politique semble abandonnée à la discussion et aux essais des hommes. Ainsi
l'esprit humain n'aperçoit jamais devant lui un champ sans limite: quelle
que soit son audace, il sent de temps en temps qu'il doit s'arrêter devant
des barrières insurmontables. (I:398)

Christianity reigns thus without obstacle, through the consent of all. The
result is that everything is certain and fixed in the moral world, while the
political world seems abandoned to human discussion and experimentation.
Thus, the human spirit never sees itself confronted by a field without limit:
whatever its audaciousness may be, it feels from time to time that it must
halt before insurmountable barriers.

The political function of the appeal to a predominantly Christian morality[15] is thus to provide a framework within which a durable link can be
established linking isolated individuals together in an indivisible and unified people or nation.

C'est ainsi qu'aux États-Unis le zèle religieux s'échauffe sans cesse au foyer
du patriotisme. Vous pensez que ces hommes agissent uniquement dans la
considération de l'autre vie, mais vous vous trompez: l'éternité n'est qu'un
de leurs soins. Si vous interrogez ces missionnaires de la civilisation chré-
tienne, vous serez tout surpris de les entendre parler si souvent des biens
de ce monde, et de trouver des politiques où vous croyez ne voir que des
religieux. (I:399–400)

It is thus in the United States that religious zeal warms itself constantly at
the hearth of patriotism. You may think that these men act solely in consideration of the other life, but you would be wrong. Eternity is not one of
their concerns. If you ask these missionaries of Christian civilization, you
would be surprised to hear them speak so often of the goods of this world,
and thus to discover politicians where you expected to find only men of the
cloth.

Or conversely, if you question democratic politicians in America, you
may be surprised to find *des religieux où vous croyez ne voir que des politiques*.
The morality of what C. B. MacPherson called "possessive individualism"
demonstrates here what MacPherson himself did not envisage: the religious roots and structure of what presents itself as a resolutely secular
enterprise.[16] But it is above all the moral code of everyday life that provides
the practical medium and relay through which the political theology of
American individualist democracy operates its practical syntheses of transcendence and immanence, collective and individual, economic and political. By virtue of this moralism, "*tout est certain et arrêté dans le monde moral,*

quoique le monde politique semble abandonné à la discussion et aux essais des hommes" ("everything is certain and fixed in the moral world, although the political world seems abandoned to human discussion and experimentation") (I:398)—or worse, abandoned not simply to discussion and experiment, but to a corruption and venality that seems to confirm the most pessimistic Puritan vision of the fallen, guilty nature of the creation.[17]

Thus, if as Tocqueville suggests at the beginning of the second volume, the Americans are "Cartesian" without having read a word of Descartes insofar as "chacun se renferme . . . étroitement en soi-même et pretend de là juger le monde" ("each one shuts himself off . . . narrowly in himself and claims from there to judge the world") (II:10), such democratic individualism implies an epistemological individualism as well. At the same time, the attempt to "chercher par soi-même et en soi seul la raison des choses" ("to look on one's own and in one's self for the reason of things") (II:9) would be condemned by the feverish and disorderly conduct of "affairs," were it not grounded and supplemented in a religiously based moralism:

> Si les Américains, qui ont livré le monde politique aux essais des novateurs, n'avaient point placé leur religion quelque part en dehors de lui, à quoi pourrait-elle se tenir dans le flux et reflux des opinions humaines? Au milieu de la lutte des partis, où serait le respect qui lui est dû? *Que deviendrait son immortalité quand tout périrait autour d'elle?* (I:405, my italics)

> If the Americans, who have delivered the political world over to the experiments of innovators, had not placed their religion somewhere outside of that world, what could it hold on to in the ebb and flow of human opinions? In the midst of the struggle of parties, where would be the respect due him? What would become of his immortality when everything all around is perishing?

But effects of such separation and isolation are not restricted to the relation of religion (and morality) to politics: they also condition the relation of religion to itself, at least in its institutional incarnation. Tocqueville, perhaps unknowingly, elaborates on Luther's maxim, *sola fides*, when he concludes that "la foi change d'objet, elle ne meurt point" ("faith changes object, it doesn't die"). This follows his observation:

> Dans les siècles de ferveur, il arrive quelquefois aux hommes d'abandonner leur religion, mais ils n'échappent à son joug que pour se soumettre à celui d'une autre. (I:406)

In the most fervent centuries, human beings abandon their religion, but they never escape from their yoke except by submitting themselves to another.

American democracy perpetuates those "siècles de ferveur" in the ostensibly secularized but fervid conduct of affairs—the business of a capitalist market economy. Such "fever" suggests that the project of self-fulfillment that informs the individual proprietor may not be separable from self-consumption, and this in turn promotes the recourse to religion. This situation leads Tocqueville in conclusion to pose a series of questions:

> La religion est beaucoup plus nécessaire dans la république qu'ils préconisent [ceux qui attaquent les croyances religieuses], que dans la monarchie qu'ils attaquent, et dans les républiques démocratiques que dans toutes les autres. Comment la société pourrait-elle manquer de périr si, tandis que le lien politique se relâche, le lien moral ne se resserrait pas? et que faire d'un peuple maître de lui-même, s'il n'est pas soumis à Dieu? (I:401)

> Religion is much more necessary in the republic envisaged [by those who attacked religious belief] than in the monarchy they attack, and in democratic republics even more than in all the others. How could society fail to perish if, while the political nexus is weakened, the moral bond would not take up the slack? And what would happen to a people master of itself if it were not submitted to God?

The Theater of Democracy

In the light of the previous discussion and above all, of the questions just quoted, it appears that the oppositions of religious and secular, transcendent and immanent, heteronomy and autonomy, individual and collective are not mutually exclusive, but collaborative and complicitous. Such collaboration and complicity, working often out of sight, sustain the conception of an indivisible identity that informs American democracy. The relation of visible (indivisible) to invisible (divisible) thereby emerges as the not-so-hidden mainspring driving the febrile fervor characteristic of the American way of life, then as now.

It is this insight that informs certain observations of Tocqueville that otherwise might seem isolated in his work. One such seeks to respond to the question, *Pourquoi les Américains élèvent en même temps de si petits et de si grand monuments?* (Why the Americans build at the same time such small and such great monuments?) To this he begins his response by observing:

> Chez les peuples démocratiques, les individus sont très faibles; mais l'État, qui les représente tous et les tient tous dans sa main, est très fort. (II: 66)

> With democratic peoples, individuals are very weak; but the State that represents all and holds all in its hand, is very strong.

It is not, however, the desire to create munificent monuments as such that interests Tocqueville, but rather the juxtaposition he discerns between ostentatious manifestation of the collective and the far more humble reality of the individual citizen:

> Les mêmes hommes qui vivent petitement dans d'étroites demeures visent souvent au gigantesque dès qu'il s'agit des monuments publics. (II:66)

> The same men that live small lives in narrow and restricted dwellings often aim at the gigantic wherever public monuments are concerned.

At the time he was writing, Tocqueville could not—or at least, did not—anticipate how the individual, or rather individualism, would take its revenge. If the monument always has a collective implication, and if moreover it is a "work" rather than living faith, there is an alternative that seems to combine monumentality with living presence and it has become perhaps the major cultural hallmark of American society: the twin cult of the Star and the Spectator.[18] Tocqueville could not foresee this cult, but he did discern a related tendency operating within the sphere of politics: the propensity of democratic egalitarianism to encourage submissiveness and its correlative, the "concentration of power." He described "l'idée d'un pouvoir unique et central qui mène tous les citoyens par lui-même," ("the idea of a single and central power leading all citizens all by itself") and ascribed that "idea" to a propensity, "in politics as in philosophy and religion," for ideas that are "simple and general." The simplification and generalization of ideas, including that of a dominant and leading "centralized power," Tocqueville traced to a certain use of the imagination and the image:

> Les systèmes compliqués repoussent [l'intelligence des peuples démocratiques], et elle se plaît à imaginer une grande nation dont tous les citoyens ressemblent à un seul modèle et sont dirigés par un seul pouvoir. . . . A mesure que les conditions s'égalisent chez un peuple, les individus paraissent plus petits et la société semble plus grande, ou plutôt chaque citoyen, devenu semblable à tous les autres, se perd dans la foule, et l'on n'aperçoit plus que *la vaste et magnifique image du peuple lui-même*. (II:355–56)

Complicated systems repel [the intelligence of democratic peoples], which like to imagine a great nation where all the citizens resemble a single model and are directed by one sole power. . . . To the extent that the conditions of a people become more equal, individuals seem smaller and society larger, or rather each citizen, having become like unto all the others, loses himself in the crowd, and all that can be seen is *the vast and magnificent image of the people itself.*

Monuments, of course, are one manifestation of this "vast and magnificent image," but they are also an inanimate one. They are resistant to temporal change and alteration, but only by virtue of their not being self-present in the way a living being is considered to be. "Live" programming of today's audiovisual media can thus be understood as a means of *presenting* "the vast and magnificent image of the people" in its indivisible unity. "Stars" are another such means. There is, however, one place where the spectacle reveals its constitutive dependence upon what at first sight seems to be external and extraneous to it: the spectator. And that place is the *theater.*

The chapter that Tocqueville devotes to this singular place bears an unusual title; for whereas most of the chapter titles in his book are encapsulated summaries of what is to come, this one announces mere "observations": "Quelques Observations sur le théâtre des peuples démocratiques" (Some observations on the theater of democratic peoples). They begin with a general remark: After a revolution has begun to transform the "social state of a people:"

> c'est en général par le théâtre qu'elle se produit d'abord, et c'est là qu'elle demeure toujours visible. . . . Si vous voulez juger d'avance la littérature d'un peuple qui tourne à la démocratie, étudiez son théâtre. (II:103)

> it is generally by theater that it first emerges, and it is there that it remains visible. . . . If you want to judge in advance the literature of a people that turns to democracy, study its theater.

In a democracy, then, theater occupies a privileged place among the literary arts—if indeed it is to be included among them: it reveals and renders visible what otherwise would remain invisible, even and above all to those most intimately concerned. Thus, spectators in a theater find themselves in a situation that mirrors the world outside: there is no time to reflect on what one sees, to consult one's memory or ask the opinion of experts. Instead, the spectator:

est en quelque sort pris au dépourvu par l'impression[s] qu'on lui suggère
. . . il y cède avant de les connaître. Les auteurs ne tardent pas à découvrir
de quel côté incline ainsi *secrètement* le goût du public. (II:101, my italics)

is to a certain extent taken by surprise by the impression[s] that are proposed to him . . . he yields before knowing them. It takes the authors little
time to discover toward what side the taste of the public is *secretly* disposed.

The "taste" of the public is thus addressed in its most intimate, but also
most *secret* dimension, which is normally under control neither of the individual nor of society.

The theater therefore tends to be a place where the laws of literature
and of society are suspended, and often in a violent manner:

Les goûts et les instincts naturels aux peuples démocratiques, en fait de
littérature, se manifesteront donc d'abord au théâtre, et on peut prévoir
qu'ils s'y introduiront avec violence. Dans les écrits, les lois littéraires de
l'aristocratie se modifieront peu à peu, d'une manière graduelle et pour
ainsi dire légale. Au théâtre, elles seront renversées par des émeutes.
(II:102)

The tastes and instincts that are natural to democratic peoples, concerning
literature, manifest themselves first in the theater, and one can predict that
they erupt there in a violent manner. In writings, the literary laws of the
aristocracy change little by little, in a graduate and thus so to speak legal
manner. In the theater, they are overturned by revolts.

But this suspension of existing laws in the theater and the revolt against
them is neither entirely chaotic nor arbitrary. The popular "taste" shared
by the dominant part of the audience may be "secret," but it is not without
a certain system:

Les peuples démocratiques n'ont qu'une estime fort médiocre pour l'érudi-
tion . . . ils entendent qu'on leur parle d'eux-mêmes, et c'est le tableau du
présent qu'ils demandent. (II:102)

Democratic peoples only have a very limited respect for erudition . . . they
intend to be spoken to themselves directly, and what they demand is an
image of the present.

Democratic peoples demand that their theater—and nowadays one can
say, audiovisual media in general—furnish them with a "tableau du présent" ("image of the present") rather than with a depiction of "history";
indeed, in popular American parlance today, the word "history" has become synonymous with irrelevance ("It's history!" means that it is over

and done with, once and for all). The withdrawal of individuals into themselves has, as its temporal correlative, a privileging of the present over past and future, and a conception of the present as self-contained. Theater has always been associated with a certain presence, but in a context of democratic individualism, this presence has never appeared to be more problematic:

> Dans les sociétés démocratiques, les spectateurs . . . aiment à retrouver sur la scène le mélange confus de conditions, de sentiments et d'idées qu'ils rencontrent sous leurs yeux; le théâtre devient plus frappant, plus vulgaire et plus vrai. (103)

> In democratic societies, spectators . . . love to rediscover on stage the confused mélange of conditions, feelings, and ideas that they see before their eyes; the theater becomes more striking, more vulgar, more true.

It is as if democratic *theater* provides a counterexample to that "vast and magnificent image" of a unified people presented by great monuments. What it presents is the "confused mélange of conditions, feelings, and ideas" that one encounters outside. This confusion is increased by the diversity of authors and audiences participating in theater:

> Une pareille multitude, composée d'éléments si divers et répandus . . . ne saurait reconnaître les mêmes règles et se soumettre aux mêmes lois. *Il n'y a pas d'accord possible entre des juges très nombreux qui, ne sachant point où se trouver, portent chacun à part leur arrêt.* Si l'effet de la démocratie est en général de rendre douteuses les règles et les conventions littéraires, au théâtre elle les abolit entièrement. (II:103–4)

> Such a multitude, composed of such diverse and dispersed elements . . . would be capable only of recognizing the same rules and submitting to the same laws. *There is no agreement possible between these very numerous judges who, not knowing where to find themselves, develop their verdicts in isolation from one another.* If the effect of democracy in general is to render literary rules and conventions dubious, in the theater they are abolished entirely.

In a democracy, the "people" that is supposed to be "sovereign" loses the attributes traditionally considered to be the indispensable condition of all sovereignty: unity and self-identity. The rules and laws that hitherto functioned to maintain that self-identity in a state of perpetual presence and self-fulfillment are no longer in force, no longer *the same*. And they are no longer the same because there is no longer any single authority capable of integrating them. In the absence of a Constitution, there is only a multitude of judges who are "too numerous" to know "where to find themselves (and each other: *se trouver*)."

This in turn calls into question the traditional conception of theater itself. It can no longer be taken for granted as a medium of literary representation, in which *spectators* are simultaneously and perhaps above all *readers*. Rather, in the theater of democracy, these *spectators* have literally become an *audience*: "On écoute les pièces de théâtre, mais on ne les lit point" ("Theatrical plays are listened to, not read") (II:104). It is this *listening* that, according to Tocqueville, constitutes the distinctive quality of the democratic theatrical *spectacle*, which is something not just to be seen or read, but to be heard.

The "rule" that informs this show is that of "moving" or "touching" the audience, less by "thoughts" than by what Tocqueville calls "les emotions vives du coeur" (II:104) ("the lively feelings of the heart"). Today we might speak of "strong emotions." But his designation is more precise: it suggests, first, that the "emotions" appealed to and touched by theater are felt by the "audience" to be as intimate and as internal as a "heart"; and second, it implies that that most intimate, "heartfelt" feeling draws its force from the way it confirms the sense of being *alive*. Such a sense of being enlivened can, but need not, entail an experience of living-on, surviving, and this is surely one of the aspects that makes the position of the spectator so seductively powerful in individualist democracies generally and in the United States in particular.

In traditional theater, of course, the spectator does not remain self-enclosed within the intimate realm of the "heart." The spectator has to leave "home," at least temporarily, to experience the "heartfelt" sensation of being alive. And in a traditional theater this experience is inevitably shared, and not entirely private. Today, by contrast, this is no longer necessary. Today, theater has come "home" as "home theater." The *home* is increasingly the privileged place where spectacles are experienced—and survived. But also the place that is ever more threatened: by child abuse, domestic violence, but also by an economic violence that is less visibly linked to the home, but upon which it depends. Against the background of such growing "domestic violence"—in all the senses of "domestic"—September 11 could only be regarded as a relief. For it enabled the "terror" to be expelled from the home and regarded as entirely alien: as the result of an Axis of Evil, against which war could be waged. The uncanniness, *Unheimlichkeit* of the home, the insecurity of the domestic economy and its social ramifications, has temporarily been eclipsed by the Office of Homeland Security. For how long remains an open question.

E pluribus unum

This expression, which goes back to a Latin poem, *In Moretum*, dealing with "habits and customs ascribed to a vigil," was chosen by Franklin, Adams, and Jefferson to serve as the motto on the seal of the newly independent United States. Almost immediately the motto found its way from the seal of the new nation to its coins. At the end of the Civil War, it was joined by the slogan, "In God We Trust," which in 1956 then became the official national motto. Since then, it in turn has been supplanted, especially in times of crisis—by the expression, "God Bless America!"

It is said that the initial motto, *E pluribus unum*, was popular among English newspapers in the first half of the eighteenth century, where it was used to recall that the newspaper was the "work of many."[19] But in face of the politico-theological ideal of the "individual," whether as person or as collective, the notion of "plurality" often assumed—and continues to assume—the aspect of an utterly unassimilable heterogeneity and alterity. This specter is then ambivalently associated with technology: ambivalently, because here as elsewhere, technology brings with it and confirms the very dependencies, the very divisibilities that are incommensurable with the ideal of democratic individualism. American literature is haunted by this specter, which indeed often provides it with its very medium. One instance among countless others: Poe's story, "The Man Who Was Used Up." The story tells of the encounter of the narrator with a retired military office, Brevet Brigadier General John A. B. C. Smith. Now although the story is situated in England and its hero is British, what drives the narrative toward its shocking conclusion is that unmistakably American transformation of anxiety into guilt and curiosity. Witness the opening paragraph:

> I cannot just now remember when or where I first made the acquaintance of that truly fine-looking fellow, Brevet Brigadier General John A. B. C. Smith. Some one did introduce me to the gentleman, I am sure—at some public meeting, I know very well—held about something of great importance, no doubt—at some place or other, I feel convinced, whose name I have unaccountably forgotten. The truth is—that the introduction was attended, upon my part, with a degree of anxious embarrassment which operated to prevent any definite impressions of either time or place. I am constitutionally nervous—this, with me, is a family failing, and I can't help it. In especial, the slightest appearance of mystery—of any point I cannot exactly comprehend—puts me at once into a pitiable state of agitation.

The story begins, then, with the recollection of a lapse of memory, concerning the "when and where," the determinate site of the initial encounter, whose "name I have unaccountably forgotten." Such forgetting suggests an "origin" that is more structural than chronological. It gestures towards the kind of indeterminacy that Henry James will explore and exploit in his fiction: the indeterminacy of a significance whose enigmaticity barely overshadows a palpable if intangible threat. For "the truth" is elusive and difficult to locate, impossible to pin down: only its effects are beyond doubt, "a degree of anxious embarrassment" that then, as once again today, is declared to be constitutional and hereditary: "a family failing, and I can't help it." Such a familial heritage has a double effect: it produces "a pitiable state of agitation" that can only be calmed, it seems, by a story: one with a beginning, middle, and above all, an end: an end that serves as a conclusion, rather than as an interruption.

The story that is then told is of a magnificent military figure, "a presence singularly commanding," not just of a person but of a body that exudes strength, dignity and confidence, almost a kind of perfect, classic statue: "unquestionably the finest bust I ever saw. For your life you could not have found a fault with its wonderful proportion." Note the familiarity that links the anxious, agitated narrator with his anonymous readers, whom he appears to know all too well.

And yet the mystery is no less palpable in "the odd air of je ne sais quoi which hung about my new acquaintance." It is as if the "odd air" that so fascinates and concerns the narrator compels him to forsake his native, familiar, domestic English idiom, even though it is with the gesture of demonstrating his cosmopolitan culture. Only such a scope can hope to correspond to the "dignity of colossal proportions" he sees in his hero, who appears increasingly as the living exemplification of the love for monumentality Tocqueville had discerned in America—and that he had shrewdly linked to a certain destitution and vulnerability in its everyday life.

The latter will, of course, constitute the great "discovery" and dénouement of Poe's story, a shock that is somewhat diminished, at least après coup, by its crassly antithetical status with respect to the magnificent, monumental expectations that precede it. The General turns out not to be a Star—not at least, in the sense of the Monument—but an all-too-vulnerable, indeed badly wounded invalid, as the narrator discovers when, with that precipitation born out of panic, recalling the frenetically fervid pursuit of happiness—goods and well-being—described by Tocqueville, he bursts into the General's "bedroom" and discovers not the colossal and majestic figure he had expected, but only:

> a large and exceedingly odd looking bundle of something which lay close by my feet on the floor, and, as I was not in the best humor in the world, I gave it a kick out of the way.

The narrator's bad "humor" and his gesture, giving "it a kick out of the way," sums up the response of a certain individualism to the "odd looking bundle" that doesn't fit in, doesn't meet the expectations of an individual always already on the run from the specter of a past that threatens to overtake the future.

When the "bundle" however cries out in protest, "in one of the smallest, and altogether funniest little voices, between a squeak and a whistle," the narrator is overwhelmed not by laughter but by terror and he seeks to run away:[20]

> I fairly shouted with terror, and make off, at a tangent, into the farthest extremity of the room. "God bless me, my dear fellow!" here again whistled the bundle, "what-what-what-why, what is the matter? I really believe you don't know me at all."

The narrator is speechless with fear and shock, but this only allows "the thing" to observe: "Strange you shouldn't know me though, isn't it?" The implication, which has been carefully cultivated throughout the text, is that despite their ostensible differences and distance, the narrator "knows" the figures whose "mystery" he seeks to elucidate. There are two aspects to this, both of which will be familiar from the previous discussion. First, the General is presented as the Man:

> The kind friend who presented me to General Smith whispered in my ear some few words of comment upon the man. He was a remarkable man—a very remarkable man—indeed one of the most remarkable men of the age.

This "remarkable man," not just Man of the Year but Man of the Age, is remarkable among other reasons because of his history and of his name. His history involves his role as "hero of the Bugaboo and Kickapoo campaign," about which we learn very little, except that it was a "savage affair" and one at the same time that the General himself links to the progress of technology as well as of empire:

> I perceived, too, that the gallant soldier preferred topics of philosophical interest, and that he delighted, especially, in commenting upon the rapid

march of mechanical invention. Indeed, lead him where I would, this was a
point to which he invariably came back.

"There is nothing at all like it," he would say, "we are a wonderful
people, and live in a wonderful age. Parachutes and rail-roads-mantraps
and spring-guns! Our steam-boats are upon every sea. . . . And who shall
calculate the immense influence upon social life—upon arts—upon com-
merce—upon literature—which will be the immediate result of the great
principles of electro-magnetics! Nor is this all, let me assure you! There is
really no end to the march of invention.

At the same time, it is what follows this rather conventional celebration of
science and technology, albeit in relation to their globalizing, and indeed
imperial effects, that turns out to be more distinctive, and strangely
familiar:

The most wonderful—the most ingenious—and let me add, Mr.—Mr.
Thompson, I believe is your name—let me add, I say the most useful—the
most truly useful—mechanical contrivances are daily springing up like
mushrooms, if I may so express myself. . . . Mr. Thompson, *about* us and
ah-ah-ah—*around us*! (my italics)

Of course, the General gets the Narrator's name wrong—"Thompson,
to be sure, is not my name"—but that is also the point. For what he has
to tell him goes beyond the propriety and property of a proper name,
beyond that which might be held to circumscribe the limits of the individual. For the technological inventions that the General describes are all the
more significant, but also more uncanny, in that they are springing up
"about" and "around us," and thereby exposing a medium in which the
bodies of individuals, which have traditionally been viewed as the physical
containers and vessels of their individualities, are now being experienced
differently: namely, as displaceable and exposed components whose significance depends upon an environment that can no longer be taken for
granted. The "individual," like Saussure's signifier, is thus increasingly
determined and defined by everything that is "about" and "around" it,
not "in" it. There "is" nothing left that guarantees the borders of that
"inside," and this is what the colonialist "campaign" against the Bugaboo
and Kickapoo seems to have irrevocably decided, at least for General
Smith. In going out beyond the traditional borders of the homeland to
conquer the world, the heroes discover that they no longer possess anything or anywhere they can securely fall back on and call their own—least
of all their "own" bodies.

Of course, this discovery is already inscribed in the somewhat less than proper name of General Smith, who is at once defined by his military title: Brevet Brigadier General, and by a first and Surname that could not be more generic: John Smith. John Smith, of course, was also the name of the Puritan youth who, in American colonial mythology, fell in love with the Indian maiden, Pocahontas, whom he then married. The encounter of Brevet Brigadier General John Smith with the "savages" is, to be sure, of quite another kind and leaves behind a very different legacy: one that mobilizes all the prosthetic forces of modern technology, science and medicine in order to enable the General to reappear as an integral, integrated individual—but only by virtue of the artificial components that now compose him. By seeking to impose the law of the homeland upon the outside world, the body of the hero survives merely as a patchwork of external elements, reassembled only by virtue of the aid of "the old negro valet," Pompey, for whom the General's dependence is exceeded only by his patronizing and presumably affectionate impatience.

In short, to conclude that the mystery of this particular General can be understood as that of "the man that was used up" is to overlook the specific historical destiny that led to his being used up. Or is it? For a major part of the specificity of that destiny seems to be inseparable from the compulsion to identify a certain Western European notion of male individuality with humanity as such, with "The Man"—a tendency whose resilience the Narrator experiences when, instead of learning more about the General, he is offered the apparently far more entertaining story of "Captain Mann." The Narrator thus feels compelled to get to the bottom of the story of the General, Man of the Age, but at the same time ignores the literal non-sense inscribed in his identifying initials: "A, B, C." Such references to the alphabet only seem to frustrate his search for more "definite information," as when he receives the following response from one of his close friends:

> "Smith!" said he, in his well known peculiar way of drawling out his syllables; "Smith!"—why, not General John A. B. C.? Savage affair that with the Kickapo-o-o-os, wasn't it? . . . By the by, did you ever hear about Captain Ma-a-a-a-n?"

The "drawling out" of the vowels, "Ma-a-a-a-n" accentuates the dismemberment not just of the proper name but also of the generic noun that guarantees the property and propriety of all names and nouns, at the same time as it demonstrates how that process of disintegration calls for yet another "story." And yet, as the friend goes on to suggest, the "other"

story, about "Captain Mann," may well be not so very different from the
story the Narrator is after:

> "Captain Mann be d—d!" said I; "please to go on with your story."
> "Hem!"—oh well!—quite la meme cho-o-ose, as we say in France.

Apparently it helps to go to France to learn that the story of Captain
Mann, and the story of that remarkable man of the age, "Brigadier-Gen-
eral John A. B. C." are "quite la meme chose." "John A. B. C.? Why,
bless me, he's the ma-a-an."

It is this bit of "ungentlemanly conduct and ill breeding" on the part
of his friend that drives the Narrator to finally call upon the General himself, and make the discovery that the Man is a Thing, a "bundle" rather
than the heroic Individual he has been seeking. Like a bundle of letters,
or a bundle of rags in a doorway, a sight that has become all too common
in recent years in the cities frequented by General Smith, Captain Mann
and Edgar Allan Poe, not to mention the Bugaboo and Kickapoo, who at
the time presumably knew little of cities.

"John A. B. C.? Why bless me, he's the ma-a-an—"
God bless Me,
the ma-a-a-n, my, or: Give me a break!

In September 2003, a leading American newspaper carried a front-page
article celebrating a new primary school established by Columbia University. Under the headline "New School is Educators' Dream" the *International Herald Tribune* reported that "the school, which opens Wednesday,
intends to develop individualized learning plans for every student." A
"unified curriculum" for the primary grades has been developed by Marc
Meyer, director of research and curriculum design. Meyer, described as a
"medievalist," said he had constructed his curriculum "around two questions: What does it mean to be a human being? and What does it mean to
be an educated person?" This then translates into the following themes,
to be dealt with progressively from kindergarten through fourth-grade:

> "Me and Myself," "Me and My Family," "Me and My Community," "Me
> and My Country," and "Me and the World." Older students will explore
> the individual's position in society, the clash of culture and civilization and
> the quest for justice and liberty.

"There is nothing new in any of this," Meyer was quoted as stating, while adding that it is "the way it comes together in an educational institution—in an integrated curriculum—that is innovative."

There will probably be little place in such an integrated and innovative curriculum for texts such as "The Man That Was Used Up"—if only by virtue of the crass replacement of the relative personal pronoun, "who" by the impersonal "that." For the "integration" that Marc Meyer, like most good pedagogues, would place at the heart of curricular "innovation" depends, today as it has for centuries, on a certain notion of the "who": of human beings as unified and integral, and therefore ultimately, as The Man, who can see everything in terms of the Self: as "me" and "my."

Perhaps there is a glimpse of hope in the fact that for the fourth grade, at least, "Me" will be confronted no longer by "my" but by "the World." Perhaps. But perhaps it is also just "the" world of the threatening, senseless others, the world of the Kickapoo and Bugaboo, that serve only to kick and bug us and ours? The world outside the homeland we seek to make secure.

The trace of the plurality that was still legible in the nineteenth-century newspaper use of *e pluribus unum* tends today to be increasingly overshadowed by the idea of unity, integrity, indivisibility, figured in the close-up images of "anchor-persons" who present the "news" of the nation and the world on national network television. Or by the carefully composed ethnically representative "teams" that present the "news" of city, state and region on "local" television. In the space-time occupied by these many "ones," little room is left for the unexpected except as the cultivated "break," which, whether as commercial or as "breaking news," reinstates the continuity it punctuates rather than suspends.

CHAPTER 2

Of Debts, Dreams, and Jokes: or, Weberian Theatricality

Simon Morgan Wortham

It might be said that Samuel Weber made his name by writing on psycho-analysis rather than deconstruction. Early texts published in *MLN* and *Glyph* in the 1970s, although by no means devoid of reference to Derrida's work, were to devote attention to various aspects of Freud's writing in particular. Subsequently, it was his two books on psychoanalysis which brought Weber critical acclaim. *Return to Freud: Jacques Lacan's Dislocation of Psychoanalysis* was originally written and published in German in 1978, while *The Legend of Freud* first appeared in 1982. Indeed, Weber's next book, *Institution and Interpretation*, which explores issues of interpretive conflict and their relationship to processes of institutionalization, includes complex and influential writings that draw extensively on readings of psychoanalytic texts. Here, essays such as "Reading and Writing—*chez* Derrida" and "The Debts of Deconstruction and Other, Related Assump-tions" offer critical readings of deconstruction by way of a return to Freud and, indeed, an exploration of Derrida's engagement with him, most nota-bly in *The Post Card*. Of the different texts included in *La Carte postale*, it is perhaps "Spéculer—sur 'Freud'" which is of the most interest, since here Derrida retraces the strategy or scenario of "making a name" for oneself: in the case of psychoanalysis, a "pseudonymic" name which Freud makes for himself, one which confuses species and genre. In various ways, across the body of his writing, Weber shows the importance the *name* of Freud holds for both psychoanalysis and deconstruction—indicating perhaps the irony that Weber's *name* has itself been made by virtue of writings which frequently dwell on the operations, implications and effects of this *other* name: Freud. How this "debt" is to be assumed or repaid, just how it is "owed" and whether indeed it is "owned," poses itself as a question which remains closely tied, of course, to the kinds of readings of psychoanalytic texts, and indeed of "deconstructive" ones, undertaken by Weber.

Since it would be difficult, to say the least, to dispense with them easily, any reader of Weber or Derrida will have occasion to return to these texts on the name and indebtedness of Freud and of psychoanalysis. In brief terms, however, they allow Weber, via Derrida, to ponder the notion that, "in contrast to more traditional sciences and disciplines, psychoanalysis is bound up with the name of its founder" since "its specificity is indissolubly linked to a fundamental indebtedness" ("Borrowing is the law," as Derrida puts it: the law of psychoanalysis, in the multiple sense of such a phrase), so that "something like a proper name is required to hold it together" (this line of enquiry opens up most especially in Weber's essay "The Debts of Deconstruction and Other, Related Assumptions").[1] "But for this very reason," writes Weber, "the 'property' of that name will be even more fragile than is ordinarily the case in regard to the sciences" (108). Indeed, Weber suggests an affinity between, on the one hand, the necessarily fragile reduction of the entire discursive practice of psychoanalysis to the proper name of "Freud" and, on the other, the "noncontingent limitation at work in the Oedipus complex" described by Derrida in *La Carte postale*, whereby the latter—the Oedipus complex—constitutes itself as a "reductive, regulative fiction, a part masquerading as the whole" of what Derrida describes as the "nebulous matrix" of the *fort-da* (106–7). As Derrida points out, what goes under the name of "Oedipus" might be said to distinguish only one of the "threads" or "sons" of this "nebulous matrix, with its chains of fusions or fissions, its permutations and commutations without end, its disseminations without return" (106).[2] Nevertheless, as Weber notes, it becomes extremely difficult to account for such apparently unavoidable or "noncontingent" reduction, when just such reduction would seem to be "the condition of the possibility of *accounting* in general" (107). This aporetical situation surrounds the oedipal reduction being discussed here, but also presumably envelops the circumstances in which the complexly and unstably interwoven matrices of "psychoanalysis" are reduced to the name of Freud. From this point onward, then, the "noncontingency" under discussion means that one cannot dispense with an account of, as Weber puts it, "the manner in which an irresistible process of repetition assumes the aspect and the allure of a *proper name*" (108). Yet such repetition is one of the *fort-da* discerned, as we have just seen, in psychoanalysis, which more specifically plays itself out in a process of doubling which ties the conditions of *possibility* of the account to the conditions of *impossibility* of accounting itself (since an account can happen only on condition of the very same reduction which the account is itself required to describe or explain). If the proper name acquires its "allure" only via a process of reduction which ties it to a repetition that must be accounted for *as a function of the reduction that gives us the proper name*, and yet for which one can never adequately account, then the fragility of the proper name in regard to the "nebulous matrix" that provides its setting suggests not just impossible possibilities, but also imposes relations of desire, debt, disavowal, possessiveness, guilt—in this "interminable story," as Derrida has put it, of the making of a name.

Derrida's argument is that Freud anticipates the fragility of the proper name in regard to this "nebulous matrix" with its "disseminations without return," and he seeks to overcome it by attempting or pretending to prepay what Derrida terms "the charges of a return-to-the-sender" (108).[3] Such a strategy nevertheless engages a disparate variety of techniques. Sometimes Freud is driven to assert his independence of mind, and thereby to confirm the self-authorizing legitimacy of his psychoanalysis, by denying or dismissing its indebtedness—to Nietzsche, for example; while, on other occasions, the debts of psychoanalysis would seem to be acknowledged so readily and entirely, assumed so radically and absolutely, that they appear quite irredeemable, quite unrepayable. For Derrida, the debt is thus rendered "either infinite or insolvent" (109),[4] so that the very notion of "debt" henceforth tends to lose its force. The distinctiveness of Weber's essay, however, consists in his attempt to dispute this idea that a debt thus generalized to an infinite degree ("Borrowing is the law") comes to be more or less invalidated and effectively inoperative. For the discussion of reduction and repetition in respect of the "nebulous matrix" and the proper name suggests that, once the notion of debt begins to lose its force, so too would the dynamic and unstable energies that impel and, indeed, compel the (impossible) process of accounting—including an account such as the one given in "Spéculer—sur 'Freud'" by Derrida himself. Debt, for Weber, is not so easily dispatched. Rather, he turns to Nietzsche's discussion of *Schuld*—debt, and guilt—in *The Genealogy of Morals*.

Nietzsche is able to uncover an historical shift from the notion of *Schuld* as redeemable debt to that of *Schuld* as unredeemable guilt. This, in turn, allows for Nietzsche's hypothesis on the origin of "the guilty conscience." The "guilty conscience" is tied to the resentment that develops out of a noble or aristocratic culture, in the process undermining the opposition between nobility and *ressentiment* that more generally structures Nietzsche's text. The transition from an "older," more "material" notion of *Schuld* as repayable debt to that of *Schuld* as irredeemable guilt occurs when an unproblematic standard of measurement or equivalence is lost. But how is it lost? "It is striking to note," says Weber, "that this loss, the key component of the genealogy Nietzsche is developing, coincides with the emergence, precisely, of something like a genealogical consciousness" (116). This perhaps gives us occasion to recall once more the aporetical condition of *accounting* in general, as that which inevitably involves a certain *repetition*—doubling itself, here, in the "genealogy of resentment" as the explanation of *loss*: from such relations unavoidably arise those of debt, loss, and guilt, as we have already seen. Such devastating loss, giving rise to the "guilty conscience," then, is to be associated with the emergence of a "consciousness" which itself partakes of and impels that which it describes: "the genealogy of resentment." The origin of this consciousness, however, is identified by Nietzsche with the self-interpretation of the identity of the community, which takes shape on the basis of an acknowledgement of a debt owed to the ancestors of the present generation. As the community develops and prospers, so the debt grows to disproportionate proportions: it becomes *immeasurable*. Far from discharging the duty owed to the forefathers, the accomplishments of the community place it ever deeper in debt, so that, as Nietzsche tells us, "in the end the ancestor must necessarily be transfigured into a *god*" (117)[5]—the origin of the self-identity of the community henceforth being located *elsewhere*—a god who is to be *feared* as much as revered. That the transition from *Schuld* to *Schuld*, from repayable debt to irredeemable guilt, is so smoothly narrativized here may serve to mask Nietzsche's complicity with the interpretive violence of a "genealogical consciousness" which itself coincides with the emergence of resentment. In this light, *The Genealogy of Morals* can be seen to partake of that which it describes, therefore becoming an example of the "phenomenon" whose origin, rather like that of the indebted and guilt-ridden community itself, is situated elsewhere. This calls us to rethink the terms in which we might approach Nietzsche's account of the origin of the "guilty conscience," of course.

For Weber, none the less, Nietzsche's interweaving of guilt and debt "should sensitize us to the possibilities of dealing with *Schuld* other than those of affirmation or resignation" (120)—*pace* Derrida. For Nietzsche's account of the spiraling generalization of unredeemable debt, and the manner in which his genealogy partakes of the structure and effects of debt-guilt that it describes, certainly does not entail, as Weber puts it, the "neutralization or nullification" (120) of debt—on the contrary, in fact! *The Genealogy of Morals* calls us to witness the interplay between guilt and debt playing itself out via "the irreducible reference to a certain alterity" (120): for instance, to the manmade gods of resentment's "guilty conscience"; or indeed, via *another* scene of origination, to the deities called forth in the "prehistorical" world so as to witness the spectacle of suffering by which "compensation" is conspicuously extracted from the indebted other; or even to the "genealogy of resentment" to which Nietzsche's "guilty conscience" may be indebted. In all these examples, the subject of debt—both "oneself" and an "other," thus acquiring the uncanny aspect of a revenant that never fully returns—must continue to participate in (although never quite "own") a guilt-debt that persists and proliferates in the very play of the affirmation and cancellation of debts. The returning force of alterities that never quite come home means that debts can neither simply be settled nor easily dispatched, but may be assumed via a movement that "retrace[s] one's dislocation by forces that one can neither determine nor identify; to 'assume,' in this sense, is both to admit an irreducible dependency, and also to refuse that dependency as a mere 'assumption': to recognize the 'other' at the very moment one tries to take hold of it" (126). Since one cannot merely "assume" debt so as to smoothly assimilate or incorporate the "other" on which one depends, debt—even, and perhaps especially, assumed debt—is always going to be, in a certain sense, the debt of another. Such "irreducible reference to a certain alterity" which structures the relations of *Schuld* therefore means that the process of assumption can never just entail "taking on," but is inevitably also one of "taking off," to borrow terms Weber has used on a number of occasions. In this sense, Weber's speculations on debt begin to translate themselves into the postal code, recasting debt as part of "a structure of alteration without opposition": one of a certain circulation that never quite comes full circle, *tele* rather than *telos*. For even if the letter is returned to the sender, this does not resolve the question of debt: who pays the return postage, if not generally the postal system itself, which therefore tends never quite to "make ends meet"? Weber's debts, Derrida's debts, Freud's debts, Nietzsche's debts, other debts, debts of the other: perhaps these may be assumed, although never quite "owned" in the multiple sense of such a term, when they are translated into the postal code, where debts never entirely devolve upon either the sender or the addressee, but remain part of a (non-totalizable) system whose accounts are ongoing, never quite achieving balance or closure.

Freud's Psychoanalysis: Conflict and Debt

What, then, of those indebted to Freud, or to Freud's psychoanalysis?

Such a question arises from the very beginning of Weber's *The Legend of Freud*. Here, Weber establishes his point of departure by tracing the history of the founding of the International Psychoanalytic Association (IPA) in 1910, the defection of Alfred Adler just one year later, and, within a further two years, the break with Jung, upon whom Freud had intended to "transfer" his authority. As the official association of those connected with Freud's psychoanalytic movement, the IPA was established, Weber tells us, primarily to act as a "supreme tribunal,"[6] committed less to challenging misrepresentations of psychoanalysis from without, than to distinguishing psychoanalysis proper from what were tended to be seen as rogue contenders or impostors within the field of psychological investigation. Weber therefore implies that the background to the establishment of the IPA might be explained less in terms of the hostility encountered by psychoanalysis at the turn of the twentieth century, than by the extent of its popularization during the prewar years. But how is it possible to account for the splits and conflicts that so rapidly came to characterize the early years of the IPA, as the very institution that was specifically intended to maintain and promote the unity, identity, and integrity of the psychoanalytic movement itself? The efforts made by Ernest Jones to explain away the frictions and increasing disunity among the psychoanalytic community as simply, in Weber's terms, "a kind of infantile malady . . . destined to disappear with increasing maturity" (36), begin to founder alongside Jones's own admission that, in contrast with the other scientific disciplines, the results of psychoanalytic investigation were in fact particularly susceptible to subjective interpretation. Here, perhaps unwittingly, Jones's insight opens up the possibility of a perspective that both surpasses and incorporates the question of the individual competencies or deficiencies of practitioners of a relatively new "science," so as to suggest that in structural terms the very institution of psychoanalysis itself gives rise to the possibility of conflict and disarray.

Attending to the question of the loss of Jung in 1913, Weber centers on the term Freud himself used to describe his intention to assign authority to his protégé: "transference." However, with the defection of Jung, such transference happens "negatively," with a concomitant reversal of roles normally expected in the analytic situation *qua* therapy. Now, it is the transferring subject—Freud himself—who acts in a conscious and voluntary way, while the "object" of the transfer—that is, Jung—remains hamstrung by unconscious drives or motives. Or so Freud would have us believe. Here, as Weber tells us, the "force of the unconscious, by implication, manifests itself . . . not in the act of transferring, but in the refusal to accept what is being transferred" (37). Yet, of course, such a "refusal" in a situation explicitly described as one of "transference" cannot help but call into question the supposedly authoritative procedures and processes of psychoanalysis itself, especially when the transferring subject here is Freud himself, and the subject of transference is nothing less than his authority. Faced with this obvious challenge not just to his supremacy but to the legitimacy of the claims of Freudian psychoanalysis, Freud nonetheless states an explicit preference for avoiding polemical denunciation of his erstwhile disciples—although, as Weber goes on to demonstrate, while Freud aspires merely to distinguishing and demarcating psychoanalysis proper in relation to variant psychological theories, unavoidably he succumbs to the temptation to devalue other, competing ideas and practices. Nevertheless, Freud's reasons for wanting to defend psychoanalysis in a more disinterested and dispassionate way could hardly be clearer. As Weber puts it, psychoanalysis, "although a theory of conflict, is according to Freud itself a most unsuitable medium of conflict" (38). Polemical exchanges, of the kind Freud ostensibly wishes to avoid, inevitably tend to reduce and confound the clear-cut roles of the analyst as "superior" and the analysand as "subordinate," as dictated by the analytical situation. As Freud himself observes, if the analyst yields to polemical interpretation, then the validity of his analytical insights risks being subsumed under the force of polemical counterinterpretation on the part of the analysand, up to the point where it is no longer possible for an impartial third party to determine the truth of the matter. Such a scenario would, of course, severely jeopardize the authority (of psychoanalysis) that is here in the process of being defended. Yet if, as Weber tells us, Freud's psychoanalysis cannot help but be drawn into the very confrontation which, for perfectly good reasons, it wishes to avoid, then the question is: Why?

Returning to Freud's project of distinguishing psychoanalysis proper from other psychological hypotheses and explanations, Weber detects—in the very effort to describe how the theories of Adler and Jung depart from the essential foundations of psychoanalytic doctrine—a more fundamental distinction at work in the Freudian text, having to do with "the very mode of thinking that produces theoretical insight" (40). Thus Freud discounts the Adlerian "system" as (in contrast to psychoanalysis) too systematic, seeking to incorporate and explain an array of "objects" and phenomena within a general and unified "theory" which, according to Freud, scarcely wishes to acknowledge the extent of its limits. For Freud, Adler's theory therefore functions along the lines of "secondary revision," of the kind to which the dream-work subjects dream-material. "Secondary revision" names the operation by which, in Weber's terms, "a semblance of rationality, a specious intelligibility" (42) is discerned in the "material" of the dream. Far from allowing disclosure or explication of the original or ultimate meaning of the dream itself, then, secondary revision works to conceal the dissimulation of the dream, "reorganizing and presenting its material in a manner that seems to conform to the logical and rational expectations of the waking mind" (42), as Weber puts it, so as to render the dream "acceptable," while at the same time throwing the dreamer entirely off the scent. Hence, so far as Freud is concerned, the "result is that precisely those dreams that seem most coherent and transparent are in reality the most deceptive" (42).

Reading across a variety of Freud's texts, Weber finds that psychoanalysis tells the story of the historical appearance of systematic thinking, first of all in terms of the rise of animism. Animism, for Freud, entails the effort to reduce the universe to a single unity, to be apprehended from the sole viewpoint of animism itself. However, as Weber tells us, the "animistic attempt to comprehend the external world in terms of unity and totality corresponds to the newly formed unity within the psyche: the narcissistic ego" (42). By organizing and interpreting the world in terms of a unifying intelligibility such as is demanded by the emergence of the ego, systematic thought reveals itself to be narcissistic as much in origin as in design. And if Adler's theory is too systematic, and thus an exemplary case of "secondary revision," for Freud it thereby suggests itself as a prime example of the narcissistic ego reacting to defend its inevitably fragile and specious cohesion against the centripetal energies or dislocating dynamics of the conflictual force-field from which it emerges: that of the unconscious. It almost goes without saying, of course, that this sounds like the most ingenious way imaginable to entirely discredit a competing psychological theory—henceforth, Adlerianism can be deemed to be not merely ignorant of that about which it speaks, but actually complicit in the kinds of deception that keep us all in the dark!

However, such an explanation or interpretation of the Adlerian "system" and its deficiencies hardly leaves Freudian psychoanalysis in a comfortable position, for a number of reasons. At the most obvious level, the theoretical aspects of psychoanalytic hypothesis or explanation henceforth become as problematic to defend or, indeed, to assume as they are impossible to eschew or discount. Moreover, the unavoidably systematic quality of psychoanalytic investigation can hardly be divorced from the unifying or integrative intelligence of "a point of view" (and in *The Interpretation of Dreams*, Freud himself does not balk at acknowledging this very same connection, although of course he is much less reflective in uncritically adopting the standpoint of the male ego in his description of the castration complex); a "point of view" that psychoanalysis itself considers a dissimulation of the kind undertaken by "secondary revision" in regard to the dissimulations of the unconscious. On the other hand, if it is Adler or the Adlerian "system" that Freud associates with "secondary revision," in contrast to Freudian psychoanalysis, which founds itself on the unconscious, then it is not just the case that the defector conceals his dependency on that which comes to be associated with the authority of Freudianism. For even if psychoanalysis proper were to be allied more closely with the unconscious than with the processes of "secondary revision" (which must nevertheless be considered indispensable to its rational and scientific disposition), then the unconscious, it must be recalled, is responsible for dissimulating its operations in the dissimulation practiced by secondary revision. As Weber notes, this would imply that, "as with the unconscious, the interests of psychoanalysis, as an institution, would depend on a certain kind of self-dissimulation, just as the dream, to fulfill its function, must dissimulate *both* its true nature, and also *that* it so dissimulates" (47). To align Freudianism with the unconscious would therefore seem to provide no more solid a foundation from which to discount the Adlerian "system," or, for that matter, any competing theoretical knowledge or analytical practice. Indeed, to follow this path would result, however paradoxical it may seem, in a similar situation to the one we might expect if psychoanalysis simply proposed itself as somehow a "better" system than that of Adler. For in either case, psychoanalysis risks acknowledging its basis in deception, concealment, duplicity. And either way (even at the point of any such self-recognition), psychoanalysis cannot help involving itself in a self-deception: whether it seeks to comprehend and master the unconscious through rational and systematic thought or investigation; or whether it pretends to forego such rationality in the interests of a closer affinity with the unconscious—which, in *The Interpretation of Dreams*, Freud himself construes less as an origin or latent content, than a "particular *form* of thinking" (102)[7] which always and everywhere dissimulates its intractably deformative character by creating a representational façade, a semblance of intelligibility.

The conflictual force-field of the unconscious, wherein unstoppable processes of deformation or decomposition are continually dissimulated, giving rise to the fulfillment of wishes that nevertheless remain hopelessly conflict-ridden and self-deceiving just where things seem to become lucid, can therefore also be taken to characterize the institution of psychoanalysis, regarding not only its structural propensity towards conflict, division, and disarray, but relating also to those effects of duplicity, blindness and ambivalence that attend the polemical cross fire by which its identity and authority come to be posited, defended, and challenged. And, of course, this returns us to the question of debt. For in the vicinity of this conflictual force-field that so characterizes the institution of psychoanalysis, *Schuld* (guilt-debt) remains and redoubles itself in the very play of the affirmation and cancellation of debts, playing itself out amid a heterogeneous series of effects: transference, defection, authority, polemic, and (underlying all these, perhaps) the wish-fulfillment of the narcissistic ego and its nevertheless ineluctable dependency on an alterity that can never satisfactorily be reduced to the image of an outsider. (Elsewhere in *The Legend of Freud*, Weber therefore succinctly observes that "psychoanalytic theory sets itself apart in an ambivalent movement that both disperses itself in categories that overlap and converge with each other, and at the same time projects its constitutive dislocation as an outward movement of heretical divergences, as a 'falling away' (*Abfallsbewegung*) it can then appear to confront and condemn" [61].) Here, then, the subject of debt in regard to Freud's psychoanalysis (both "oneself" and the "other") acquires, once again, the uncanny aspect of a revenant which, like the unconscious itself, never quite succeeds in returning (to itself). The force of alterities that *remain* yet never quite come home (and the "unconscious" may be only one among a possible host of names we could assign here), mean that the debts of "psychoanalysis," the debts to or of "Freud," can neither easily be settled nor simply renounced. Psychoanalysis, in a certain sense, is more or less nothing other than *Schuld*. To assess Weber's debts to Freud, entailing a reading of his work on Freudian texts, involves us in—obliges us to draw upon—a line of thinking about psychoanalytic theory and writing, in which the question of such indebtedness only registers itself in an account of the debts of psychoanalysis—an account which, as we've just seen, could never be closed or balanced. That is to say, Weber's debts to psychoanalysis can hardly be accounted for, without acknowledging an intractable obligation to account for the debts *to*, *for*, or *of* psychoanalysis "itself"—debts which, since they can never be entirely "owned" (possessed or repossessed, held or withheld, admitted, submitted or acknowledged, construed as "property" or a "property" of) can hardly hope to be settled (settled up, settled upon). Once more, then, such debts devolve neither simply upon the sender nor the addressee, but remain part of a (nontotalizable) "system"—a postal code—whose accounts are always ongoing. And since, if we want to assess Weber's debts to psychoanalysis, we are obliged to draw upon or to credit the line (a line of credit?) Weber takes in relation to the question of psychoanalysis's debts (for on what account could there be foreclosure here?), our "indebtedness" must become an inextricable part of the accounting that is going on.

Which is to say, such indebtedness cannot be overlooked; although, of course, neither can it be overlooked in the "other" sense that it cannot ever be definitively grasped, located, comprehended, mastered, acknowledged or accounted for from a single or transcendent "point of view." In the vicinity of debates about the debts of or to psychoanalysis, that much is clear. So that the (structural) necessity and impossibility of overlooking our indebtedness here only repeats and renews, rather than resolves, the (entire question of) debt.

Indebtedness: To and of the Joke

As everyone knows, the joke is pretty much over the moment someone tries to explain it to you. If, as Freud contends, the essential characteristic of a joke remains inseparable from the burst of laughter it occasions, then what is distinctive about it simply cannot be done justice, cannot adequately be accounted for, in the aftermath or absence of the laugh (which itself radically interrupts the capacity of explanation so far as the conscious, rational subject or individual is concerned). Yet, if a joke is genuinely a joke, its true measure is that we cannot help *but* laugh—although, in that uncontrollable instant, we cannot ever truly know exactly what it is we are laughing at. In structural terms, therefore, the joke bears some of the hallmarks we've associated with debt or indebtedness. When it happens, our laughter implies that the joke can no more be affirmed than it can be denied. It simply cannot be overlooked, in the double sense of this term. If the joke is, necessarily, over in an instant, the necessarily impossible prospect of overlooking it means that it must nevertheless somehow remain or persist: the joke is in fact far from exhausted when the laughter dies away. Yet this "persistence" of the joke cannot be construed along the lines of the kind of repetition that would permit recognition of the joke's self-identity. For, far from impelling a renewed explosion of laughter, the repetition—in a conventional sense—of the joke would cause it to implode. If it is never quite exhausted by the laughter it occasions, and without which, Freud tells us, it simply cannot *be*, the joke somehow *goes on*, precisely at the expense of closure, balance, accounting, and recounting (in other words, at the expense of its own self-identity). Which is to say that the joke—if it is a joke (which, of course, it can never simply *be*)—depends irredeemably upon a situation of incalculable debt. And that such a situation of debt (the debts of, to or for psychoanalysis, for instance) may, likewise, be considered a joke.

But at whose expense *is* the joke? And who does it leave in debt? Freud? Weber? Another, us, anyone? If we've already suggested that debts such as those of psychoanalysis can never be "owned," but that the subject of debt is always both "oneself" and an "other," let us recall nonetheless that Weber disputes the idea he finds in Derrida, that the radical generalization of debt tends to neutralize or nullify indebtedness so far as anyone is concerned. Notwithstanding the finally unaccountable movement or spiraling circulation of indebtedness (somewhat akin to the amplifying volume of spasmodic explosions of laughter, to which one is forced to attend but which one can never really "understand"), the debt, like the joke, must always be "on" someone. Although upon whom exactly the joke (or, indeed, the debt) actually *is*—since it never quite *is*—may not ever be entirely clear.

Weber's writings on Freudian texts pay a great deal of attention to Freud's treatment of the problems associated with laughter and joking, so that the issue of Weber's indebtedness to Freud can no more overlook the question of the joke in or for psychoanalysis, than that of debt itself. (Of course, the joke doesn't just crop up "in" psychoanalysis or, indeed, "in" Weber's writings "on" Freud. Jokes are always "on," in the sense that they are "at the expense of.") Essays on laughing and joking in *The Legend of Freud* can be related to a wider body of work on the topic, including articles such as "The Divaricator: Remarks on Freud's *Witz*,"[8] published in the very first edition of *Glyph* in 1977, and "Laughing in the Meanwhile," appearing in *MLN* in 1987. In "The Divaricator," Weber examines Freud's theory of the *Witz* so as to ask: "does meaning constitute *an* or even *the* essential dimension of the joke?" (15). Initially, Freud wants to insist that what is fundamental to the joke concerns its form rather than its content, not least since jokes reactivate "the childish pleasure of pure play" (15), as Weber puts it, seeking liberation from the restraints of the order and logic of "meaning." Meaning, indeed, only comes into play as a ruse of the joke, distracting or assuaging the forces of reason so as to eliminate the obstructions posed by reason's inhibitionary character. Elsewhere, in "Jokes and Their Relation to the Unconscious," however, Freud draws a distinction between the jest and the full-blown joke in terms of the "substance and value" (16)[9]—the meaning—which may be accorded the latter. In the context of this apparent tension underlying the Freudian conception or determination of the joke, Weber turns to the phenomenon of nonsense jokes. The nonsense joke, argues Freud, is less hostile than merely indifferent to the laws and logic of meaning. However, in a footnote to this particular discussion, Freud asserts both that the joke draws its force simply from a frolicsome style of play that is nonchalantly indifferent to meaning, and that it continues to be motivated by the ruse or lure of a semblance of intelligibility, which deliberately panders to reason's demands in order more radically to subvert or suspend its inhibitions. At this point, Freud turns to the kinds of jokelike productions that seem to present us with mere "silliness in the guise of wit" (18).[10] Such quasi-jokes, to which Freud assigns the name *Aufsitzer*, serve, he tells us, to "rouse the expectation of a joke, so that one tries to find a concealed sense behind the nonsense. But one finds none: they really are nonsense" (18).[11] Nevertheless, as Weber points out, such jokes cannot be entirely nonsensical, due to the very fact that they can be attributed a purpose: to dupe the audience, not merely to convey the joke but to play one upon the listener. Furthermore, for Freud, this purpose may even be related to that of an intention on the part of the teller of the joke, who achieves a certain degree of pleasure in "taking in" his audience, irritating the hearer by purposefully leading him up a blind alley. The teller of the nonsense joke, therefore, would seem to have no "object" other than, as Weber puts it, "the calculated deception of another subject, who has only the possibility of recouping his losses by himself repeating the tale" (19). This obviously has consequences for a psychoanalytic theory of jokes, especially since the *Aufsitzer*, in seeming to combine an ultimate indifference to meaning with the aggressive deception of reason, cannot merely be relegated to the sidelines of Freudian theory, but instead might be considered the best, rather than the worst, of all possible jokes. For if the nonsense joke is, in a sense, "the" joke par excellence, nevertheless psychoanalysis simply could not help but be "taken in" if it were to take the *Aufsitzer* as a privileged or exemplary "object" (in the classical sense) of theoretical knowledge and rational description. The *Aufsitzer* would have the last laugh at the expense of psychoanalysis, which itself could only hope to recoup its losses by repeating the tale in a way that ensured its audience was similarly "taken in." Yet, of course, the costs of such a strategy would be as incalculable for psychoanalysis as they would remain unavoidable. Here, as Weber tells us, the "most conspicuous effect would be to reinscribe the subject of theory, and of interpretation, in the charged context of an operation of storytelling, which splits the unified subject of theory into the duplicity of the narrator and the delusion of the listener: each, in some sense, a mirror-image of the other and each engaged in a most ambivalent game" (19).

If the operations and effects of the *Aufsitzer* are strongly reminiscent of the processes of secondary revision that characterize the self-deluding aspects of all systematic thought or theoretical discourse, then the relation of the *Aufsitzer* to psychoanalysis carries implications and importance going far beyond the particular concerns of Freud's theory of the joke. The *Aufsitzer*, impossible to relegate to merely a supplementary consideration or specific region of psychoanalytic investigation, once more involves psychoanalysis in incalculable expenditure or expense, interminable recouping, irredeemable debt, beyond all possible recounting, accounting, balance, or closure. Yet, as should be obvious by now, the question of indebtedness in regard to the *Aufsitzer* cannot be confined to the concerns of psychoanalysis alone. Debts of the kind incurred by the *Aufsitzer* cannot so easily be accounted for.

In *The Legend of Freud*, Weber suggests that the closest translation in English for the *Aufsitzer* is "shaggy-dog story," and he ends a long chapter devoted to this very topic by retelling what appears to be just such a "story," one that, he informs us, "I heard many years ago and at which, if I remember correctly, I once laughed" (156). However inconclusive it may be to finish with such an anecdote or joke—especially, as we shall see, given the "substance" of the tale—the *Aufsitzer*, as we know, invites reasoned explanation or the attribution of conclusive meaning only to have a last laugh on the listener or interpreter, reinscribing theoretical description, determination or formulation as merely storytelling, and leaving the recipient or subject of the *Aufsitzer* little choice but to recount the tale amid (or, indeed, *as*) incalculable relations of expense and expenditure, recouping, debt. Perhaps it is no wonder, then, that Weber's chapter "ends" in this way. In this context, the "substance" of the "story" with which Weber "concludes" is as pertinent as the timing of its delivery:

A Jew and a Pole are sitting opposite one another in a train. After some hesitation, the Pole addresses the Jew: "Itzig, I've always been a great admirer of your people, and especially of your talents in business. Tell me, honestly, is there some trick behind it all, something I could learn?" The Jew, after a moment's surprise, replies: "Brother, you may well have something there. But you know, you don't get anything for nothing—it'll cost you." "How much?" asks the Pole. "Five zlotys," answers the Jew. The Pole nods eagerly, reaches for his wallet and pays the Jew. The latter puts the money away and begins to speak: "You will need a large whitefish, caught by yourself if possible; you must clean it, pickle it, put it in a jar, and then bury it at full moon in the ground where your ancestors lie. Three full moons must pass before you return to the spot and dig it out. . . ." "And then?" replies the Pole, puzzled: "is that all?" "Not quite," smiles the Jew in response. "There are still a few things to be done." And, after a moment's pause: "But it will cost you." The Pole pays, the Jew speaks, and so it goes on from Cracow to Lemberg. The Pole grows increasingly impatient, and finally, having paid all his money to the Jew, he explodes: "You dirty Yid! Do you think I don't know your game?! You take me for a fool, and my money to boot—*that's* your precious secret!" And the Jew, smiling benignly: "But Brother, what do you want? Don't you see—it's working already!" (156)

Since Weber merely narrates rather than interprets this shaggy-dog story, I will forego close analysis or thoroughgoing interpretation of my own, which in any case would inevitably fall foul of the snares and ruses of the *Aufsitzer* as much as it might hope to shed light upon the meaning or "substance" of the tale. If indeed there is any ultimate "substance" or meaning, independent of the form the joke itself takes. (Although, for one thing, it should be noted that tales of Jews, Poles, and trains certainly seem to demand shrewd and careful analysis in the politico-ideological field, analysis of a kind Weber clearly does not feel prepared to venture at this particular point, undoubtedly because of the immense complications involved in approaching such a task precisely in the vicinity of the *Aufsitzer*.) For the story undoubtedly involves and recounts incalculable relations of expense, indebtedness, and recouping of the kind we might associate with the *Aufsitzer* itself: the duplicitous recounting of the Jew leaves the Pole both completely out of pocket, and yet utterly indebted for the lesson, which tells him how to "recoup"—and perhaps better—his losses at the expense of another (although also, by implication, to the ultimate *benefit* of this other). The "meaning" or "substance" of the story may therefore be nothing other than that of the *Aufsitzer* itself; and yet what the story shows us, if anything, is that the *Aufsitzer* proceeds (and profits) only by way of a series of red herrings (conveying a semblance of meaning, substance or intelligibility) designed to throw the listener off the scent. If we are tempted to suggest the meaning of the story is somehow an "economical" one, then not only are its precise economics far from simple to account for, but they constitute the proceeds of the *Aufsitzer* itself, which no one can easily calculate or recount.[12]

No less pertinent, however, is the question of just who recounted this story, first heard by Weber "many years ago." It was, we are told in a footnote, none other than Jacques Derrida. At least, if Weber remembers correctly—for by his own admission he cannot be sure of the circumstances surrounding the joke, told him so very long ago, including whether or not he laughed. (To recall laughter is also, in a sense, to acknowledge its irredeemable loss amid the transitoriness that characterizes at least one aspect of joking, so that such recollection must necessarily also entail a certain lapse of memory or forgetting, albeit of that which was never truly "known" or "understood" on the occasion of laughter.) And how do we know Weber is even *trying* to tell the truth about this tale? He prefaces its delivery by acknowledging (or, at least, by *feigning* to acknowledge) "my frustration at so much uncertainty" (156) surrounding the joke and the *Aufsitzer*, and he resolves to "mute" this very same frustration precisely by retelling the tale. If he were indeed being serious or artless here, this assertion would place Weber firmly in the position of one upon whom the *Aufsitzer* has had the last laugh, and who can only vent his irritation by recounting the shaggy-dog story in a way that allows the loss to be recouped (or bettered) at the expense of another. Indeed, the entire import of his discussion of the *Aufsitzer* seems to allow for no other conclusion. And yet, if Weber is, indeed, now cast in the role of the storyteller of the *Aufsitzer*, just how easy would it be to separate and distinguish his genuine purpose or intent from the ruse or lure that characterizes the *Aufsitzer* itself? Is Weber serious or is he only joking when he implies that, due to his frustration with the subject-matter at hand, he would prefer the last laugh of the *Aufsitzer* to be on us rather than him (albeit a last laugh from which, like the Pole, we might ultimately benefit)? To convey as much, in a spirit of utmost honesty or sincerity, would hardly be the best preparation for a "good" joke, which as we know depends on the lures and traps associated with the *Aufsitzer*. Indeed, since we know that the *Aufsitzer* involves a situation in which the duped listener soon turns duplicitous storyteller, we may wonder whether the joke has already started before it has begun—right here, in the midst of apparently genuine acknowledgement or sincere revelation of the *Aufsitzer*'s "frustrations." In the most obvious sense, Weber is joking during the recounting of this little shaggy-dog story; but as the recipient or subject of the *Aufsitzer*, isn't he also, in a necessary or structural sense, joking beforehand? In this respect, Weber's retelling of "Derrida's" shaggy-dog story as obviously a joke may, unless we are careful, throw us off the scent of another joke being played here. Of course, where the *Aufsitzer* is concerned, we can never really know for sure. But the undeniable possibility of this opening of the borders of the joke or of joking certainly casts doubt upon Weber's apparently ingenuous claim (which comes afterward, in a footnote) that the joke was told him by Derrida. Which causes us to wonder what sort of acknowledgment of debt would it be (unless one were joking), to name or identify Derrida as the— necessarily duplicitous—joke-teller, and perhaps even to imply that Weber's indebtedness to Derrida might somehow be bound up with the latter's aptitude for joking as a species or instrument of duplicity? Clearly, one might be prompted to take this "moment" in Weber's writing less as a naïve reinscription of the grounds and terms by which Derrida has been criticized, condemned, or dismissed (laughed at?) over "many years," than as a playful and irreverent response to more simplistic versions of the master-disciple relation, according to which the connection of these two thinkers might otherwise be understood. Yet even here, in asserting this explanation or interpretation, we should beware of the ruses and lures that constitute the *Aufsitzer* as a perhaps more elaborate joke, one that is played precisely at the expense of intelligibility's self-delusions. That is to say, one cannot take for granted the possibility of determining the indebtedness of Weber to Derrida according to the motif of the *Aufsitzer*, since the intelligibility of this motif may itself be a ruse of the *Aufsitzer*. For this very "reason," the notion impresses itself upon us once more that Weber may be joking (whether or not, indeed, he means to) when he declares Derrida to be the one who told him the joke.

Yet if the *Aufsitzer* is nonetheless at play here (and we could never be sure, once and for all, since the *Aufsitzer* can no more be determined as a clear-cut "object" of recognition, than the relations of the "sensical" and the "nonsensical" which ostensibly constitute its specific form can ever be convincingly demarcated or stabilized), then this play has, as perhaps its most telling consequence, the effect of reinscribing "the subject of theory, and of interpretation, in the charged context of an operation of storytelling, which splits the unified subject of theory into the duplicity of the narrator and the delusion of the listener: each, in some sense, a mirror-image of the other and each engaged in a most ambivalent game" (19).

Such a game would be all the more tellingly ambivalent since it does not function to posit two clearly differentiated participants engaged in a tactical struggle, however complex this may be: the duplicitous narrator on the one hand (Derrida, perhaps, or Weber), and the deluded listener turned storyteller on the other (Weber, perhaps, or even ourselves). More fundamentally, it "splits the unified subject" in a "highly charged context" of storytelling's manifold operations, in which duping and duplicity, fooling and being fooled, can never quite be articulated or defined as distinct and separate qualities, properties, or intentions, but remain intractably entangled in and by one another. We can never finally tell who is being duped and who is being deceitful, since (to return to the language and problematic of debt) any such recounting or accounting is itself always incalculably split. Amid the effort of such tale-telling, "one" may well dupe "another" but also (inseparably) deceive, delude and divide "oneself."[13]

Theatricality and Parergon

The ultimately undecidable limits or deconstructible framework of the joke recalls the Kantian problem of aesthetic form, such as it is treated by Derrida in *The Truth in Painting*, which in fact remains decisive for Weber in unraveling the relations of form, technics, institutions, and theater. The delineation and hence the demarcation of an object, upon which the very conception of aesthetic form depends, requires the contour or frame (of the "work," for example) to be clearly distinguished, and to remain distinguishable. Henceforth, however, the frame itself appears to have a constitutive function, serving as the very enabling limit of the work. Kant, of course, wishes to downplay the importance of the frame as neither proper nor essential to the form of the aesthetic object. Yet in attempting to distinguish between "frame" and "form" so as to be able to take the latter as a standpoint or basis from which to judge—and from which to dismiss—the aesthetic value or pertinence of the frame, Kant alludes to an a priori conception of form, the legitimacy of which remains in question since its form as a concept cannot yet have been properly delineated, preceding as it does the supposedly secondary term of the "limit," border, or frame. The "frame" must therefore remain an indispensable element in the composition of "form," and thus cannot be distinguished or excluded so decisively in relation to the formal properties of the aesthetic object. The very concept of form, and, indeed, the very form of the concept, cannot be exempted from that which would appear to set it apart. Yet the fact that the "limit" or "edge" of the work irreducibly partakes of and participates in the "form" which it would otherwise serve to particularize means that, as Weber tells us in his essay "The Unraveling of Form," "just this participation would require another frame"[14] for the aesthetic object to be comprehended as such. And then, presumably, as this frame once more partakes of its constitutive function as an indispensable element in the composition of form, *another*. And then *another* . . .

The limits of aesthetic form, and indeed of the aesthetic judgment which is called for in this portion of Kant's critical philosophy, must henceforth be construed rather differently. The conception of the frame as an outer edge or margin, a continuous perimeter or unbroken contour, now gives way to the problem of the parergon, in which the "limit" unstably and unavoidably proliferates, traverses and dislocates (itself) in the very *taking place*, the very division or setting apart, of the aesthetic object or form. The limit continually divides and redivides (itself). Such unstable and ongoing processes of division do not merely indicate the always provisional and precarious nature of the borders of the aesthetic object; more fundamentally, they would seem to "internally" divide ad infinitum our very notions of "inner" and of "outer," putting into perpetual deconstruction the conceptual opposition of the two. Indeed, one effect of such far-reaching deconstructibility is, obviously, that it becomes much less satisfactory to speak merely of an "internal" division which might be found in our conception of what is "inside" or what is "outside" aesthetic limits, as if the problem could be reduced to a matter of logical contradiction or dialectical interplay. Rather, (the problem of) aesthetic form and judgment is subject to the dislocating force of an alterity not reducible to those categorizations of otherness which continue to operate on the basis of some more sustainable, more workable distinction—or even interplay—between "outside" and "inside."

Such problems prove enormously productive as they find their way into Weber's writings on a number of different occasions, and in view of a variety of topics. For example, one can see that the question of the parergon is crucial for Weber's thinking regarding the question of technics. Via Weber's discussion in *Mass Mediauras* of what he terms "emplacement" in Heidegger—as a movement which both opens up and closes down, secures and unsecures, places and displaces, locates and dislocates—the impossibility of determining "technics" as simply a question either for "the sciences" or for "the arts" becomes evident; and indeed, rather than simply being suspended or dispensed with here, the question of the borderline and interplay between the two continues to remain a tenacious and complex issue. It should come as no surprise, then, that the problem of determining "form" which arises both in the vicinity of aesthetic judgment and technical knowledge is never far from Weber's wide-ranging reflections upon the conflictual aspects of the processes of institution. And since institution and interpretation remain indissolubly linked for Weber—in the sense that the institution (of literary criticism, of the humanities, or indeed of psychoanalysis) arises only on condition of interpretive conflict—the parergon is called to mind throughout Weber's explorations of the struggle to establish a comprehensive theory of "aesthetic response": the term Wolfgang Iser adopts as a label for his theory of reading. As Weber is able to demonstrate in a long essay on Iser, "Caught in the Act of Reading," included in *Institution and Interpretation*, theoretical description cannot avoid the activity of reading it seeks to describe, transcend, or position securely as an "object" of knowledge outside itself. Proving itself partial to that it would seek to particularize or set apart (that is, reading), the "theoretical" effort that remains indispensable to the processes of founding, consolidating or reorienting the disciplinary space of literary study exemplifies the particular and nontotalizable character of the institution's "systematicity." The institution, that is to say, is ultimately unable either to fully incorporate or absolutely exclude those forces at play in its own institutionalization. Instead, since a comprehensive theoretical description of reading as an "object" of knowledge, such as is attempted by Iser, must entail resorting to somewhat partial and partisan practices of reading in order to found itself, the general system or framework uncannily (re)doubles itself in the *particular* it wishes to transcend or surpass. Once more, far from simply drawing the line, the "limit" redivides (itself), doubles, dislocates. It doubles and dislocates not just the "internal" space of that which it is supposed to demarcate. Its effects don't just stop there. For in doubling, dislocating, and continually redividing the very limit that is supposed to separate or hold apart such a space from the "outside," the parergon exposes us to a more radical alterity. Here, the coming of the "other" is not just the coming of an outsider.

It may appear, therefore, that the problem of the parergon or limit is put to *unlimited* use in Weber's work, spanning his discussions of institutions, interpretation, disciplinarity, technics, psychoanalysis, deconstruction, and, as we shall see, theatricality. And yet, paradoxically enough, if the limit was indeed simply unlimited here, it would hardly be possible even to begin distinguishing, describing, particularizing such a "work." Nevertheless, if we might wish to "frame" in some wider way the "work" of Samuel Weber by alluding or resorting to the problem of the parergon, this must obviously be considered quite inappropriate or improper: the parergon hardly offers the possibility of a simple framework, in view of which the characteristic features, orientation and bounds of a "work" might decisively be comprehended and articulated. The parergon calls us to radically question traditional conceptions of the "work" itself. When addressing questions of the limit in Weber's "work" and the limit of his "work," of what distinguishes certain parts of his writing in relation to others, or indeed what characterizes his texts in general in regard to the work of others, the parergon therefore emerges as an indispensable yet necessarily improper "framework" which subjects us to the thought and force of the "other" *as* or *at* the very limit of such categories, distinctions or oppositions. And we must ask whether Weber's "work" assumes, iterates, performs such limits, and, if so, how?

Theatrical Limits

The parergon also offers an "improper" framework for approaching the question of Weber's interest in theatricality. For what can be considered inside or outside theater? What bounds the theatrical scene? How and where can we trace its edge? Describing the performative dimensions of deconstruction in the interview "Goings On,"[15] a performativity that Weber associates with highly focused practices paying detailed attention to the singular and sometimes oblique or obscure aspects of an issue or a text, he points out that

> "performance" should . . . not be understood to deny the "reality" of power
> relationships that characterize the world in which we work and live. We
> have to make judgments, "take" decisions, evaluate situations. But such
> efforts are not simply means to an end independent of them. They are
> caught up in what they seek to grasp, discern, transform; and that involve-
> ment can perhaps best be described in terms of the relation of "perform-
> ance" and "play." Does such a theatrical perspective take reality too
> lightly? Or, on the contrary, does it do justice to the complexity—and in-
> deed, to the *ambivalence*—of our involvement in the world? (229–30)

If the performative quality of deconstructive practice often leads to de-liberately playful readings and writings which seem to flout the protocols and propriety expected of academic scholarship—just because, as Weber notes in another discussion, "Catching Up with the Past": "it is not considered 'serious' [for academics] to use language as anything other than an instrument for the communication of meaning"[16]—then for Weber it is far from a simple matter to distinguish this playfulness and theatricality from what might in fact be most "serious," going beyond the confines of theater—at least, as it is more narrowly conceived. Indeed, it is by way of a "theatrical perspective" such as that Weber associates with deconstructive writing and practice that the more wide-ranging experience or situation of being "caught up" in what we seek to "grasp, discern, transform" is reflected, replayed, redoubled. This situation of being "caught up" is something that, as we have seen, Weber discerns in the attempt to establish a theory of reading or aesthetic response, and which he detects in the effort to found and defend an institution such as psychoanalysis. But it is also by means of this description of the theatrical situation as one of being "caught up" that Weber allows himself to speak further of "the complexity—and indeed . . . the *ambivalence*—of our involvement in the world." (Here, the limits of the analysis are obviously opened up, although the complex and specific dynamics of ambivalence that Weber frequently investigates arrest any simple movement towards totalization or universality in view of the question of theatricality.) Going further still, Weber suggests it is by means of such a "theatrical perspective" that the question or possibility arises of "doing justice"—although to "do" justice, not least insofar as deconstruction is concerned, remains a highly complex and perhaps irresolvable issue. At any rate, these remarks concerning the performative aspect of deconstruction suggest that theatricality, for Weber, names the experience or situation—the *performance*—of an unavoidable yet always partial and specific participation in that which we variously attempt to comprehend, describe, delimit, delineate, observe, identify, objectify, interpret, or analyze. Here, then, the unstable processes of repetition and dislocation that occur on condition of the deconstructibility of "frames" or frameworks give rise to scenarios that, for Weber, can be explored most interestingly in terms of "theatricality."

But let us ask again, even in view of a more narrow idea of the "theatrical": What can be considered outside or inside theater? What are its bounds? How and where can its limit be marked or its edge be traced? For example, is the theatrical boundary synonymous with the borders of the stage, or can it be located instead at the outer limits of the audience? In light of the ambivalent relations or the conflictual dynamics of performance, participation, apartness, and setting apart to which Weber continually draws our attention, is it possible to secure or stabilize either of these "limits" quite so easily, or indeed to uphold a distinction between the two? Furthermore, where are the limits of scene and play, when each "frame" would seem inexorably to call for another? Stage, audience, scene, and play immediately suggest a number of spatial and temporal limits; but just how do these supply the frames or the framework for theatricality? How do they combine or contrast with one another, or indeed do they conflict with or dislocate (double, redivide) themselves and one another? As has been suggested a number of times already, theatricality is the term we might associate with the kinds of questions and effects that Weber wants to explore when the supposedly autonomous, coherent or self-contained structures or domains of "form," "work," "theory," "discipline," "institution," and "knowledge" are exposed to the constitutive yet dislocating force of the "other." But are the very *limits* of theatricality themselves subject to this alterity which, since it is not reducible to the binary opposition or dialectical interplay of inside-outside, can no more be considered the "inner" trait or essence of theatricality than it can be described as a sort of "outsider" intruding upon the supposedly "nontheatrical" domains listed above?

Taking Place, Dislocating Theater

These introductory comments and questions, then, inevitably serve to frame a discussion of theatricality in Weber's writings, but they also continually work to exceed, destabilize, and dislocate any framework in which the question of theatricality as such might be put. If the problem and the effects of theatricality cannot be reduced to detached theoretical description of the kind entailed in positing a coherent and self-contained concept or object of cognition and knowledge, then it remains to be seen how Weber's writing partakes of the kinds of theatricality he wishes to explore, and how this theatricality is at work in his own texts. To begin to approach this question, I want to turn to two essays by Weber, on opera and on psychoanalysis respectively.

In "Taking Place: Toward a Theater of Dislocation,"[17] Weber describes the Frankfurt Opera's staging of *Aida* in January 1981. Although heralded as signaling a "decisive 'breakthrough'" (108–9) for the Frankfurt Opera Company, the initial performances of *Aida* were met with "intense indignation" by those sections of the audience committed to traditional operatic dramaturgy. In his essay, Weber pays particular attention to the opening scene—"or, rather, the scene that preceded the opening of the drama, since it accompanied the overture" (107). Such a "scene," upon which Weber wants to place a great deal of emphasis, therefore seems to usher in the "work" itself. Yet, while this scene takes place at—or, indeed, *as*—the very threshold of the opera, it remains difficult to place in relation to the "work" proper: does this scene stand inside or outside the "work"? Does it "precede" or "open" the opera, or, somehow, both? In this "opening" scene, we find Ramades, captain of the Egyptian palace guard, "dressed in the civilian clothes of a nineteenth-century European businessman" and "in what appears to be a dream, he seizes a shovel (implausibly located in what appears to be an office) and begins to dig the earth, or, rather, to tear up the floorboards of the stage, bringing to light first sand, then a sword, and finally the sculpted head of Aida" (107). For Weber, Ramades—in a scene that seems bizarre enough to resemble a dream—acts to call into question the space in which theatrical representation takes place. Indeed, by digging into the very foundations of that space, Ramades "opens" the opera with a gesture that is at once undeniably self-referential yet which, at the same time, precludes the scene's self-containment. If the violent and seemingly deranged shoveling of Ramades works profoundly to disturb rather than to convey the reassuring "'dreamy' quality" (120) a traditional audience might expect of Verdi's prelude, it is nevertheless precisely because this dream-scene dislocates the work as a self-contained structure (one thereby possessed of determinable, authoritative, univocal meaning) that it replaces, according to Weber, "the traditional aesthetics of *Darstellung*" with "a theater of *Entstellung*" (121).

Ramades's digging, then, undermines—by exposing and calling into question—the hitherto taken-for-granted foundations of dramatic representation. It disorganizes the "traditional, self-contained" (117) space of theater (rather than just dismantling it—for in digging up the floorboards, Ramades nevertheless does not move outside the space of this dream-scene); and it does so, first and foremost by drawing up and including in the scene the enabling limits or foundations of theater. Far from remaining "neutral," then, these "limits" become "an integral part of the show itself" (118). Weber is quick to point out that the foundations which thereby become an irreducible component of the performance are, above all, material. That materiality, he tells us, "includes not merely the actual floorboards of the stage, but the entire social system upon which theater depends" (117). This social system is underpinned by a variety of attitudes, practices, and institutions which, Weber tells us, can be characterized in terms of "nostalgic idealization and identification," whereby the "exotic—the distant, heroic, sumptuous Golden Age of the Bourgeoisie—is made familiar" (111). Such effects occur by way of an "exercise in recognition," as Adorno puts it.[18] Yet if "exotic artificiality is built into operatic form"

(116), and if it is very much expected by the more conservative operagoer, then, for Weber, an alienation effect along Brechtian lines will be insufficient to call into question traditional operatic dramaturgy. For, Weber asserts, "if audiences identify with opera today, it is precisely because of its distance, not in spite of it" (116). To the extent that it is shocking, Ramades's violence cannot simply be reduced to a strategy of *Verfremdung*, since what the conventional operagoer generally expects to be foregrounded and celebrated during the performance is a highly contrived and self-conscious theatricality, tied to the lavish rendition of a now-remote historical epoch. Since opera's "exotic artificiality" is irreducibly linked to effects of identification and illusion which are promoted so as to secure the ideological disposition of the spectator, it remains questionable whether this "exotic artificiality" should be distinguished quite so decisively in relation to the conventions of naturalistic drama. According to Weber, of course, such a decisive distinction between operatic and naturalistic theater is what forces us to rule out *Verfremdung* in the opera as a meaningful strategy or source of critique and resistance. Nevertheless, Weber is right to point out that, in one sense, Ramades's digging profoundly disorganizes the space and foundations of theater often taken for granted by "reactionary" and Marxist dramaturgy alike. He writes, "as generally understood, the notion of *alienation* supposes precisely the traditional, Euclidean notions of space that stagings such as the one we are discussing seek to problematize: a space in which distance and proximity are mutually exclusive" (116–17). That is to say, when comparing the dramatic theory and practice of naturalism with the theater of alienation, relationships of detachment and engagement are obviously configured very differently; yet in each case they are imagined to be subject to the controlled and calculated design, or intention, of a theatrical strategy that rests upon the conceptual coherence of the distinction between what is proximate and what is distant in spatial terms. In the opening scene of the Frankfurt Opera's *Aida*, however, "something far more disquieting takes place, something which can no longer be understood in terms of the ultimately reassuring opposition of 'outside' and 'inside.' What is represented onstage is an act that calls the space in which it 'takes place' into question" (117). The spatial relationships and distinctions presupposed by a more traditional and secure conception of *place* are subjected to the maddening force of their own deconstructibility, since the import of those (material) foundations which Ramades puts (or folds) back into (the) play as an "integral part" can be determined only by reference to the theatrical context

that they had hitherto served to delimit, but that they now come to disorganize and dislocate. In a similar vein, although the objects that Ramades
brings up along with the floorboards of the stage—namely, the sword and
the sculpture—are normally taken to embody the traditional and reassuring connotations of glory and art, power and love, this interpretation depends upon a taken-for-granted conception of the operatic "work" and
event, the *taking place* of which is now thrown into disarray just as the
"integral part" of the theatrical limit or foundation is exposed or revealed.
Henceforth, the opera simply cannot be contained, simply cannot contain
itself; and it is, in the widest possible sense, now "no longer a suitable
object of identification" (116). (Indeed, this remains true even in view of
the nineteenth-century costume and setting in which we find Ramades.
This might seem to conjure up the "Golden Age of the Bourgeoisie" and
hence provide a "suitable object of identification." Yet, as Weber writes:
"Like the stage floor, the historical context of . . . emergence is inscribed
in, or rather *as*, the scene that 'ushers in' the work; once again the enabling
limits of the opera are folded back into the spectacle itself" (121). Once
more, then, this reinclusion of the "enabling limit" happens in a way that,
for Weber, both opens up and dislocates the framework of theatrical representation.) If the opera is "no longer a suitable object of identification,"
let us recall that such identification—providing the grounds for "nostalgic
idealization"—is, of course, an enabling feature of "an entire social system" having its own material basis. Thus, where the material foundation
of the opera becomes "an integral part of the show itself," a better description of this theatrical "limit" would be of a *disintegral* part. For, Weber
tells us, "this part is one that calls the whole into question" (118): the
authoritative intentionality of the "work," the coherence and self-containment of the operatic event, and the (self-) recognition of the audience.
Hence, if the framework according to which theatricality is conventionally
understood itself breaks down or divides into a series of structuring parti-
tions or "frames"—the stage, the theater, the audience, the scene, the
play—then far from combining harmoniously as self-consistent elements
in order to allow the whole to come full circle, these "frames" dislocate
themselves and one another in the Frankfurt Opera's *Aida*:

> Once the limits of the scene, the foundations of this site, are thus included
> in the scene itself, the space of representation can no longer simply be
> taken for granted or unequivocally delimited. Who is to say where it starts,
> and where it stops? The audience, finding itself on the spot and yet unable
> to determine where that spot is located, is put out: exasperated by a space

in which it is not entirely at home, and yet which it knows all too well. The opera house has ceased to be a home. (118)

It is this, above all, that disorganizes the desire of the audience for (self-) recognition: for how can it hope to recognize what it cannot definitively locate? Once the limits of the scene are no longer neutral, the spectacle is no longer securely in place, nor are the spectators.

For some, Weber might be digging too deep in order to imbue Ramades's shoveling with a greater degree of importance than it deserves. For in order to confirm the value of a "theatrical perspective" such as is offered or practiced by deconstruction, whereby "performance" and "play" are seen as inseparable from the "complexity" and "ambivalence" of "our involvement in the world," is it enough to celebrate the "decisive 'breakthrough'" of the Frankfurt Opera Company in unsettling the assumptions and expectations of the traditional operagoer? In Weber's own terms, "does such a theatrical perspective take reality too lightly?" Despite Weber's remarks concerning the material basis of a specific social system and group for which opera is traditionally an important tool of self-recognition, does the operatic "performance" and "play" that he wishes to dwell upon here in fact lead us away from, rather than towards, "involvement in the world"?

The attention paid by Weber in regard to the Frankfurt Opera's *Aida*, and to Ramades's digging in particular, calls to mind his own depiction of deconstructive reading and practice. The "small detail" (if we may call it that) of this opening or preceding scene, which might be construed as of minor significance when compared to the grandeur and seriousness of the operatic "work" proper (let alone in relation to important issues in the "outside world"), is not merely taken to exceed its own, particular limits. Since it "takes place" at the very threshold of the opera, such small detail calls into question the very limits that delimit aesthetic form, "work," dramatic unity, and indeed the identity of the audience. And, as these limits come to be "included" so as to disorganize and dislocate the very forms and spaces which they are supposed to delineate and demarcate, it becomes all the more difficult to decide how and where to delimit aesthetics in regard to politics, representation in relation to reality, elitism as distinct from what might be termed the "everyday." As Weber puts it: "Who is to say where it starts, and where it stops?" Just where Ramades digs, there is no longer a stable basis to assume that the importance of this little "scene" stops with the question of operatic dramaturgy or, indeed, the particular cultural proclivities of a hugely privileged social elite.

A Theater of Entstellung

But what, then, *is* the wider importance of this little scene? And in what ways does it help us return to the questions with which we began? If, in regard to the opening scene of the Frankfurt Opera's *Aida*, one might indeed ask: "Who is to say where it starts, and where it stops?" then exactly how does Weber's writing itself partake of the kinds of theatricality he wishes to explore? How is this theatricality at work in his own texts, and with what effects? Perhaps most important, when considering these effects, what is the extent of their significance?

When Weber tells us that "what is represented onstage [when Ramades digs] is an act that calls the space in which it "takes place" into question," he is guilty of a rare lapse in precision. For Ramades's deranged and violent shoveling dislocates and disorganizes the scene in a way that allows Weber, elsewhere in his essay, to speak of a shift from "the traditional aesthetics of *Darstellung*" to "a theater of *Entstellung*"—one of distortion, disfigurement, dislocation. It is therefore inappropriate to speak of Ramades's gesture in terms of an *act*—and here the implication is of a deliberate "political" strategy and rationale at work in the opening sequence of the opera—not just because it takes place during something like a dream-scene, in which conscious ideas and decisions are all but confounded by unconscious processes and drives. More importantly, if the disorganizing and dislocating force of Ramades's digging ushers in not the "work" but instead a theater of *Entstellung*, then we should never expect to excavate an original intention that organizes the meaning (or indeed, the narrative) one might elaborate in terms of the scene's significance. For his violence to be considered an *act* in the sense of prosecuting an explicit and deliberate "political" intention, decision or strategy, surely Ramades would need to attain a degree of exteriority, however minimal, in relation to the "dream"? He would surely need, in some sense, to move or operate voluntarily, "outside" the dream-scene, especially one that ushers in a theater of *Entstellung*. Yet not only does Ramades *not* move outside this theatrical space; his digging serves to disorganize the "reassuring opposition of 'outside' and 'inside'" that would seem to provide the basis and orientation for a traditional conception of the voluntary or volitional (political) act. This also means that the audience, while they are undeniably "put out" by his highly contentious and shocking gesture, can no more act independently of it (for it is the dislocating part of a "scene" that defies identification and re-cognition) than Ramades can intervene to control or determine its meaning by adopting the standpoint of an intentional agent.

The dream's structure as *Entstellung* therefore provides something like "an allegory of the Freudian unconscious," as Weber, in a footnote to the essay, puts it. Here, "the position of the spectator is revealed as both specious and unavoidable."[19] It is unavoidable, in the sense that the spectator unavoidably *dreams* the dream of Ramades: the audience is exasperated, somehow put on the spot or, rather, put out, but bewilderingly they seem unable to act, or to escape, in relation to that which they cannot definitively recognize or locate. The operagoer *as* dreamer, then, "appears to be a mere observer of the dream." Yet as Weber in the same footnote explains, this turns out to be "merely part of the dream's structure as *Entstellung*," in which the audience cannot help but be included, so that the spectatorial standpoint is at the same time "specious." As Weber therefore tells us of the dream's structure as *Entstellung*, the perspective of the spectator is "ineluctable," but nevertheless "it remains inscribed in a spectacle that no glance can oversee." As one particular theatrical limit or "frame," one structuring partition of the general framework that gives us our traditional conception of theater, the audience here do not merely trace out the "edge" of the drama in terms of a spectatorial vantage point from which the "work" can be definitively comprehended, or the opera appraised. Instead, since this very same liminality turns out to be "specious," "merely part of the dream's structure as *Entstellung*," the audience are also drawn into the theatrical (and theatricalized) space precisely by means of the specious impression of mere spectatordom. But does "just this participation . . . require another frame," and *another*, and *another* . . . as the characteristic or condition of a "spectacle that no glance can oversee"? Is this the theater's, or the dream's, structure as *Entstellung*? And, if so, how might the "structure" of *Entstellung* also describe (although not in the sense of marking out or drawing a line around) the scene or the staging of Weber's own writings, taking his speculations concerning a variety of phenomena, issues, and texts "beyond" mere spectatorship of the kind associated with more traditional conceptions and renditions of knowledge?

Weber's essay "The Blindness of the Seeing Eye" offers a succinct yet illuminating discussion of *Entstellung* in Freud's writing.[20] As has been indicated, this term signifies distortion, but, according to Weber, carries the sense of dislocation as much as of disfigurement in Freud. For Freud, dreams cannot be considered in terms of their latent content ultimately to harbor a single, determinable meaning; nor, therefore, are they reducible to a self-contained object of cognition that is susceptible to "a hermeneutics that defines its task in terms of *explication* or of *disclosure*" (79). Instead,

dreams constitute themselves, as Weber puts it, "through, and as, interpretation" (77), which must itself be conceived in terms of a process that
is closer to *Entstellung* than *Darstellung* (the latter signifying presentation
or exposition). Freud tells us that the dream manifests "a particular *form*
of thinking" (79)[21] which Weber describes as "that of a de-formation
which serves to dissimulate its deformative character by creating a representational façade" (79). While Freud insists that all dreams are in principle liable to interpretation (although not general theoretical categorization
or reduction as such), the dream's dissimulation should therefore not be
construed as a veil to be penetrated by the interpretive effort of a traditional hermeutics, so as to reveal a fully determinable object, the ultimate
meaning of the dream itself. Instead, the "representational façade" dissimulates the "essence" of the dream-work as a form of "thinking," interpretation, distortion, or dislocation occurring as the effect of conflictual wish-
fulfillment. In *The Interpretation of Dreams*, Freud therefore writes: "It is
true that we distort dreams in attempting to reproduce them . . . but this
distortion (*Entstellung*) is itself no more than a part of the elaboration
which the dream-thoughts regularly undergo as a result of the dream-
censorship" (78).[22] The interpretation of dreams is thus a dislocating repetition and a repetitious dislocation of the dream: it should be construed in
terms of *Entstellung* as discerned by Freud in the dream-work, arising on
condition of a conflictual wish-fulfillment that cannot be set apart as simply a characteristic feature of dreaming when asleep, for example. (Indeed,
in "The Meaning of the Thallus," one of the subsections of *The Legend of
Freud*, Weber takes Freud's insight further, so as to write: "The logic of
identity takes its place in the dream's strategy of displacement as that
which dissimulates the distortions that have taken place, have taken *the*
place of the conscious mind precisely by seeming to yield to it" [103].) If
the interpretive effort of the audience of *Aida* founders when "confronted"
with the dream scene in which Ramades disorganizes the foundations of
stage (and, thereby, those of dramatic representation), it is because, far
from shedding light upon an original intention, a fundamental meaning,
and hence a separable object of cognition, Ramades's digging entails a
kind of "dream-work" that ushers in a theater of *Entstellung* in which all
must participate and which none can simply oversee. And if "just this participation . . . require[s] another frame" in order for such a theater of
Entstellung to be recognized or distinguished at all, then the interpretive
effort of the critic—Weber himself—can no more be divorced from the
effects of dislocating repetition or repetitious dislocation that it wishes

(and yet does not wish) to "describe." For these effects are not only pervasive, but always already at play.

How, then, might we read Weber's texts so as to discern an alternative
to the long-standing model of interpretation, predicated upon *"explica-*
tion" or *"disclosure,"* that is associated with traditional hermeneutics; an
alternative which cannot merely be proposed, but which must be assumed
as already at work or at play in his writing (on theatricality, for instance,
the limits of which are far from certain)? Such an alternative interpretive
practice would necessarily be less recognizable in terms of conventional
academic scholarship, although perhaps (like Ramades) it might serve to
replace it, less in the sense of seeking to dismantle or move outside its
space than by serving to disorganize and call into question the assumptions
and distinctions that would otherwise serve to distinguish and demarcate
such "scholarship" from charlatanism, amateurism, intellectual imposture,
and so forth. On the basis of the previous discussion, this "alternative," as
bizarre as it might sound, would therefore be more closely allied to dreaming, to theatricality, indeed to the theatricality of the dream and the
dream-work of theatricality—although it should be obvious enough by
now that such "dreaming" cannot simply be opposed to the ostensibly
"serious" and "sober" efforts and activities of more "reputable" scholars.
Yet on the surface, at least, Weber's books and essays do seem much less
performative or theatrical in style than, for example, Derrida's *Glas* or his
writing on Mallarmé—so in what sense exactly are they "theatrical"?

In "Taking Place," Weber turns his attention to the Frankfurt Opera's
staging of Wagner's *Ring of the Nibelung*. Here, his discussion draws upon
Freud's conception, in the *Interpretation of Dreams*, of the "navel of the
dream," wherein:

> one notices a tangle of dream-thoughts arising which resists unraveling but
> has also made no further contributions to the dream-content. This then is
> the navel of the dream, the place where it straddles the unknown. The
> dream-thoughts to which interpretation leads one are necessarily intermi-
> nable *and branch out in all directions into the netlike entanglement* of our world
> of thought. Out of one of the denser places in this network, the dream-
> wish rises like a mushroom out of its mycelium. (133)[23]

Dream-thoughts, as the *entstellte* "fulfillment" of conflictual and hence
unresolvable and ongoing desires, therefore unavoidably "branch out in
all directions." They become an entangled and spreading expanse in which
the dream-thoughts exceed their "contributions to the dream-content,"
thereby inevitably dislocating the dream and its interpretation alike. As

the "netlike entanglement" thickens or intensifies, then, it also spills out and into "our world of thought," as Freud puts it, and in particular, as Weber notes, into "our waking thoughts" (133). Yet if such a dislocating movement or process were permitted to continue without impediment, presumably the dream would become so swept into this "navel" as to no longer simply "straddle" the unknown. Instead, it would surely be entirely engulfed by it, to the point where even the most minimal degree of coherence or recognition would be lost. The dream would no longer be liable to any interpretation whatsoever. Equally, since the "netlike entanglement" of dream-thinking would also engulf waking thought, nothing could stop conscious life becoming so drawn into the navel of the dream that it would be utterly incapable of establishing or maintaining any focus of attention. However, since (as Freud asserts) dreams do remain susceptible to interpretation, albeit of a specific and provisional kind, and since conscious life never seems to give itself over entirely to the "navel of the dream," the dissipating movement of *Entstellung* must somehow be held in check. Freud's suggestion is therefore that this "mycelium" not only proliferates and extends its "netlike entanglement" but that it in fact give rises to a "mushroom"—at last, a recognizable form found growing among this most fecund organic matter, somewhat akin to decomposing compost—to which Freud assigns the name of the "dream-wish." The dream-wish is, as Weber puts it, "a new phenomenon rising above the proliferation of shadows to provide the badly needed bright new center of attention" (133). Yet, as Freud himself insists, the dream as the fulfillment of a wish cannot be construed in terms of the expression of a latent content, which might endow it with integrity as an intentional and objectifiable phenomenon. Rather, the dream-wish "fulfils" itself only as it arises from the always conflictual and hence irresolvable play of desire(s) that give it its specific force or structure. As Weber tells us:

> The dream-wish, then, which arises out of the dream-navel, endows the interminable proliferation of dream-thoughts with a certain structure. But at the same time this structure recenters the dream around the "unknown," around the overdetermined conflictuality of which the dream is a self-dissimulating dissimulation. The emergence of the phallic dream-wish therefore does not abolish . . . the thallic dynamics of the dream—it merely gives its dislocation a focus. (134)

Dream-thoughts (imbued with a "thallic dynamics" wherein, as the dictionary definition of *Thallus* suggests, the "true roots are absent") unavoidably proliferate, spread, traverse and exceed their bounds, branching out and breaking into conscious life (as sensible, rational, voluntary). Yet the dissipating and decentering force of the dream-thought is somewhat held in check by what Weber calls a "structure" or "focus" conferred by the fulfillment of the dream-wish, which in turn "recenters" the dream around the "unknown," here conceived in terms of "overdetermined conflictuality" and "self-dissimulating dissimulation." While the latter—"self-dissimulating dissimulation"—recalls the irreducible *theatricality* of the dream, "overdetermined conflictuality" takes place not only in the dream or the unconscious, but finds its way into "waking thought" or conscious life: for example, in the conflictual play of forces that, as Weber's work shows us, give rise to technologies, "works," institutions and interpretations of all kinds. The dislocating movement of *Entstellung* associated with dream-thoughts plays itself out, then, through the specific form—the "mushroom" or reef—of the dream-wish, the fulfillment of which both decenters and recenters, structures and destructures the dream around the "unknown" as the dream-navel, as the unconscious, as theatricality, as the "overdetermined conflictuality" that gives rise to (always deconstructible) institution and interpretation.

As has already been noted, Weber's thinking and writing thereby cannot help but assume or partake of "dream-thought," although, as should therefore be obvious, this could not just happen as the result of an intention, decision, strategy, or rationale on Weber's part. As it branches out or breaks into conscious life, however, dream-thought not only submerges and sweeps focused or structured thinking into the entangled and dissipating space—the black hole—of the dream's navel. Instead, it gives rise to wishes which provide a "center of attention," but one which nevertheless draws us back towards or into "overdetermined conflictuality" and theatricality alike, and which therefore replaces or recenters this "center" around, or at the (decentering) limit of, the "unknown." While such "themes" or "ideas" could be said to constitute the abiding interest of Weber's work, explicit everywhere at the level of its "content," it also seems fair to say that the very procedure or practice of this "work" is bound up with the dislocating movement of *Entstellung*, a movement which we are here associating with both dream-thinking and theatricality. This *entstellte* "work" of Samuel Weber could be described as a play or a "goings-on" of destructuring structuration, in which the center of attention is continually displaced, replaced, and displaced once more in turn, at—or, indeed, *as*—the very limit (never just a dividing line) of the "other" or the "unknown." Just this *entstellte* participation on Weber's part means that each "frame" calls for *another*, and *another* ("no glance can ever over-see") . . . so that Weber's "work" is itself theatrical in the sense of staging a "series" of scenes that dislocate themselves and each other. In turn, this theatricality would disrupt or, indeed, dislocate any simple attempt to cor-relate, reduce, and explain Weber's writings in terms of a continuous, con-sistent body of scholarship or a distinguished instance of philosophical "development," accessible to its readership as an "object" of knowledge or cognition to be grasped and mastered by an autonomous subject of reason or thought (the independent individual). The "structure" or the "focus" we might discern not only in particular texts by Weber, but link-ing his writings in general, undeniably reactivates the wish for a kernel or "center" (of attention) that is liable to interpretation. But such a "center" can be and *is* always dislocated or replaced by yet another frame, which in turn enters into the analysis only on condition of *another* . . . (indeed, on condition of a frame that must, in a sense, be *other* than the "frame": a necessary yet also impossible condition). Hence, the reprises, repetitions, linkages, and connections in Weber's work, to which this essay has, at times, drawn attention, constantly invite or require rephrasing, reiteration, reformulation—and hence, inevitably, transformation—of the questions or problems under discussion, undermining attempts at reduction, gener-alization, systematization, or totalization.

Theatricality and Uncanny Thinking

The second edition of Weber's *The Legend of Freud* includes a new essay, "Uncanny Thinking," with which the book opens. Here, Weber describes his original project as an attempt to "explore how Freud's writing and thinking are progressively caught up in what they set out primarily to describe and elucidate" (1). To this extent, the Freudian text continually calls into question the "assumption of an extraterritorial position with re-spect to the matter being considered" (1). Detachment or "safe distance" in regard to an object of interest, investigation or knowledge is jeopard-ized, for example, where either the patient or, indeed, the doctor come to reject a perception that doesn't fit in with their expectations. Such a rejec-tion does not amount simply to "a *lack* of consciousness with respect to an object" (the object is not just "missed" or "overlooked"); but, more pre-cisely, it entails "a blindness of consciousness with respect to its own activ-ity (of dissimulation)" (4). If what we are therefore describing is nothing other than the advent of the unconscious in conscious life, here it is marked by a (re)doubling of consciousness's blindness—a blindness, that is to say, which can be described in terms of a twofold process that concerns both the inadmissible "perception" which confronts consciousness to begin with, and the dissimulating "activity" of consciousness by which such a rejection remains unacknowledged. The unconscious, then, ushers in a scene that is characterized by relations of ambivalence, conflict, and struggle; for here the subject is split off from itself, dispersed in an action which, while it may indeed be inaccessible to consciousness, nevertheless establishes the conditions for the emergence of a particular kind of knowing. And, far from being able simply to observe or comprehend such a phenomenon from the vantage point of psychoanalytic interpretation or "knowledge," Freud's own text implies that "knowledge" itself may well be little more than the name we assign to the effort consciousness makes in trying to deal with processes it can never really come to master or, indeed, to know. This scenario, then, is one into which psychoanalysis itself must inevitably be drawn.

The rejection of a perception that does not fit in with one's expectations is, of course, how Freud tells the story of "castration." The perception of sexual difference is rendered compatible with the "expectation" of male identity through the recounting of a story which, as Weber puts it, "temporalizes" difference so as to redefine it "as a modality of identity" (5). Hence, the immediate perception is not merely rejected outright ("I must be wrong, there has to be a penis there"). Instead, the fact of sexual difference is rejected by way of recasting variation in terms of lack, so as to confirm the positive self-identity of the male ("there must have been a penis there once, I'm right after all"). Here, once more, the "blindness" of the conscious mind can be described in terms of a double process that concerns, firstly , the inadmissible "perception," but that also entails the dissimulating "activity" of consciousness in relation to itself, by means of which the rejection remains unacknowledged *as such*, as it must do if the story of castration is to serve its purpose. And, as Weber points out, one of the main purposes of this story is to confirm the extraterritorial position of the storyteller himself. Since the story of castration is intended to render the perception of difference compatible with the narcissistic "expectation" of a (male) self that wishes to consider itself "intact, whole, autonomous" (6), then it is related precisely so as to propose that the ego can assume a position that is sufficiently separate and self-contained, in respect of the events being recounted, that it ultimately remains unaffected by them. "The 'I' that tells itself this story thereby strives to secure its position as mere 'observer,'" Weber tells us, "situated at an ostensibly safe remove from the disturbing possibilities it seeks merely to describe or re-tell" (6). Yet while "the separation it sought to dominate" is apprehended by this ego as something like "an obstacle to be overcome," nevertheless as the trait of a rejected perception and, indeed, of consciousness's double and (re)doubling blindness, it remains as the "constitutive force" of a self that is "irrevocably scattered" and dispersed in the action or scene of the unconscious, from which the subject of the narrative or of "knowledge" can only impossibly hope to emerge unscathed.

This other story of "castration," then, is best retold not in the idiom of theoretical description or positive, empirical knowledge, but via the language or thinking of the dream, with all the effects of theatricality this entails ("the 'I' of the dreamer . . . finds itself scattered throughout the dream despite its apparent distance from it" [7]). Weber's "Uncanny Thinking" therefore turns to E. T. A. Hoffman's uncanny tale, "The Sandman," upon which Freud's essay on the uncanny concentrates. Here, one uncanny story, one (dream) scene encounters another, or is staged within or alongside another. And, perhaps, yet another, and, right here, look, another: my recounting of Weber's recounting of Freud's recounting of a tale by Hoffman that concerns . . . recounting. But of what? As we shall see, the array of difficulties this very question occasions means that these various retellings cannot so easily find a stable or secure "center of attention" so as to be construed in terms of a series of concentric circles, each fully containing the other. Instead, our attention is drawn to the patterns of dislocation that repeat themselves throughout this "series."

Since, as Weber tells us, the Sandman "names the violence of a certain disassemblage," what we are doubtless in the midst of here is a retelling (*otherwise*) of the story of castration. (The Sandman eats dismembered parts of bodies, and his appearance "medusizes" the transfixed child, whose gaze is itself threatened by the Sandman's particular taste for eating eyes.) But how is this story to be recounted, or *dreamed*, and by whom?

In Hoffman's tale, or rather within a letter to his fiancée's brother, the young student Nathanael conveys a recent, seemingly trivial occurrence, whereby an eyeglass vendor enters his lodgings, taking him unawares. Nathanael not only rejects the wares the eyeglass vendor offers him, but threatens him with violence unless he leaves immediately. By way of an explanation of his own, apparently excessive reaction, Nathanael recalls another scene, this time from his childhood, when his household was frequented by the portentous "Sandman," whose identity remained a long while shrouded in mystery. Like the eyeglass vendor, then, the Sandman

unexpectedly arrives upon the domestic scene (although he does so repeatedly) with a sudden, intrusive force which indicates the fragility of its de-
fenses and the vulnerability of its borders. If the coming of the eyeglass
vendor only repeats this pattern of repetition, the fact that he nevertheless
takes Nathanael unawares suggests the curious state of knowing *without*
knowing that Freud associates with the subject who rejects a perception
that does not fit in (the subject, for instance, of the story of castration). As
a child, Nathanael responds to this threat by seeking, as Weber puts it, to
locate it. (Indeed, several years later, he tries once again to overcome the
intimidating episode of the eyeglass vendor's startling and unforeseen intrusion by *locating* it, this time in terms of childhood memories that themselves only repeat, rather than resolve, the attempt to locate the threat.)
This entails an effort to visualize the Sandman, to find out what he looks
like. But, as Weber points out, "the name and the story of the Sandman
already anticipates this effort and incorporates it, as it were, into the
threat" (8). For the very coming of the Sandman is marked not so much
by his appearance (which, in any case, only threatens to devour the eye)
as by an irresistible drift toward sleep and dreaming, one that is accompanied by the wholly unwelcome yet entirely irrepressible drawing down of
heavy lids, which makes the child's eyes feel as though sand had been
thrown into them.

To the extent that "the very name and story of the Sandman" radically
impedes the attribution of an origin or intention insofar as the meaning
or identity of the Sandman is concerned—and indeed, since the story in
fact reincorporates this very same effort so as to redouble the threat—the
Sandman only *is* insofar as he is *coming*. Never does he come, arrive, or
appear definitively, once and for all (he will always come again, no doubt
in unexpected guise); nor can his identity *as* such (for example, as a subject
or agent in the traditional sense) ever be definitively postulated as anterior
to the processes and effects that surround his coming. The Sandman's
coming, then, powerfully recalls the comedic theatricality of the posse
actor Beckmann, whose distinctive talent, Kierkegaard tells us, resides in
his ability to "come walking."[24] Via Weber's work on Kierkegaardian experimenting as a possible (impossible) model for the future of humanities,
Beckmann's (experimental) theatrical style can be linked (perhaps by
means of a kind of dream-thinking) to Derrida's "vision" of the university
after Kant, as an institution that is deeply unsure of its foundations, or of
its point of origin; an institution which therefore finds, founds, foots itself
as a body continually off balance, always already coming, however un-
steadily or uncertainly.[25] Such a university is therefore impelled to "walk

on two feet" (neither left nor right), in order to exert a kind of leverage on the basis of an "other" that is not merely one of a pair. Beckmann's coming could thus be taken to "improvise the whole scenic setting" of the university institution after the Enlightenment. As a repetitious act without definitive origin or conclusion, his comically off-balance "walking" repeats the coming of the Sandman, blinding the vision of, in this case, the university itself: as Derrida, following Heidegger, shows in "The Principle of Reason: The University in the Eyes of Its Pupils," the vision of the university proceeds from what remains concealed in that vision, since the institution built on the principle of reason is also constructed upon "what remains hidden in that principle."[26] Here, the strange familiarity and uncanny repetition that connects the Sandman and Beckmann might lead us to dream of new ways to reframe debates regarding the university institution—indeed concerning institutions of all kinds—in terms of the scene of the unconscious and the story of castration. For instance, we might then be able to retell somewhat differently the story of the "impossible" emergence of knowledge from (the theatricality of) the dream. Equally, the *unheimlich* pathway that leads from Beckmann to the Sandman might allow us to restage the scene of the unconscious, and to recount the story of castration, in terms of the question of (the) institution—of psychoanalysis, for example. Here one finds an inextricable tangle of traits that one could never hope to exhaust or master. Each frame calls for another, dislocates and re-places itself and the other (or, indeed, "in" the other) via a movement that continually circulates but never comes full circle, never allows us to achieve balance or completion (and now I could speak of the extent to which Weber's own "work" itself comes walking, in the style of Beckmann, or indeed just like the Sandman, so as to deal with all sorts of interesting and hitherto unforeseen consequences and effects that this might imply. But to take such a turn would only imply another frame, and "who is to say where it starts, and where it stops?"). In the midst of a kind of dream-thinking that leads us from the Sandman to Beckmann, then, we become drawn into the movement of destructuring structuration that we have associated with the theatricality of Weber's own writing, a theatricality that always leaves us teetering precariously at the limits of the unknown.

A theatricality that therefore compels us, somewhat off-balance, somehow to move, to take a plunge. So that if we get back to the story that Weber is telling us (that Freud is telling us that Hoffman is telling us that Nathanael is telling us) pretty soon we are off elsewhere. In *The Legend of Freud*, Weber writes:

The Sandman *is* insofar as he is *coming*. Nathanael's problem is related precisely to the ubiquitous possibility of this coming, an eventuality that cannot be foreclosed by any of the borders with which we seek to wall in our spaces and control access to them.

The power of the Sandman, then, inheres in his ability to invade and occupy what in the modern period is considered the most sacred of spaces: the private space of the family, the *home*. At the same time, however, as he turns the home inside-out, he also reaffirms domestic space, but in a way that transforms it from a place of security. (9)

By alluding to the Sandman's coming in terms of "an eventuality that cannot be foreclosed by any of the borders with which we seek to wall in our spaces and control access to them," Weber recalls the "goings-on" of technics, in which the irresolvable interplay of "opening up" and "closing down" (for Heidegger) puts *place* continually into *play*. Here, another frame suggests itself. Of course, in picking up such threads, a great deal more could be said on the subject of technics, interpretation, reading, or indeed institution, in the context of this discussion of the uncanny, the unconscious, and the story of castration. But whether we continue in this vein or that (and "who is to say where it starts, and where it stops?"), the writing here suggests a variegated and proliferal structure or movement not dissimilar to the "thallic dynamics of the dream." This entails a theatrical movement (uncanny thinking?) in which each scene is continually called into question, dislocated and replaced by an *other*.

But let us get back to the story once more. As we have said, the name and the tale of the Sandman together anticipate Nathanael's effort to visualize and hence definitively identify the threat he poses; and indeed such an effort is incorporated so as to redouble this threat (the child's eyes are transfixed by that which will medusize, blind, or devour them). Far from becoming merely the object of an identification or recognition on the part of a detached observer who is placed, unseen, at a safe remove, the Sandman comes to confound or, rather, to disorganize the spectacle the child wishes to make of him; and it is therefore also in this sense that the Sandman "names the violence of a certain disassemblage" akin to that of Ramades digging up the foundations of the operatic stage. Unable to maintain—or to *stand*—the extraterritorial position of the unseen spectator, since it is his very eyes that the Sandman threatens to blind or devour, Nathanael is driven by the Sandman's "appearance" to leap from his hiding place, to take the plunge "from the ostensibly hidden and protected security of an unseen viewing position onto a stage whose borders are difficult to define, since they change in function of movements they cannot simply contain or situate" (14). As the Sandman takes center stage, what actually takes place is, as we have seen, an indefinite and unpredictable number of shifts and repetitions (from the eyeglass vendor to the Sandman, from the Sandman to Beckmann, from Weber to Freud to Hoffman to Nathanael, from the story of castration and the scene of the unconscious to the advent of theatricality, to the question of institution, to the problem of technics, to that of reading and writing—*chez* Derrida, and so forth) that neither begin nor end with the Sandman's coming, and that therefore serve thoroughly to disorganize the borders of the stage he inhabits. At this point, where such a scene "ceases to be mere story and spectacle and becomes a theatrical scenario instead" (14), the possibility that anyone could ever simply recount the tale falters. For who *could* recount it? Certainly not Nathanael, who in taking the plunge acts out his part in the story he otherwise wishes to relate and, indeed, interpret. Not Freud, who cannot exempt himself from rejecting those inadmissible perceptions that do not fit in with one's expectations and that therefore repeat themselves, in unexpected guise, precisely in the vicinity of consciousness's unacknowledged blindness (so that "intellectual uncertainty" cannot be reduced merely to the "anxiety" occasioned by the tale, as Freud would have us believe [15]). And not the Sandman, with whom the story never quite begins or ends. Not any one in the "series" of storytellers—Weber, Hoffman, Freud, Nathanael, myself included—whose various recountings "center" upon a childhood memory that itself only repeats, rather than resolves, the attempt to locate and define the identity, intention, or meaning of the Sandman. All of us, like Nathanael, take the plunge onto the stage, "in both senses," as Weber tells us: "taking a fall and being thrust or thrown off balance" (15). For this stage is itself the "place" where the body "as a matrix for the ego: self-contained, unified, integrated" (15) is violently disassembled or disorganized. Just as Nathanael's limbs are unscrewed, and his body dismembered, he therefore loses consciousness in a sudden spasm. The dream itself theatrically dislocates and replaces the conscious life. And hardly for Nathanael alone, but for anyone who would try to tell this story:

> Hidden behind his curtain, Nathanael believes he has discovered, with his own two eyes, just *who* the Sandman really *is*. He believes he has replaced the figurative destination "Sandman" with an authentically proper name. But the name he comes up with turns out to be a link in a signifying chain that unravels what it is intended to close up: "Coppelius" [the old lawyer

who occasionally dines with the family] becomes "Coppola," the vendor of
Perspektiven, whose name . . . signifies "socket" or "hollow," but also recalls, phonetically, *copula*. The Sandman "is" the lawyer who "is(st)" [or
"eats."] The lawyer "is" the vendor of prostheses, whose name recalls the
operator of predication itself. But . . . in thus consuming its univocal meaning, this *is(s)t* emerges as the disjunctive junction of that which diverges
and yet coexists, as a part that never becomes a whole. (21)

CHAPTER 3

Technica Speciosa: Some Notes on the Ambivalence of Technics in Kant and Weber

Peter Fenves

When did a *techne*-term first become a technical term of philosophical discourse? This question can be easily answered: after the ancient Greek philosophers, who adopted the word *technê* from everyday speech, *techne*-terms first entered the lexicon of "first philosophy" in the extensive introduction to the *Critique of Judgment* that Kant carefully prepared and soon discarded in favor of a shorter introduction that largely does without these terms.[1] The fact that Kant discarded his most complete exposition of the critical program as a whole indicates that he was ambivalent about *something*, and the name of this something is, in all likelihood, *Technik*, which, as Samuel Weber's suggests, should be translated as "technics."[2] The two introductions to the *Critique of Judgment* differ in several respects, but none is more important than this: the discarded introduction makes copious use of the terms *technisch* and *Technik*, whereas the published introduction speaks of *Technik* only once, almost in passing. The question to which this essay addresses itself is therefore: why does Kant erase *Technik* from his exposition of the systematic aims of the critical program, even as he recognizes—at least for a moment—that it captures the capstone of the entire critical program more successfully than any other? The guide for the response to this question will be the work of Samuel Weber, who, more than anyone else since Walter Benjamin, has combined an intense study of the *Critique of Judgment* with an acute awareness of the ambivalent "goings-on" of "technics"—and has, in addition, made *ambivalence* into an ambivalent term of art for the predicament around which the third *Critique* revolves.

Kant Shrinks Back

The erasure of *techne-terms* from the introduction to the *Critique of Judgment* is a remarkable occurrence—not least because the introduction establishes and divides the general territory covered by the critical project. If one of the principal terms of demarcation is dropped, the terrain itself may not be changed, but access to the principle of its articulation surely is. And this is what happens to *techne-terms*. Just as Kant begins the discarded introduction by distinguishing practical reason from technical reasoning— the former is based on freedom under laws, whereas the latter remains a matter of cognition—he opens the published version of the introduction by distinguishing "technically practical" from "morally practical" (5:172). Yet, even here, in the sole place where Kant grants a *techne*-term a significant role in the outline of the critical project, an erasure of "technics" can be glimpsed. For, as he makes clear in the opening section of the original introduction, an insuperable distinction must be made between practical and technical imperatives. Kant even faults himself for failing to draw this distinction sharply enough in the *Groundwork for the Metaphysics of Morals*. Technical imperatives are not based on transcendental freedom, and for this reason they belong to theoretical philosophy despite their "practical" character. *Technik*, however, cannot be entirely integrated into theoretical philosophy; the extent of its independence is the preliminary subject, so to speak, of the third *Critique*—which, for its part, will have the same relation to "technics" as the second *Critique* has to practice. Or so one would conclude from the original introduction. In the published version, however, the assimilation of technical imperatives under the misleading rubric "technically practical" gives the impression that "technics" could not enjoy any degree of independence: by virtue of its nomenclature, *technisch* is tied to practical philosophy; consideration of its systematic function, by contrast, assigns it to theoretical philosophy.

The analogy that guides Kant's introduction to the last *Critique*— "technics" is to the *Critique of Judgment* what practice is to the *Critique of Practical Reason*—does not depend on either the erasure of the term "technical imperative" or the alteration of emphasis expressed by the phrase "technically practical." Kant is explicit about this analogy in the opening section of the discarded introduction. And for anyone who doubts that such is the case, the final words of this section emphasize that the very faculty under scrutiny, namely *Urtheilskraft* (the "force" or "power of judgment"), is not only bound up with *Technik* but is itself "*technisch*" through and through—whatever these techne-terms may mean: "we will not call the judgments themselves technical [*technisch*] but, rather, the power of judgment [*Urtheilskraft*], on whose laws they are grounded, and in accordance with [this power] we will also call nature technical; moreover, since it contains no objectively determining propositions, this technics [*Technik*] does not constitute any part of doctrinal philosophy but only a part of the critique of our faculty of cognition" (20:201)—precisely the critique that goes by the name *Kritik der Urteilskraft*. An alternative title for the final *Critique* is, therefore, *Critique of Technics*.

Or more accurately: an alternative title of the *Critique of Judgment* prefaced by its original introduction could be *Critique of Technics*, for the revised introduction gives no hint that the "power of judgment" is thoroughly and fundamentally "technical." In *Kant and the Problem of Metaphysics*, Heidegger proposes the gothic thesis that Kant "shrinks back" from the dismaying insight upon which he had originally laid the groundwork for metaphysics. This insight consists in a projective awareness of the abyss upon which human finitude grounds itself in absence of intellectual intuition—an abyss that Kant almost inadvertently captures under the title of the "transcendental synthesis of the imagination," from which, according to Heidegger, the twin stems of finite cognition (conceptuality and sensibility) owe their origin.[3] *Kant and the Problem of Metaphysics* thus becomes a philosophical oddity—even among Heidegger's texts—for its central claim is expressed in narrative terms. "Something happened" is the formal version of the claim; its material version reads, "In unveiling the subjectivity of the subject Kant shrank back [*züruckweicht*] from the very ground that he himself had laid down."[4] Heidegger finds the evidence for this thesis in the numerous alterations Kant makes to the *Transcendental Deduction of the Categories* from its first version, published in 1781, to the second version, which appeared six years later. During these six years, according to Heidegger, Kant was driven by a self-imposed desire to lay the groundwork for the metaphysics of morals in order to protect philosophy from "popular philosophizing." As a result, instead of laying out the abyssal "ground" on which *metaphysica generalis* can be glimpsed as a problem in its own right—the essential problem of the *Dasein* "in" the human being—he latched onto reason as the unshakeable bedrock for the accomplishment of the critical program.[5] Without a detailed exposition and analysis of this claim, at least this much can be said concerning the status of its textual evidence: the place where, according to Heidegger's argument, Kant concludes his project of laying the groundwork of metaphysics in the *Critique of Pure Reason* is the section devoted to the schematism of the categories, where the transcendental imagination plays an indisputably decisive role in the constitution of what Heidegger calls "transcendence": the ability of the self to encounter something other than itself. Yet, strangely enough, the schematism section is the only one that Kant left entirely unchanged from the first edition to the second.

Contrast this situation with the revision of the first introduction to the *Critique of Judgment* into the second: the first is the sole contribution to transcendental philosophy for which, as far as anyone knows, Kant prepared a fair copy and yet decided not to publish—as if, for some reason, he had sensed something startling, unnerving, or perhaps even uncanny. An oblique expression of this fright can be found in the retrospective comment he made about his decision to withdraw the original introduction: he did so, as he explains to Jacob Sigismund Beck in 1792, "merely because of its extensiveness disproportional to the text [*für den Text unproportionierten Weitläuftigkeit*]" (11:396).[6] Where else does Kant worry about being excessively prolix, especially when, as he writes in the same context, that it can contribute "much" to a "more complete insight" into the problem at hand?[7] And what does *Weitläuftigkeit* indicate other than something that "runs" away from those who pursue it? If one were to suppose that Kant "shrank back" from a disconcerting position he momentarily advanced, considerations of textual evidence alone might very well lead to the conclusion that such a withdrawal occurred in the context of the original introduction to the third *Critique* and, more precisely, in response to its use—for the first time since the ancient Greeks—of *techne-terms* as technical terms.

The reference to Heidegger's analysis of Kant's retreat—or diagnosis of his failure—would be otiose were it not for an odd coincidence: the principal evidence to which Heidegger draws his readers' attention returns to the suppressed introduction of the *Critique of Judgment* with only a slight alteration. The evidence is the appearance of a new name—indeed, a proper name—for the transcendental synthesis of the imagination in the second edition of the *Critique of Pure Reason*: specifically, the name *synthesis speciosa*. It reappears in the original introduction to the *Critique of Judgment* as *technica speciosa*. From *synthesis* to *technical*: such is the course of *species* that Kant tenuously charts from the revised version of the first *Critique* to the suppressed version of the third. It is as if "technics" replaces "synthesis" as the name for the original act of bringing order to appearances—"as if" only because "technics" is not exactly an act and cannot be entirely captured in either a critique of cognition or a critique of action. This subtle yet remarkable replacement can then be seen in retrospect as an uneasy recognition that something has indeed happened: the "technical" ordering of appearances gains a certain independence from intellectual syntheses imaginative synopses in which the unity of experience is rooted. This independence expresses itself in the absence of a "technician" to whom the "technical" ordering of appearance can be *unambiguously* attributed. Ambivalence, then, is built into this question: why do appearances as a whole appear to be technically ordered? Which is to ask: who, after all, is the technician if it cannot be the subject who must judge the world to be organized in a technical manner? The ability of the subject to see itself as both completely different from the technician and strangely like it— especially in its exercise of the reflective power of judgment—generates an insuperable ambivalence whenever the specter of "technics" arises. As an expression of this ambivalence, Kant discards the conclusive introduction in which he, for the first time, makes *techne-terms* into technical terms of first philosophy.

Entitlement

It is worth proceeding at a slightly slower pace, however, in keeping with the difficulty of the terms under discussion. Heidegger's endorsement of the first Transcendental Deduction over the second is hardly new; it corresponds to a preference expressed by post-Kantian philosophers from Hegel to Husserl. And contrary to many of the responses to *Kant and the Problem of Metaphysics* among Kant scholars, from Cassirer onward, Heidegger's endorsement of the first version of Deduction does not devolve into the thesis that Kant simply ignored or overlooked the transcendental synthesis of the imagination in the revised version. His proposal is far more complicated—and much more broadly implicated in Kant's invention of technical terms for the description of his unprecedented project. The crucial lines of the second version of the Deduction, according to Heidegger, are the following:

> The synthesis of manifold of sensible intuition, which is possible and necessary a priori, can be called figurative (*synthesis speciosa*), as distinct from that

which would be thought in the mere category with respect to the manifold of an intuition in general and which is called combination of the understanding (*synthesis intellectualis*). . . . That which determines inner sense is the understanding and its original faculty of combining the manifold of intuition, that is, of bringing it under an apperception (as that on which its very possibility rests). . . . It [the understanding] therefore exercises under the nomination of a *transcendental synthesis of the imagination* [*unter der Benennung einer transzendentalen Synthesis der Einbildungskraft*] that action [through which it can determine sensibility] on the *passive* subject, whose *faculty* it is, about which we rightly say that inner sense is thereby affected. (B 151, 153–54)

According to Heidegger's line of argument, this passage demonstrates that, for Kant, the imagination is no longer the original faculty of synthesis; all combinations are now said to owe their origin to the understanding. The imagination can claim a transcendental "use" only under the condition that its every action be authorized by the power of the understanding, which is to say, in the end, the transcendental unity of apperception. The principal action that the transcendental imagination is entitled to perform, as Kant notes moments earlier, cannot fail to appear "paradoxical" (B 152), for its "object" is the passivity of the "subject" it constitutes by thus acting. Only in the 1787 edition does Kant invent a technical term for the agent that performs this seemingly paradoxical act, namely *synthesis speciosa*. Such a synthesis consists in the determination of the *species*: the "aspect," the "look," or the "figure" in which things are knowable as the "species" of the very thing they are. From the perspective of *Kant and the Problem of Metaphysics*, the act of giving the transcendental imagination its own name repeats at the level of philosophical discourse the paradox that the term *synthesis speciosa* is supposed to capture, for, as Heidegger proceeds to explain—although he does not draw out the implications of his own formulation—the imagination gains a *proper name* only by losing its *proper standing*. Only insofar as something is independent and therefore has a standing of its own, in other words, can it garner a "proper name" in the proper sense: "in the second edition the transcendental imagination is there only in name. . . . And even if Kant in the second edition introduces an apparently characteristic proper name [*Eigenname*] for the transcendental imagination under the title *synthesis speciosa*, this expression proves precisely that the transcendental imagination has forfeited its earlier independence [*Eigenständigkeit*]. It is thus named only because the understanding relates to sensibility in it and is without this relation *synthesis intellectualis*."[8]

The term *synthesis speciosa* grants the imagination its own place in the lexicon of philosophical discourse at the very moment that it, according to Heidegger, cedes its place to the faculty from which it otherwise seeks to distinguish itself. Entitlement is therefore at stake in this conflict of the faculties. And the entitlement of the various faculties of the mind to legislate in their own domains is the initial concern of both introductions to the *Critique of Judgment*. That Kant seeks to sort out the claims that the "higher" faculties make in the course of writing the third *Critique* is hardly surprising from the perspective of *Kant and the Problem of Metaphysics*, for this effort can be seen to solidify the "shrinking back" that takes place in the second edition of the first *Critique*: neither introduction grants the imagination the "proper standing" that the "proper name" *synthesis speciosa* would seem to suggest; both emphasize that the *Critique of Pure Reason* is only a critique of the claims of the understanding alone—not a laying the ground of the being of "to be." This retrospective retitling corresponds to the project of deciding which faculty is entitled to dominate a part of the territory and therefore make this part into a domain, properly speaking. The first *Critique* turns into the "critique of the understanding," while the second becomes the "critique of the faculty of reason." And the third? Does it, too, have another title—not, of course, one that suggests itself to Kant as he completes the critical project but, rather, a title that would become legible only in the light of later developments? To these questions, which Kant himself elicits by renaming his previous *Critiques* at the moment in which the "critical business" is declared complete (5:170), the idea of a "critique of technics" naturally responds, for the decisive act by means of which Kant divides the two parts of the final *Critique* revolves around what he call *technica speciosa* (20:234)—perhaps in remembrance of the previous time he had sought to capture his own insight into, or flight from, the abyssal foundation of the critical project by introducing the technical term *synthesis speciosa* into the heart of its founding doctrine:

> The aesthetic judging of natural forms, without a basis in a concept of the object, was able to find certain objects occurring in nature purposive in the mere empirical apprehension of the intuition, that is, merely in relation to the subjective condition of the power of judgment. Aesthetic judging therefore requires no concept of the object nor did it bring one forth; thus, it explained these objects not as *natural purposes* [*Naturzwecke*], in an objective judgment, but only as *purposive* [*zweckmäßig*] for the power of representation, in a subjective relation, which purposiveness of forms can be called figurative [*figürlich*], and the technics of nature [*Technik der Natur*] with regard to such forms can also be thus named *technica speciosa*.

Teleological judgment, by contrast, presupposes a concept of the object and makes a judgment about its possibility in accordance with a law of the connection of cause and effects. This technics of nature could thus be called *plastic*, if it had not already become fashionable to use this word in a more general sense, namely for natural beauty as well as natural intentions; hence it may be called the *organic technics* of nature. (20:233–34)[9]

The difference between the two parts of the *Critique of Judgment* thus come down to the distinction between "figurative" and "plastic" technics: the former is solely concerned with the "aspects" or "species" of nature that appear to its judge, whereas the latter is concerned with the form of the apparent object itself. The primacy of the first part of the third *Critique*, which Kant emphasizes in both introductions, follows from the fact that it alone makes an independent contribution to transcendental philosophy. The analysis of organic nature is doubtless an indispensable element of systematic science, which critical philosophy seeks to secure; but only the analysis of the figural character of the technics of nature has anything to do with the question first posed by the *Critique of Pure Reason*: how is nature in general possible? The answer provided by the first *Critique* revolves around the idea of a *synthesis speciosa*; the answer provided by the third—at least in its original introduction—veers toward the technical term *technica speciosa*. Here, however, the parallelism between the two *Critiques* breaks down, for the idea of a *synthesis speciosa* represents the culmination of a complex argument about the power of the imagination in its "transcendental use," whereas the idea of a *technica speciosa* marks the absence of an argument that begs to be developed. If it were possible to justify the claim that something in nature is beautiful by seeing it as a "species" or "figure" of the "technics of nature," then Kant would have accomplished the goal he sets himself in the preface to the third *Critique* and put the "entire critical business" (5:170) behind him.

But Kant does not proceed in this manner. It would be more accurate to say, however, that he does not want to complete the critical project by resting its final claim about the conditions of possible cognition in the idea of a *technica speciosa*. And there is at least one good reason for his diffidence in this regard: if the estimation of a phenomenon in terms of its beauty is based on the idea of a "technics of nature," then the analysis of aesthetic judgment must be subordinated to a wider inquiry into the *nature of technics*. The first introduction to the *Critique of Judgment* represents a tentative step in this direction, from which Kant ultimately withdrew. Instead of grounding aesthetic judgments in the idea of a *technica speciosa*, Kant decided to base it on another idea, namely that of a specifically "aesthetic common sense," in which the accord of the two higher cognitives generates a feeling that is qualitatively different from all others and corresponds to the "transcendental" concept of feeling as such, namely that of state of mind which maintains itself on the basis of its own causality. With this alteration, Kant doubtless reemphasizes the subjective character of aesthetic judgment and allows for a transition between theoretical and practical modes of thinking; but at the same time he loses what he had momentarily glimpsed in the tenth section of the original introduction: that aesthetics—which is characterized by a singular combination of singular cases and universal claims—is, after all, only a tributary of the unexplored territory entitled "technics."

"Ambivalent Demarcations"

To assert, without further ado, that aesthetics is a tributary of technics is, however, to assume that technics is a properly demarcated territory in its own right—a territory that could somehow be discovered among the "field of concepts" that Kant tries to demarcate in the preface to the *Critique of Judgment*. And the journey of discovery would follow the lead of aesthetics. But such an assertion is faulty to the precise extent that it captures something about the relation between aesthetics and technics from the perspective of the critical project. Technics is not the title of a specific territory within the "field of concepts" that is divided into two domains, one subordinated to the concepts of nature (the highest of which are the categories of the understanding), the other subordinated to the concept of freedom (which is the basis for categorical imperatives). Rather, if technics is the title of any territory, which is by no means certain, it is that of the rift that divides the field from itself, a rift that the *Critique of Judgment* is charged with bridging without actually repairing lest the two domains that otherwise cover the same field lose their constitutive autonomy. To be sure, Kant wants to ward off the suggestion that technics belongs to *both* sides of the field. By a process of exclusion—technics does not belong to practical philosophy pure and simple despite the fact that everyone thinks of technics as a species of action—Kant hopes to maintain the integrity of the division in question; but the very fact that the territory of technics can be demarcated principally by way of exclusion indicates that it partakes of the kind of ambivalence that Samuel Weber describes in and by this name.

This peculiar ambivalence is then acted out, as it were, in the act of discarding the first introductions to the last *Critique*. About "the ambivalence of demarcation," Weber writes, "the marks of distinction imperceptibly but inexorably *demark* themselves. The particular concern with the particular, the unpredictable, the unexpected, defines itself through a heterogeneity from which it can never entirely extricate itself. Such marks thus remain determined by what they are not even when they seek to conceal this unrequitable indebtedness."[10]

In order to delineate the characteristics of ambivalent demarcation Weber turns to the account of reflective judgment that can be found in the published introduction to the *Critique of Judgment*. Kant distinguishes the determinate "power of judgment" (*Urtheilskraft*) from its reflective counterpart by representing the latter as the direct inversion of the former: whereas determinate judgment subsumes the particular under the universal, to which it enjoys immediate access, reflective judgment holds onto the particular with a view toward discovering the universal under which it can be retrospectively subsumed. Understood in this way, the power of judgment per se does not require a critique of its own: only insofar as it is merely reflective does the situation change, for under this condition the power of judgment is detached from the telos of subsumption and thereby gains a certain—highly indeterminate—freedom. According to standard interpretations of what follows from this freedom, merely reflective judgment is purely regulative: it establishes rules for empirical research into nature; but these rules, which must not be mistaken for laws, are valid solely as guidelines for those who engage in such research. For Weber, by contrast, merely reflective judgment is principally *deregulative*, for the rules established under its auspices rob the judging subject of any assurance that they are anything more than singular instances—representations, events, or acts. If this is the case, however, then these rules are constitutively incapable of being regulated. Or more exactly: the only universally valid rule is that every rule is in the process of being altered to the point where it no longer functions as a rule. The *deregulative* character of merely reflective judgment is a direct consequence of the "ambivalent demarcation" by which the subject matter of judgment is generated: the only way to mark a concept that is "given" for judgment in its merely reflective capacity is by way of exclusion: not a flower in general, for example, nor a flower in the botanical sense of the word, as the sexual organ of the plant, not even "this" flower, insofar as "this" is taken to be a predicate of a peculiar kind, which applies to more than a single instance, but only a flower whose very exemplarity is bereft of the universal term it is supposed to exemplify. None of the marks by which a "given" concept can be delimited, if not determined, are free from the same process of demarcation. They, too, can be known only by way of exclusion—the exclusion, namely, of the general mark of which they would be particular cases under the condition that they were indeed "cases" and not singular, unruly instances: wild markings, say, which doubtless mean something, but do so only under the condition that this "something" not be determined with respect to what someone wished to say, even if this "someone" is another kind of understanding altogether— which is the case with Kant but not for Weber.

Kant is clear about this point: the "technics of nature" suggests that the figures of nature we judge to be beautiful ultimately owe their origin to another kind of understanding, which would produce the objects it intuits simply by virtue of the intuition itself. This suggestion expresses itself in the form of an "as if": we are to regard the "technics of nature" as if it were produced by a form of understanding about which we know nothing other than the negative fact that it is altogether different from our own. In this way we are justified in applying the word *technics* to nature in the absence of any insight into the corresponding "technician." As Weber writes near the end of "Ambivalence," the fictional character of the "tech- nician" who is supposed to stand behind the "technics of nature" compro- mises whatever cognitions are gained on its basis: "The fictionality of the Kantian *als-ob*, the 'as-if,' thus becomes the condition of all knowledge of the particular. But it is a singular condition, one we 'assume' without 'really' assuming it, since it is 'only' what we might call a 'heuristic device.' And yet, can we be sure that the discoveries made possible by such a device are themselves more reliable or any less fictional than the 'assumption' from which they proceed?"[11] For Weber, the answer to this question is unambiguously "no." Kant's account of merely reflective judgment doubt- less suggests *something*; but this "something" is not the existence of an "intuitive intellect" or "intellectual intuition" who creates nature in such a manner that we judge it be purposive. Rather, it suggests that the very idea of cognition must be transformed. Instead of reconfirming the tradi- tional idea of cognition as static recognition of underlying reality, the pub- lished introduction to the third *Critique* comes close to acknowledging that the act of cognition is inseparable from a transformation of what it means to know: "What Kant's notion of reflective judgment suggests, without stating it as such, is a situation in which 'given' concepts do not suffice to identify or 'subsume' the particular case, and hence in which the latter requires a reorganization and reworking of these concepts. If such a reworking is what constitutes the a priori principle of judgment, then its product, whether it is cognitive or aesthetic, will always entail an element of *change*, of *transformation*. This notion of transformation, never mentioned by Kant, is nonetheless what might be called the *deregulative idea* of the third *Critique*."[12]

Once the "technics of nature" is no longer seen as a different kind of understanding—whether it be called "intuitive intellect" or "intellectual intuition"—then it can be understood as the transformation of the sole kind of understanding with which we are familiar, namely our own. But there is undeniable cost to this transformation: it is no longer possible to say, with conviction, that we are familiar with our own kind of understanding; on the contrary, understanding—not only the "higher faculty" of the mind analyzed in the first *Critique* but also the most elementary act of taking something for something else—is irredeemably unfamiliar, perhaps even uncanny. This self-division of the understanding thus becomes the lesson of the third *Critique*. The "official" part of this lesson expresses itself in the discovery of an independent, a priori principle for merely reflective judgment, which disengages itself from its subservience to the understanding, namely the principle of the formal purposiveness of nature. Beauty forms a primary part of this lesson, for it demonstrates that nature is indeed sometimes favorable to us: our cognitive faculties are felt to be made for nature, even if—or more exactly, precisely because—the purposiveness in question is without purpose. Another version of the same lesson says something very different, however. It expresses itself in the thought that *technics is, as such, without a corresponding technician*. The absence of the technician is not a dogmatic absence, which would correspond to the thesis of dogmatic metaphysics and would express itself in the formula "It is absent." Or, more pathetically stated: "God is dead." No, the absence of the technician means the absence of a given rule by which "the" technician—divine, human, or neither human nor divine—can be ascertained. Without such a rule, there can only be a conflict over who "in fact" made whatever appears to be made for us. This is, as it were, the remarkably simple insight toward which the original introduction to the *Critique of Judgment* moves and from which Kant apparently shrinks: the insight that technics always already operates independently of "the" technician to whom it supposedly owes its origin. This independence can be quickly cast in terms of "aesthetic freedom," but it is originally something else—and something far less reassuring: it amounts to the constant and unpredictable transformation of the subject who is supposed to gain knowledge of things on the basis of a synthesis of unmediated intuition and discursive concepts. The tendency of technics—beginning with the *technica speciosa* about which Kant momentarily writes, only to forget his own remark—runs counter to this definitive synthesis, as it begins to insert itself *between* these two sources of knowledge without presenting itself as the root from which they both develop.

Technica Speciosa *Yet Again*

"Ambivalence" is not an essay on the problem of technics. Instead, it is concerned with the relation between "institutions and interpretation"—to cite the title of the volume in which it can be found. Weber presents the *Critique of Judgment* as something like a critique of "institutional think-ing," which is to say, the mode of thought on which institutions rest and which presupposes, in effect, that the act of instituting can be clearly de-marcated from the actual institution thus created. By reflecting on the idea of the institution from the perspective of those sections of the third *Cri-tique* that frame its discussion of aesthetic judgment—specifically the pub-lished introduction and the final reflections on the absence of any conceivable "methodology of taste"—Weber shows that institutions are necessarily caught up in the same "embarrassment" (*Verlegenheit*) that generates the need for a critique of judgment. In both cases, a singular instance remains the principal point of reference for the generation of the rule under which it is supposed to fall, with the result that the rule—the concept in the case of aesthetic judgment, the set of authoritative regula-tions in the case of institutional thinking—is always only surmised, which is to say, fictionalized. Aesthetic judgment has the advantage of emphasiz-ing the fictive status of the rule: it is not entirely "made up," to be sure, but it is always a matter of dispute. Reflection on institutions—which is inseparable from specific institutional practices—could take a lesson from Kant's analysis of reflective judgment. The point of this lesson is not to "aestheticize" already formed institutions but, on the contrary, to recog-nize that the apparently straightforward act of founding an institution is structurally equivalent to the convoluted act of merely reflective judgment that Kant analyzes in the third *Critique*.

But there seems to be a fundamental disparity between the act of aes-thetic judgment and that of forming an institution: in strictly Kantian terms, the former is primarily "receptive," whereas the latter is a function of its opposite, namely "spontaneity." If the third *Critique* were *solely* con-cerned with the nature of aesthetic judgments, this disparity would dimin-ish the structural similarity between aesthetics and institutionalization.

Such is not the case, however, because the third *Critique* also tentatively takes into consideration the "productive" dimension of aesthetics, especially in its discussion of "aesthetic ideas." Weber quotes the following passage from section 49 in Bernard's translation, in which an aesthetic idea is described as "a representation of the imagination associated with a given concept [and] bound up with a multiplicity of partial representations in its free employment that for it no expression marking a definite concept can be found."[13] As Weber proceeds to explain, inquiry into the nature of institutions is comparable to reflection on aesthetic ideas, insofar as both require the exploration of "the processes and mechanisms by which a certain degree of unity—of names or terms—is imparted to that 'multiplicity of partial representations' which Kant described as characteristic of aesthetic ideas."[14] The *partiality* of representation is doubly important: in the context of aesthetics, it means that there is no complete representation of the idea, which implies, in turn, that only certain "names or terms" are appropriate for its exposition; in the context of an inquiry into the nature of institutionalization, it means that there is no *final* form in which an institution fully expresses and affirms the founding act by which it was instituted.

Aesthetic ideas, unlike the "free beauties" of nature, are made. But—and this is, for Kant, the decisive point—they are not a matter of "mere technique." On the contrary, only a "genius" can create an aesthetic idea. Since the term *genius* is defined as the ability to "give rules to nature," this famous proposition from the third *Critique* could be reformulated in the following fashion: "genius" is the name of an instance in which technique, as it is generally understood, makes way for the "technics of nature," which the understanding can under no condition comprehend. "Genius," in other words, is not the origin of the idea but only its *medium*. And the medial character of "genius" means that aesthetic ideas cannot be seen from the perspective of their putative origin but must, instead, be analyzed only in light of the entire spectrum of "media" by which they come to be known—a spectrum in which the supposed "individual genius," whose name we might be able to identify, is only an evanescent moment. A remarkable ambiguity thus accrues to aesthetic ideas: it marks the passage from the idea of "fine art" to the problem of "technics as medium." Of course, for Kant, only geniuses are capable of enriching the "fine arts." But his definition of genius, taken literally, points elsewhere, for "geniuses" are not ultimately responsible for the things they create—nature is. And here the nature to which these things owe their origin is exactly the same nature that generates the "appearance of technics" (*technica speciosa*). In the opening chapter of *Mass Mediauras*, after conducting a thorough examination of the problem of form in the "Critique of Aesthetic Judgment," Weber returns to the problem of aesthetic ideas and emphasizes again—pace Bernard—that they are precisely not "ineffable" but, rather, "unnameable" (*unnennbar*): "This is not to say that aesthetic ideas, as the effect of form in the process of becoming unhinged, cannot make use of names or of nouns but rather that such ideas will never be able to be named properly. Aesthetic ideas are by necessity 'overnamed,' to cite a term of Walter Benjamin's, and as such they are also *undernamed*."[15] Understood in this manner—which draws on Benjamin's analysis of the medial character of language—the idea of aesthetic ideas gives rise to a long series of questions, all of which point toward the intimate relation between mediality and technicity:

> If "aesthetic ideas" can no longer be rendered by a univocal and proper name, how will they ever permit anyone to know with any certainty just who is speaking or writing? And if it can never be established beyond the shadow of a doubt just what is being said, how can anyone be held definitively accountable? How will it be possible to attribute or restore a statement to its legitimate owner if the statement does not stand still long enough to be unequivocally *identified*? And are not such questions pertinent for visual representation as well as for verbal discourse? With the emerging awareness that neither *name* nor *form* can be relied upon to provide a reliable point of reference, the status of the *object* itself is no longer certain.[16]

At this point in his reflection of the "unraveling of form" Weber turns to Kafka's "Sorge eines Hausvaters" (Cares of a family man)—not least because the only apparent "care" of the "family man" is the potentially ever-unraveling form of something indeterminate that calls itself "Odradek." But the wider arc of *Mass Mediauras* points to another unraveling phenomenon, namely "the aura," as it appears in Benjamin's "The Work of Art in the Age of its Technical Reproducibility." In the discussion that concludes this book Weber emphasizes the relation between Benjamin's inquiry into the work of art and Kant's analysis of merely reflective judgment: "The ambiguous, even ambivalent, notion of an 'aura' elaborated by Walter Benjamin in his effort to rethink the aesthetic in the light of modern technologies of representation is very indebted to this Kantian tradition."[17] It is not as though the notion of the aura is a descendent from that of the aesthetic idea—although this may very well be the case. The point is, rather, that there is something like an "elective affinity" between the two: on the one hand, the aesthetic idea is at first simply a matter of human "spirit," which lifts it above all merely "technical" skill, whereas the aura is decidedly not the creation of any individual human being but is, on the contrary, a function of certain practices; on the other hand, the aesthetic idea cannot in the end be attributed to any individual creator other than the indeterminate "no one" whose improper name is *nature*, whereas the aura is inseparable from the experience of the particular "hands" that work on the thing from which it emanates. What unites these two notions is what appears to destroy them both: "too much" technics. The aura "declines" in conjunction with the intensification of technical reproducibility; the production of aesthetic ideas is incompatible with too great a reliance on transmissible techniques.

As Weber emphasizes, however—so much so that this emphasis can even be called one of the primary lessons of *Mass Mediauras*—Benjamin does not have a *single* theory of the aura, and he does not simply say that "too much" technics results in its "decline" (*Verfall*). On the contrary, Benjamin's theory of the aura "disintegrates, falls, *verfällt*, into at least two theories."[18] And: "*aura thrives in its decline.*"[19] Something similar can be said of aesthetic ideas: it is not simply that they are incompatible with mechanically reproducible techniques; "too much" is a function of "not enough"—not enough *nature*, which is to say, not enough *technics* of an entirely unknown kind. The theory of aesthetic ideas disintegrates into two theories as well. On the one hand, it is an almost tautological exposition of what geniuses are capable of producing by virtue of the fact that they are geniuses and not merely skilled artists. On the other hand, and in abstraction from the dubious concept of genius, the theory of aesthetic ideas recapitulates and intensifies the ambivalence that expresses itself in the term Kant carefully eliminated from the published version of the *Critique*, namely *speciosa technica*. The term cannot be translated as "the appearance of a technics *of* nature," for nature can be considered the origin of the "technical" appearance only under the fictive condition of an "as if." Still less can the term be understood, in reverse, as "the appearance of technics in the traditional, namely mechanical, sense of the term," in which case an identifiable human being, namely a genius, would be inextricably associated with its production. The theory of *technica speciosa* can be adequately developed only under the condition that it is clear from the start that there is no unambiguously nonfictive agent who can be held accountable for the appearance in question: it is not "nature" that gives rise to this *species*, since the attribution of authorship to nature is only a function of reflective judgment; nor it is a "genius" who can be called its author, since the idea of genius is dependent on the "actual"—which is to say in this context, fictive—attribution of authorship to nature.

As Weber also emphasizes at the conclusion of his reflection on Benjamin's "Artwork" essay—and this can be considered another of the primary lessons of *Mass Mediauras*—the fact that the aura not only fails to disappear when it is in "decline" but positively thrives under this condition does not mean that the phenomenon of "declension" is illusory. Something indeed collapses—not the aura around but, rather, the artwork: "What is condemned in the age of technical reproducibility is not aura as such but the aura of art as a work of representation, a work that would have its fixed place, that would take its place in and as a world-picture. What remains is the *mediaura* of an apparatus whose glance takes up everything and gives nothing back, except perhaps in the blink of an eye."[20] Kant doubtless had no knowledge about such an apparatus, especially if it is identified with the camera, which *literally* makes possible purely "technical appearances." Nevertheless, the idea of *technica speciosa* can be understood as a precise response to the collapse—or as Weber suggests, the "condemnation"—in which it discovers its function. This much is clear: the "thing" that appears as technical in the ambivalent phenomenon of *technica speciosa* is not a *work*. Kant calls it a "figure," in contrast to a "plastic" object like an organic being; but the difference between "figure" and "plastic" cannot be reduced to a matter of dimensionality. "Figure" as opposed to "plastic" means, rather, that *the whole is never present*—only an "aspect," in other words, a "species." Because a work of art cannot appear in this manner, without immediately destroying its art-character, Kant apparently has no choice but to affirm that *technica speciosa* must be seen as phenomenon on *nature*. But he could just as well be heard to say: "here is the phenomenon of the *mediaura*, the apparatus of which I am as yet utterly unaware." Because he does not want to say this—or perhaps because he simply wants to say that the apparatus in question is not only unknown to *him* but unknowable *in principle*—he dispenses the original introduction to the third *Critique* and replaces it with an introduction that makes no mention of *technica speciosa*. To be sure, he does not thereby overcome the ambivalence of this term; he only makes sure that it will not be taken for what it says, namely that the fundamental problem of aesthetics is neither that of "natural beauties" nor that of "fine art" but, rather, of *technical appearances*. These appearances do not call for aesthetic reflection. Rather, they call *apparatuses* in and through which they can take place as such. What can be seen from the perspective of Weber's analysis of third *Critique* in conjunction with Benjamin's "aesthetics" is that this is perhaps what Kant meant by "merely reflective judgment" all along—a merely technical apparatus for the taking-up of *technica speciosa*.

CHAPTER 4

Surfing Technics: Direction and Dispersion in the Age of Information

R. L. Rutsky

Samuel Weber's writings generally take as their point of departure the most significant works of Continental thought, from Freud and Lacan to Derrida and Heidegger, Kant and Hegel, Benjamin and Adorno, and others. Yet, what is unique about his work is that, in the course of careful readings of "high theory," Weber frequently moves from these theoretical texts to topics such as the Gulf War, the "War on Terror," the media, and contemporary technologies, topics that are generally regarded as involving more pragmatic, "real world" issues than the supposedly airy heights of Continental philosophy. Indeed, Weber's work is, in large part, a sustained effort to disrupt such distinctions between the theoretical and the practical, the philosophical and the political, and between the ingrained figures (for instance, "the heights" versus "the down-to-earth") that support them.[1] This is also to say that Weber's work is not a matter of applying theory to "objects" in the world[2]—an approach that inevitably represents the relation of theory to practice as a unidirectional passage from high to low, thereby reinforcing the distinction of theory from practice.

If Weber's work takes its departure from theoretical considerations, it never indulges in metatheoretical pretensions; neither does it, on the other hand, pretend to have moved outside of theory, beyond theory, to some more authentic locale. Rather, it is theory itself that moves: a theoretical movement that proceeds not toward a particular destination or end, but that "takes off from" its "objects," so that its own trajectory is continually deflected, displaced, by what it encounters. If this movement may be said to have a direction, it is not a direction that is predetermined, plotted in advance. This "indeterminate" quality has in fact led some critics to depict deconstruction—and theorists influenced by deconstruction—as aimless or lacking in direction, particularly in regard to social and political issues (politics being defined precisely in terms of clear positionality and direction of movement toward a known end). Such criticisms, however, inevitably return to the entrenched binary positions (politics versus theory, direction versus lack of direction) that deconstructive work such as Weber's attempts to disrupt, to unsettle. Indeed, one might say that the theoretical movement of Weber's work is unsettling because it neither relies on a fixed direction nor lacks all direction. Rather, Weber's work moves, not simply at the direction of a subject presumed to know, but through a process of interaction: an interaction with the other, with alterity, that continually displaces, redirects, and detours it.

I have taken up this question of—or perhaps, as Weber has suggested, this "quest after"[3]—movement and directionality because I believe that it has an important bearing on contemporary issues of technology and media. Weber has, of course, written extensively on these issues, and his writings repeatedly move around and through a rhetoric in which place, movement, direction, and dissemination are "brought-to-the-fore." His texts are strewn with terms and concepts such as emplacement and displacement, setting-in-place and unsettling, bringing-forth and going-on, destination and dispersion. Yet, in his work, these concepts are themselves unsettled, cast into ambivalent and shifting relations. In taking these works as my own point of departure, I hope to point out how our notions of media and information technologies continue to be defined by figures of direction and becoming lost, navigation and drift, solidity and fluidity, concentration and dispersion. I also hope to show how—following in what Weber refers to as "the wake of deconstruction"—we might figure our relation to the world of information and new technologies not simply in terms of our ability to navigate it, to place or secure ourselves in relation to it, but in terms of movements that, like those of information itself, are complex, fluid, and often unsettling. What follows will, therefore, necessarily be disjunctive and partial, shifting from one direction to another, much as one might attempt to surf on a wave—or in this case, on a wake—as it moves across the water.

Information

The figures of directionality and its conventional opposites, drift and dispersion, are present in the very formations of information theory, on which our current conceptions of information continue to rely. It is hardly coincidental, for example, that Norbert Wiener's use of the term "cybernetics" was based on the Greek for steersman.[4] In Wiener's formulation, cybernetics was indeed a matter of steering: of controlling or organizing information in a self-regulating system, a system in which information becomes the "feedback" that the system uses to adjust its behavior—to steer its course. Here, information becomes precisely a matter of having direction, a purpose, a destination or end. Information that does not have this sense of direction or purpose is not information at all; it is merely random, meaningless noise—the opposite of information. In Claude Shannon and Warren Weaver's theorization, on the other hand, information becomes a measure of the degree of statistical uncertainty or randomness in the communication situation. Information, in other words, is equated with a lack of organized direction, with random diffusion or entropy as opposed to purposeful, directed communication.[5] Less information exists in a communication situation that is highly organized or directed. By the same token, any decline in the level of organization involves a corresponding increase in the amount of information present. Thus, in Shannon and Weaver's model, one might say, information is presented as a kind of drift. Yet, as Weaver himself notes, Shannon and Weaver's concept of information as a measure of uncertainty leads to the rather counterintuitive conclusion that noise must itself be considered as information:

> If noise is introduced, then the received message contains certain distortions, certain errors, certain extraneous material, that would certainly lead one to say that the received message exhibits, because of the effects of the noise, an increased uncertainty. But if the uncertainty is increased, the information is increased, and this sounds as though the noise were beneficial! (109)

Faced with this situation, Weaver hastens to reestablish a distinction between "good" and "bad" information:

> It is therefore possible for the word information to have either good or bad connotations. Uncertainty which arises by virtue of freedom of choice on the part of the sender is desirable uncertainty. Uncertainty which arises

because of errors or because of the influence of noise, is undesirable uncertainty. (Ibid.)

At first glance, it may seem that Weaver's distinction is simply a means of restoring the idea of direction or steering to the communicational equation; the sender's intention or meaning becomes the directing principle of the communication, and as such, it is favored over the undesirable uncertainty of errors or random noise. Yet, what is actually preferred here is not the sender's intent, but the sender's "freedom of choice." What makes uncertainty desirable—that is, what makes information good as opposed to bad—is not that a sender chooses a particular message (in which case it would no longer be uncertain), but the possibility that one of several messages could be chosen. The "choice" or information in a given situation would be greatest when there is an equal probability that any of the possible messages will be chosen. If one message is more likely to occur, the situation becomes more directed, and the choice, or level of information, declines. If only one message could be sent, there would be, as Weaver remarks, "no uncertainty at all—no freedom of choice—no information" (105).

Why is informational freedom of choice more desirable than the information involved in random noise? At the most obvious level, of course, this privileging of choice reflects the typical assumptions of Western and capitalist individualism, where the discourse of individual freedom often seems indistinguishable from the rhetoric of personal or consumer choice. Freedom of choice is, in fact, often figured as the equivalent of "free will," the freedom to choose one's destiny, one's destination. An individual who has no choice—whether of message or direction—is not considered free. Thus, to be without informational choice is presented as having a direction, and therefore destination, imposed upon one. It is to merely "follow directions," to lose one's "free will," to be an object rather than a subject.

Much of the appeal of capitalism has rested on this ideology of "free" choice. In capitalism, consumer choices are portrayed—and this applies as much to the consumption of information as to the consumption of goods—as a form of self-expression or individual freedom. The availability of such choices allows us, as consumers, to feel that we have made our own decisions, that we have chosen a particular direction or lifestyle over another. Here, informational freedom of choice is presented as desirable for precisely the same reasons that being able to choose freely from among such commodities as clothing or cars is supposedly desirable: it gives us the sense that we are directing our lives, choosing our own course.

Weber has pointed to the important role that the sense of freedom and directional mobility plays in the constitution and "securing" of the modern self. Contrasting mass transportation to the automobile, he notes that "the lure of the private automobile is associated with the greater 'freedom' it promises with regard to such predetermined circuits. It holds out the hope of escaping from established tracks and routes, the promise of being able to displace oneself at will: of being truly auto-mobile."[6]

This dream of uninhibited mobility and choice serves to confirm the self-determining, self-directing capacities of the individual subject. Here, freedom of movement, and of choice, become a means of securing the self, proving the self's mastery over the world. This sense of mastery is—as Weber, drawing upon Heidegger, points out—made possible through technology's "emplacing" of that world in instrumental terms, for the subject's use. Today, this placing or enframing is, I would argue, increasingly figured in terms of "digitization" and "information."

With the increasing digitization of the world, the promises of mobility and choice also seem to have been amplified. Much of the celebratory rhetoric of information technologies is founded upon the liberation of the self that they supposedly make possible. Yet, this liberation remains dependent on the self's sense of mastery and direction. Ironically, however, as the world of information grows in density and scope, this sense of mastery and direction often seems increasingly in doubt.

This concern with direction and control helps to explain why Shannon and Weaver must distinguish noise from freely chosen information. Unlike messages, noise has no particular point of origin, direction, or destination. It cannot be located, for noise has no particular site, no fixed address. Noise can appear anywhere, at virtually any time. Noise is a matter of movement, but its movements are not stable, intended, or predictable. Rather, the movements of noise are random, chaotic, accidental. They take place, one might say, on their own terms, without regard for senders, receivers, or channels. Noise may be information, but it is not instrumental information; it does not exist for the human subject's use, nor can it simply be chosen. The possible messages in Weaver's example of "good" information, on the other hand, require the existence of someone or something capable of choosing among them, directing them. Without this mechanism of decision, all information would be random. It makes little sense, though, to think of noise as chosen or directed by a subject—unless, of course, we have recourse to magical, spiritual, or extraterrestrial discourses. UFOs and aliens, for example, are often associated with various sorts of noise: static, electrical disturbances, unexplainable random lights.

Thus, while the uncertainty among possible messages is figured in terms of human choice, the uncertainty of noise is, it seems, often regarded as inherently inhuman. It is inhuman precisely because it is not chosen, controlled, directed to human ends. It therefore disrupts the fantasy of unrestricted freedom and mobility that is the promise of modern technics generally and of information technologies in particular.

Yet, according to Shannon and Weaver's theories, noise is information. There is, therefore, a notable similarity between these figurations of information and noise and that ambiguous dynamic that Weber traces in Heidegger's thinking on technology. Heidegger sees modern technics as a form of emplacement or setting-in-place that enframes or directs our view of the world. As Weber notes in his essay "Upsetting the Setup," this technical emplacement is linked to information, for it treats "objects as calculable data, as information to be taken into account" (73). Yet, if modern technics (and information) can be figured in terms of emplacing, Heidegger also sees the essence of technology as an ongoing process or movement, which Weber reads as "a movement of unsecuring" (70). This unsecuring movement is, in the enframing or emplacing of modern technology, resecured, given a set direction or destination. Yet, this unsecuring tendency is not simply effaced or removed; it continues to be part of the movement of modern technics—and of information culture. Indeed, I would suggest that this unsecuring movement corresponds closely to the dispersive movements of noise. With its lack of articulable direction, its unsecuring tendency, its entropic dissemination, noise can be seen not only, as Shannon and Weaver argue, as a matter of information, but as the very essence of information.

Channels

Figures of direction and dispersion are not, of course, confined to information theory, but appear throughout information or media culture. Informational and media technologies in fact present themselves as means of "channeling" what are taken to be aimless movements (of, for example, electrons, photons, bits), directing them to purposive, "human" ends. The term "channel" has traditionally referred to navigable passages of water, and by extension to figurative routes or passages through which messages are conducted, through which information flows (for instance, "diplomatic channels"). In radio usage, "channels" came eventually to refer to specific bands within the frequency spectrum—for example, "clear channels"—

that were allocated by governmental regulation for particular purposes. In radio, however, the term *channel* did not designate, as it later would with television, the broadcast frequency of a particular station. It was only with the rise of television that channels came to be a way of specifying the "place" of a "station," fixing its "location" within the frequency spectrum. In this sense, channels served as addresses for television broadcast stations. Indeed, in most locales in the United States, television stations are known less by their names (that is, their "call letters") than by their address within the frequency spectrum, as indicated by their channel number. Thus, people tend to speak of Channel 4 or Channel 7 more readily than they do of KNBC or WABC. With the growth of cable and satellite television, channels may no longer refer to "actual" frequency locations, but they have become an even more crucial means of specifying the place of stations and networks amidst the plethora of available programming. On the Internet, too, the terminology of channels has been employed to designate virtual locations where flows or streams of information can be found and accessed.

This emphasis on location, number, and addresses makes clear one of the most basic assumptions underlying the idea of channels: channels represent an emplacement of a previously unlocatable virtual space—whether in the frequency spectrum or within the space of computer networks. Moreover, this placement is figured not merely as a matter of place, but, frequently, as a commercialization and privatization of space: channels, in other words, become a kind of real estate—or, rather, a kind of virtual estate. Like commercial property, broadcast channel space is, for example, "leased" through an agreement that gives stations exclusive rights to "tenancy" and protects them from "poaching." The scarcity of frequency bandwidth has meant that these channels have become extremely valuable properties. Indeed, many broadcast stations are now attempting to use digital technologies to "subdivide" their spectrum space, so that they can provide several simultaneous channels instead of only one. Here, channels have become not only a means of marking and fixing location, but also of fixing the value of those locations as a form of property.

At the same time, however, that channels are set in place both in terms of location and property values, the idea of a channel continues to serve as a figure that necessarily involves a displacement, a movement from one location to another. In "Television: Set and Screen," Weber takes note of this basis in movement when he argues that "television is perhaps first and foremost a method of transmission; and transmission, which is movement, involves separation."[7] Yet, in Weber's view, television implies not only the separation or displacement involved in transmission; it also involves the sense of "presentness" that "takes place" in reception. Indeed, Weber argues, "television takes place in at least three places at once: (1) In the place (or places) where the image and sound are 'recorded'; (2) in the place (or places) where those images and sounds are received; and (3) in the place (or places) in between, through which those images and sounds are transmitted" (117). Channels, of course, are a name for this "in-between" location, through which the movement or displacement of information occurs. Channels, however, imply that this transmissive movement is not a matter of random drift or dispersion, that the "messages" transmitted are not a matter of mere noise. Channels, rather, are a figure for the routing of information; they are supposed to serve as a means of imparting direction to the undirected, dispersive, or entropic movements of fluids, electrons, or data. If, for example, information flows through a channel, its movements are limited, its direction is set. It cannot, supposedly, go astray or become lost, but must, rather like water in a canal or pipeline, follow a predetermined course to its destination. Indeed, the goal of a channel in this sense is to direct the fluidity of information, so that data arrive at their locus of reception unsullied, pure, with no loss, no drift. In this sense, channels aspire not simply to transmit information (or entertainment), but also to give that information an address, an end, and, ultimately, a sense of meaning and presence. Thus, Weber argues, "What television transmits is not so much images, as is almost always argued. It does not transmit representations but rather the semblance of presentation as such, understood as the power not just to see and hear but to place before us" (117). For Weber, this "setting in place" is fundamental to televisual presentation, which is why he maintains that "what television sets before us is first and foremost the television set itself" (119). From this perspective, channels may be seen as the means—or perhaps the medium—through which transmission is "set in place." Channels serve to secure the movements of information, to place the dissemination of information within "proper," locatable boundaries. They might therefore be said to "inform" these movements. Without channels, or some similar figure, the fluidity of information would in fact be indistinguishable from the random distributions of noise.

Of course, as Derrida has observed of writing (another information technology that has often been figured as an empty channel for messages), efforts to impart a set direction or proper place to information often seem to go astray, to lead not to a predetermined destination, but to drift in unforeseen directions. Something always becomes lost in the transmission and reception of information, overspilling the technological channels and guides that would present information merely as a matter of calculable vectors and verifiable coordinates. Weber observes a similar ambivalence between setting in place and displacing in television: "television brings the most remote things together only to disperse them again" (125). Television, like technology more generally, therefore becomes caught in a kind of vicious circle, with its dispersive, unsettling qualities provoking ever more intense efforts to resecure or rechannel information, to reestablish a sense of (remote) control and direction. In Weber's view, "the more technology seeks to put things in their proper places, the less proper those places turn out to be, the more displaceable everything becomes and the more frenetic becomes the effort to reassert the propriety of the place as such" (124). It would seem that these efforts must grow increasingly desperate as information and channels proliferate (not only on cable and satellite, but also on the Internet), and as devices for recording, time-shifting, and customizing viewing become more common. Yet, as Weber argues, "the more the medium tends to unsettle, the more powerfully it presents itself as the antidote to the disorder to which it contributes" (126).

Navigating

If television continually attempts to position itself as a secure, unifying space amidst the unsettling disorder that it "sets up," this tendency is perhaps even more pronounced in information and networking technologies. This ambivalence is especially apparent on the World Wide Web, whose very name promises a space of inclusive totality that is, at the same time, dispersed and decentralized. This decentralized status is in fact crucial to the web's supposedly liberatory potential. No longer concentrated in large, mainframe computers, or constrained by "mainstream" media channels, information on the web is spread across many locations, making it freely available for the public to access and use. This "freedom" of information on the web is therefore presented as a freedom of movement—which applies both to the movement of information and to the subject's ability to move freely among informational "sites." Thus, the web presents itself in very much the same terms of mobility and choice that Weber observes in regard to the private automobile. If the automobile represents an escape from the timetables and established routes of mass transport, the web represents—or, rather, is represented as—a similar break from the channels and schedules of traditional media. As I have already suggested, this promise of "free" movement and choice reinforces the subject's sense of autonomy and mastery over the fluidity of information. Even more than the automobile or the television, the web highlights this ability to move anywhere, to obliterate distance. Here again, however, this freedom of movement, will, and choice is caught in a cycle of securing and unsecuring. As Weber notes of the automobile, in his essay "Objectivity and its Others," "this hoped-for mobility of the self . . . is in turn driven by the striving to secure oneself, as well as by the correlative fear of not being able to reach a position of complete security."[8] On one of the rare occasions when he writes explicitly about computers and computer networks, Weber makes a similar argument in "Theater, Technics, and Writing": "the hand that strikes the keys or moves the mouse is, even in the apparent solitude and safety of a well-insulated study, inextricably implicated in a network of alterity which no safety lock or protective device can ever definitively control."[9]

As regards the web, this insecurity is generally figured in terms of a complex and confusing fluidity, which threatens to overwhelm or engulf us in a flood of data, making us lose our bearings, our sense of direction. Amidst these seas of information, we become lost, adrift, unable to chart a course. These fears of informational fluidity explain why the rhetoric of the web, and of information technologies generally, is so frequently cast in terms of the ability to locate and direct information, to chart a course through its hyperabundant fluidity, to move easily across or through it (as in the figures of information superhighways, thoroughfares, traffic, and the like). Through this rhetoric, our interactions with the world of information are figured precisely as a matter of navigability. Thus, for example, moving across the web is represented as becoming a "Navigator" or "Explorer."

Navigating and exploring imply not only movement, but a directed movement or steering. To navigate is to be able to chart your direction, to map your destination, in advance. Navigation, in other words, requires knowing where you are and where you are going. Without the ability to navigate, we could only drift, borne by currents and flows beyond our control. It is no coincidence, then, that many web developers have been particularly concerned with issues of navigability and mapping, which has led them to include "navigation bars" and "site maps" as a standard feature of most commercial web sites. These attempts to provide a clear sense of place and direction on the web have become increasingly necessary as information has continued to proliferate and disseminate itself ever more widely. However much we try to make information navigable, to secure it in terms of well-demarcated sites and boundaries, we inevitably feel a sense of insecurity, a fear that not only our data, but we ourselves, are in danger of becoming lost, immersed within the immense quantities of information that surround us.

To be unable to navigate is, by definition, to be lost—not only in terms of place, but also as subjects. For our very notion of ourselves as subjects—not only individually, but collectively—has traditionally been based upon our ability to know where we are and where we are headed. Indeed, this inability "to grasp our positioning as individual and collective subjects" has been cited by some cultural critics as exemplary of not only "information culture" but also "postmodern culture."[10] Here, the perceived loss of direction is figured not only in spatial terms, but in social or political terms as well. As, for example, Fredric Jameson has argued, a lack of spatial direction leads to a loss of the "capacity to act and struggle." Thus, Jameson, like many other cultural critics, casts politics (and theory) as precisely a matter of directed movements, of navigation. Weber has, in fact, critiqued the teleological pretensions of Jameson's work, noting that its presumption of "a single, selfsame narrative . . . a movement of identity and presentation" assumes a position "detached from and outside of what it seeks to contemplate."[11] This detached position is, I would suggest, precisely the position of the navigator who charts a course by the stars; it is only from such a position that Jameson's idea of a "global cognitive mapping" of postmodern space can be achieved. Here, the figure of navigation becomes a means of securing the unsettling fluidity and alterity of the postmodern world (as well as the world of information), locating a direction, a narrative, amidst its wild and confusing plethora of data. Indeed, this narrative in many ways follows the course of an older narrative of exploration, navigation, mapping, and conquest: that of European colonialism and imperialism. For the idea of navigating and exploring the "new world" of the web cannot help but recall the explorations of the "great navigators" of Europe and their voyages of "discovery," through which they mapped the alterity of oceans and "new" lands, cataloguing and colonizing the "others" that they encountered. It is worth comparing these movements to the movement of representation that Weber observes in his explication of Heidegger's "Die Zeit des Weltbildes." This movement, Weber argues, "embark[s] upon a project of conquest in which the heterogeneity of beings is accepted only insofar as it can be objectified and represented." It therefore serves to confirm "the place" of the Navigator—and, indeed, of the Western subject—in the world.[12]

Surfing

In a world, or ocean, of information, navigation becomes increasingly necessary to maintain the location and course of the subject, but it also becomes increasingly difficult. In many ways, this situation—or perhaps, this difficulty of situating ourselves—replicates and follows from the movements described by Walter Benjamin in "The Work of Art in the Age of Mechanical Reproduction." As is well known, Benjamin argues that this process of reproduction results in a withering or decline of the aura of the artwork. As Weber emphasizes in *Mass Mediauras*, however, Benjamin figures this process of reproduction not simply in terms of a multiplicity of copies, but also "as a mass," as "massive or mass-like—*massenweise*" (84). Weber links Benjamin's use of this term to "mass movements":

> whatever else is meant by "mass" in his writings, it entails a dynamic element that demands attention. Mass movements are the result, or rather, the corollary, of that movement of detachment, *ablösen*, that marks the decline of aura. For aura relates to mass . . . in spatial terms, as a fixed location does to one that is caught up in an incessant and complex movement. (84–85)

It does not seem to me to be "going too far" to suggest the similarity of these "mass movements" to the also incessantly moving—and certainly massively complex—ocean of data in which we now so frequently feel ourselves immersed. For Weber, the movements that Benjamin discerns are linked to the notion of *Zerstreuung*, which, in the English translation of Benjamin's text, is usually rendered as "distraction." Yet, as Weber observes, translating *Zerstreuung* as distraction overlooks its "strong spatial overtone," its sense as a scattering or dispersive movement (92). Here, too, the dispersion effected by film in Benjamin's essay—its ability to "burst asunder" the world—seems to parallel, or perhaps foreshadow, the digital reproduction that unsettles and displaces the world as "bits" of data. Yet, as Weber also notes, these movements are profoundly ambivalent: it is the very fact of this unsettling dispersion that enables a sense of "direction and meaning" to be "reimposed," that allows the aura to be "reproduced in and by the very media responsible for its 'decline'" (101).

This reassertion of direction or rechanneling is, as Weber implies, a matter of figuration—of the figures by which we represent the media (including digital media) and our relation to them. I want, therefore, to turn to a well-known, but certainly ambivalent, figure that has come to describe our relations to the channels of television, the world of the web, and to information culture more generally: the figure of surfing. Like navigation, surfing is a figure of movement that also involves a relation to a complex and massive fluidity. If the figure of the navigator/explorer perpetuates the position and mastery of the subject through its emphasis on an instrumental and directed movement, the figure of the surfer (much like the driver of an automobile, as well as the flâneur) is often employed to position the subject in terms of a mobile mastery, a freedom of movement that is not bound by instrumental concerns. In this sense, the figure of surfing gives form and direction to the dispersion of the media and of information. It allows the subject—like a surfer on the crest of a wave—to feel an exhilarating sense of control, without aiming at a particular destination.

Yet, surfing—unlike the idea of navigation—is never entirely a matter of mastery over the world, or the World Wide Web. Even the most masterful of surfers cannot entirely control their path, or the waves they ride on. They can, at best, act in concert with them. Thus, as Gilles Deleuze has noted, surfing requires becoming involved, caught up in, movements where the human being is no longer the source of action: "All the new sports—surfing, windsurfing, hang-gliding—take the form of entering into an existing wave. . . . The key thing is how to get taken up in the motion of a big wave, a column of rising air, to 'get into something' instead of being the origin of an effort."[13] In "Upsetting the Setup," Weber makes a similar point with regard to Heidegger's views of modern technics, in which "places and placing can no longer be taken for granted. Rather, they must be taken as granted, that is, as the consequence of a granting that cannot be reduced to or derived from a subject. At most, subjectivity responds to this granting, which, in giving, opens up a way that can never be entirely secured" (74).

Yet, if these movements are not predicated simply on human actions or mastery, neither should they be figured merely as a matter of passivity, of losing direction, or of aimless drift (although these are precisely the figures that Western colonialism has attempted to impose on the Pacific Island cultures from which it appropriated the idea and practice of surfing). Surfing instead suggests the possibility of a "distracted" or "dispersed" movement that takes place not by moving toward a predetermined destination or an instrumental end, but that is instead performative. Surfing, after all, is not a matter of "getting somewhere," but of the performance itself. This performance, however, is not simply enacted by a subject; rather, the subject participates in the performance of surfing.

Surfing, then, is not just a matter of "reception in a state of distraction," but of a distracted, unsettling interaction that proceeds, as Benjamin suggests, in an "incidental fashion." Surfing, in this sense, figures an interaction with alterity, with an otherness that, however much we might wish to direct it to our ends, can never be simply navigated, channeled, or secured. If we have come increasingly to see information, or even technics itself, as other, it is perhaps because the "essence" of information, like that of technics, is not only purposeful and directed, but also massive, fluid, ambivalent, and dispersed. The figure of surfing allows us to imagine an interaction with this complex and unsettled fluidity—an interaction that cannot be reduced to the opposing figures of direction or drift, an interaction that is never simply a matter of mastery or its lack. For as most serious surfers know, surfing is always, to some degree, dependent on where the waves take us, on what the ocean grants. A similar relation is perhaps necessary in regard to the web, to information, and to technics more generally. Here, it is perhaps only fitting to grant the last word on these issues of direction, drift, and movement to Weber himself:

> I consider it more accurate to speak not of making or taking decisions but of being taken—even overtaken!—by them. A decision, in the strong sense at least, is often something that catches up with you. . . . That's why writing, as a process, seems so paradigmatic. You can "decide" to move in a certain direction, in a certain way, make an outline, do your research and all the other preparation you want. The actual process of writing, however, almost always leads somewhere other than where we expect.[14]

CHAPTER 5

IT, Again: How to Build an Ethical Virtual Institution

Gary Hall

"IT, Again" arises out of a long-standing engagement on my part with questions of digitization. Fittingly for a text composed and concerned with what, for shorthand (and for reasons that will soon become clear), I will call *information technologies* (IT), this essay is woven out of the links and connections between a number of nodal points of interest: capitalist neo-liberal economics, the knowledge economy, deconstructive pragmatics, papercentrism, the crisis in tenure and publishing, the academic gift economy, ethics, politics, disciplinarity, judgment, cognition, and the institution of the university. "IT, Again" is experimenting with these points and issues in the sense Samuel Weber has given to the term "experimenting," whereby "the present participle involves a movement that is first of all, repetitive, second of all, never conclusive or contained, third, on-going and futural, and fourth and finally, actual and immediate."[1]

My reading of Weber's work here does not therefore aim to come "full circle to produce a concept of itself," but rather "doubles up into a language that can no longer be assigned to a single, authoritative speaker or to a reliable, truthful voice."[2] In other words, I will not be attempting to capture the "meaning" of Weber's work in this chapter; nor to engage polemically with other interpretations of it; nor even to produce a "deconstructive" reading that shows how Weber's texts put forward irreconcilable positions that are different from, and in many ways opposed to, those they are generally portrayed, or portray themselves, as espousing. I will rather be experimenting, by analysis and performance, with the way in which Weber's own "concepts . . . operate in a singular situation"—in this case, that of the development and institution of a cultural studies open access electronic archive. It is with a certain "deconstructive pragmatics" arising out of Weber's ideas on how to (re)think the institution of the contemporary university that this chapter will be experimenting in particular. Weber's writings will thus be treated much as he himself treats those of Jacques Derrida and Paul de Man: as texts "whose import only is accessible to a reading that moves [them] elsewhere"—not least through the notions of repetition, iteration and iterability Weber discusses in a number of books and articles, among them his own early essay, "It."

Experimenting with the University: Weber on Instituting the Institution

What kind of "experimenting" with the institution of the university can be undertaken in the current politico-economic climate, in which the forces of capitalist neoliberal economics are increasingly transforming higher education into an extension of business? Rather than propose a return to the kind of paternalistic and class-bound ideas associated with Matthew Arnold and John Henry Cardinal Newman that previously dominated the university—ideas that view it in terms of an elite cultural training and the reproduction of a national culture, with all the hierarchies and exclusions around differences of class, race, gender, ethnicity, and so forth that those terms imply—I want to raise the following question: "How can we think the university otherwise?" This is more than a casual or even "theoretical" (in the more usual sense of the term) query. For all the complaints about the marketization of the higher-education system, their inability to articulate an effective "alternative" vision for the future of the university appears to have left the majority of academics and institutions with very few options as far as resisting or even redirecting such changes is concerned. It is with ways of answering this question—how is it possible to think the university otherwise, beyond the neoliberal and elite cultural models?—that I have been experimenting for some time now. Weber's work on institutions and institutionalization has been instrumental for me in this process.

In what remains his most influential book, *Institution and Interpretation*, Weber shows how institutionalization can be construed rather differently from the way in which it has traditionally been conceived. "The dominant tendency," he writes, following the work of René Lourau, "has been to reduce the concept to only one of its elements: the maintenance of the status quo, and thereby to eliminate the dynamic, transformative aspect."[3] In other words, institutionalization has been taken for granted; it has been perceived as something that already exists and that just needs to be described, rather than as a *process* to be understood. Weber, by contrast, puts forward a notion of institutionalization "in which *instituted* organization and *instituting* process are joined in the ambivalent relation of every determinate structure to that which it excludes, and yet which, qua excluded, allows that structure to *set itself apart*" (xv).

Weber's analysis of the process of institutionalization, expounded in a number of books and articles, including a recently reprinted and expanded version of *Institution and Interpretation*,[4] has become absorbed into the mainstream of literary and cultural theory (even if the "origins" of this kind of institutional analysis with Weber are, ironically enough, not always explicitly acknowledged or even recognized). Of particular interest for a project involved in "rethinking the university," however, is the way in which—in a procedure he identifies as being "highly characteristic of the organization of knowledge in modern society," and that "has developed with problematic intensity in what we call the humanities" (137–38)—a discipline for Weber institutes itself by distinguishing itself from other disciplines, from what is different from it, what it excludes or expels from its limits. Significantly, this process of demarcation does not entail complete and total rejection; "*rather, the exclusions persist qua exclusions,* and they must be so maintained if they are to delimit what falls within the scope of [the discipline's] determinations" (145). Unable to forget about what it has expelled and carry on with its assigned tasks, then, the discipline has to continually refer to that which lies outside its limits. This results in what Weber terms the ambivalence of demarcation: "The demarcation is ambivalent because it does not merely demarcate one thing by setting it off from another; it also de-marks, that is, defaces the mark it simultaneously inscribes, by placing it in relation to an indeterminable series of other marks, of which we can never be fully conscious or cognizant" (145).

At this point it becomes possible to detect a certain instability in the process of institutionalization. For if a discipline delimits its internal coherence as an identifiable, recognizable, and autonomous body of thought by means of this exclusionary activity, if it is dependent for its identity on what is different from it, on what it expels outside its borders, then it cannot be self-identical, independent, autonomous, *or* self-contained. What is more, this irreducible complication in its identity does not come along *after* the formation of the discipline in its ideal, self-contained purity and unity. Rather this relation, this contamination by the other, by what is positioned as being outside and heterogeneous to it, is *originary*: it comes *before* the establishment of the discipline and is in fact what makes it and its founding possible (and simultaneously impossible). The discipline is thus always opened to its others: other academic disciplines and other forms of knowledge, both legitimate and illegitimate or not yet legitimate; but also forms of what, for short, might be called "non-knowledge" (although this term is not without problems, as we will see later).

Now, according to Weber, this process of *demarkation* effectively never ends. Nevertheless, if it is to take place at all it must be brought to a halt: "We must both refer the defining terms to other marks that can never be fully defined for us and at the same time—but this precisely fractures the Sameness of that Time—we must 'forget' this irreducibly undefinable vestige, this set of exclusions that is neither entirely indeterminate nor fully determinable" (145). In this way, Weber's analysis helps us to recognize that any such differentiation or demarkation as goes to institute a discipline—the judgment or decision as to what to include and what to exclude, what should be gathered inside and what expelled—is an inherently unstable and irreducibly violent one: the violence inherent in this demarkation, the forceful arrestation of the inherent instability of the discipline's limits, can never be disarmed. The instability can never be removed once and for all; only degrees of control are possible.

What we can also see from the above is that at the discipline's founding origins lies an *aporia of authority*. For where does the authority to stop this endless process of demarkation and establish—or institute—a discipline by setting itself apart from others, from what it is not, come from? A discipline cannot found itself, as that would require it to already possess such authority. This authority *must* come from somewhere else, somewhere outside the discipline and which precedes it. A discipline is thus indebted to some other, external authority for its authority. And yet the search for origins does not end, or begin, there, since even if this external authority were examined it would not enable the discipline to escape the aporia that lies at its heart. For where would *that* authorizing authority gain *its* authority? It would have to come from outside that authorizing authority, whose authorizing authority would in turn come from outside its authority, in a process leading to a series of infinite regressions. (As far as the university is concerned—which is where academic disciplines do gain much of their authority—its accreditation, its legitimacy as a seat of learning, its power to award titles of competency, does comes from elsewhere, from outside: this authority is granted to the university by the nation-state, via accrediting agencies. But from where does the nation-state gain its authority?)

In order to function as a legitimately instituted field of knowledge the discipline must therefore overlook or "forget" its foundational violence, and act instead as if it is beholden to no one but itself for its authority (although it cannot forget its indebtedness entirely, since it is upon the ambivalence of demarcation and the aporia of authority that the discipline is founded). The discipline thus seeks to overcome its unstable and violent nature by performatively producing a set of "founding" principles and procedures for the institution and reproduction of itself and its original guiding idea. These principles and procedures form the basis of the various rules, regulations, laws, norms, protocols, and conventions concerning the identity of its founding thinkers, their followers and interpreters, its canon and pedagogical techniques, as well as its various forms and styles of writing, publication, research assessment, and so on, which go to make up the discipline, defining its sphere of competence and providing the means by which it develops. The problem is that as the discipline does proceed to develop, increasingly little attention is paid to the violent and paradoxical authority on which it is based. Describing some of the distinctive features of the "culture of professionalism" as they appear within the university, Weber puts it in the following terms:

> The university, itself divided into more or less isolated, self-contained departments, was the embodiment of that kind of limited universality that characterized the cognitive model of professionalism. It instituted areas of training and research which, once established, could increasingly ignore the founding limits and limitations of individual disciplines. Indeed, the very notion of academic "seriousness" came increasingly to exclude reflection upon the relation of one "field" to another, and concomitantly, reflection upon the historical process by which individual disciplines established their boundaries. (32)

It is not surprising that professional scholars and academics have for the most part followed these procedures with regard to founding principles and disciplinary borders. After all, as Weber shows, to do otherwise would require them to bring their own legitimacy, based on what he analyzes as the *"professionalist paradigm of knowledge,"* into question. For

Weber, "[t]he regulative idea of this paradigm is that of the *absolute auton-omy of the individual discipline*, construed as a self-contained body of investi-gative procedures and of knowledge held to be universally valid within the confines of an unproblematized field" (147).[5] As a consequence, little attention is paid to the irreducibly paradoxical and inevitably violent na-ture of the discipline's own foundation. Whenever the issue of its legiti-macy is raised, the discipline merely resorts to narrative myth-making of one sort or another, telling the story of its foundation, and thereby gener-ating effects of legitimacy through repetition that can only ultimately be maintained through violence and force.

From Knowledge Economy to Academic Gift Economy

The mythical narrative of the foundations of disciplinary authority is im-portant in the context of this chapter because one of the issues I myself have been experimenting with, in an attempt to articulate an effective "al-ternative" vision for the future of the university, is precisely the question of how to institute a university or discipline that would take on, rather than merely act out, the effects of the ambivalence Weber describes in *Institution and Interpretation*. Obviously, I have not been able to establish my own university—but I have set up some smaller experimental projects; projects which may enable us to make what Bill Readings (himself greatly influenced by Weber's work on institutions) referred to as an institution-ally pragmatic "tactical use of the space of the university," and so begin to think the institution differently. One of these is *Culture Machine* (www.-culturemachine.net), the open access electronic journal of cultural studies and cultural theory I co-founded in 1999. But it is a more recent project, which has involved establishing the first (to my knowledge) digital, open access archive for cultural studies and cultural theory, CSeARCH (www.culturemachine.net/csearch), that I want to concentrate on in my attempt to "think the university otherwise."[6]

The electronic reproduction and publication of academic research and scholarship in open access digital journals and archives is particularly in-teresting in the context of the paradigmatic shifts that are currently taking place within higher education. As is now well known, modern govern-ments worldwide have come to regard the management of knowledge and information as increasingly important. Whereas previously economies were understood as being driven by the manufacture of goods and services, nowadays it is knowledge and its successful commercial exploitation by business that is held as the key to a society's success and future economic prosperity. Joseph Stiglitz, a Nobel Prize winner for economics and ex–senior vice president and chief economist at the World Bank, describes the situation as follows: "Knowledge and information is being produced today like cars and steel [were] produced a hundred years ago. Those, like Bill Gates, who know how to produce knowledge and information better than others reap the rewards, just as those who knew how to produce cars and steel a hundred years ago became the magnates of that era."[7] As Stiglitz's reference to Bill Gates indicates, IT is regarded as playing a vital part in the development of what has come to be known as the "knowledge economy," helping to transform traditional modes of production, consumption, and distribution, and creating in their place new types of firms, products, and markets based on the commodification and communication of knowledge and information. Universities and academics are assigned an important role in this new vision of society: both in producing economically "useful" knowledge and research, which can then be commercially exploited through the establishment of links with business and industry; and in educating and training the more flexible, constantly creative, imaginative, and dynamic entrepreneurial labor force of "knowledge workers" that this economy requires.

One effect of this marketization of the university has been the radical change in the nature of academic publishing. Here, severe cuts in funding brought about as a result of successive governments' attempts to compete in the global marketplace by reducing their state budget deficits through decreases in public spending, not least on higher education, have created a situation in which it is increasingly difficult for libraries to be able to afford to stock books, and for students to be able to buy them. To provide just one example from the United States: whereas previously the University of California would have bought a copy of a particular book for each of its eight campuses (UCLA, Berkeley, and so forth), in 2002 it was reported as having made a decision to purchase only one copy to share across all of them. The response of many academic publishers has been to cut back drastically on their lists, and to concentrate on producing readers and introductions for the relatively large undergraduate core courses. Consequently, although more books are being published now by international university and trade presses than ever, many academic titles are merely repeating and repackaging old ideas and material. All of which means that it is getting harder and harder for "junior" members of the profession to publish the kind of research-led books and monographs that are often going to enable them to secure their first full-time position, let alone establish a reputation for originality of thought. Yet it is not just those in the early stages of their careers who should be concerned. The current state of academic publishing makes it difficult for nearly everyone in those fields where the full-length book is the most valued mode of publication (apart from a relative few "stars" perhaps) to continue to produce certain kinds of research that might otherwise be associated with the university: research that is intellectually ambitious, challenging, even if at times difficult and time-consuming to read, and that is therefore not always particularly accessible or student- (or indeed government-) friendly. If publishers cannot sell it in sufficient amounts, they are increasingly making the decision not to publish it at all and to focus on "products" that are more financially profitable instead. As a result, not only are the careers of a generation of younger scholars in danger of being damaged, but the whole of academia also risks being intellectually impoverished, as research that breaks new ground and develops new insights and understanding is rejected for publication (and hence dissemination among peers) in favor of that which merely introduces or collects the work of previous generations.

Digital publishing and archiving, however, is one area where academics *have* challenged the forces of neoliberal economics in a reasonably effective manner (even if this has not always been as a result of conscious or overtly "political" intention on their part). They have done so by developing open access archives of electronically reproduced academic research. Perhaps the best known of these is the arXiv.org E-Print Archive (www.arXiv.org), which was founded in 1991 by Paul Ginsparg and originally based at the Los Alamos National Laboratory before moving to Cornell in December 2001. Initially established for high-energy physics—although it has since expanded to encompass other areas of physics, as well as mathematics, computer science, and quantitative biology—arXiv.org has (by August 2006) over 379,940 submissions, deposits of a further 54,000 a year, and receives 270,000 connections daily at fourteen mirrored sites worldwide. It works as follows: whenever a scholar in one of the fields covered by the archive is about to submit a paper to a refereed scholarly journal for publication, the journal sends a preprint copy to this archive. This self-archived preprint is then made available to any researcher, scholar, or student without charge. All the reader has to do is download the file from the archive.[8] Open access archives thus furnish academics with a means of publishing their research, and making it widely available, immediately upon completion, to anyone who can access it, regardless of how much particular publishers decide to charge for their books and journals, and how much individual institutions and libraries can afford to pay for them. Accordingly, open access archives, together with open access electronic journals, are seen as offering a solution to many of the problems currently confronting scholars as a result of the decline in government funding for higher education and the increasingly market- and profit-driven nature of academic publishing. They do so by providing an alternative model for the sharing and exchange of knowledge to that afforded by capitalist neoliberalism: one in which participants are able to give and receive information at comparatively little cost, and in which decisions over the publication and distribution of research can be made, not on the basis of a text's ability to make a commercial profit for its author or publisher, but according to other criteria, not least its intellectual value and quality.

One of the ideas behind the development of the Cultural Studies e-Archive (CSeARCH) I have been involved in has therefore been to create a space where research in the field *can* be published, disseminated, and accessed for free. However, the advantages offered to academics by the digital mode of reproduction are not the only reason this "academic gift economy" is worth exploring. The ethical and political questions open access archiving raises for academic and institutional authority and legitimacy (that is, the basis on which decisions regarding intellectual value and quality can be made), are just as important here. Indeed, I would argue that archiving promises to transform and redefine our relationship to knowledge, and thus helps us to begin reimagining the university. Even though many of the issues I want to address regarding the ethics and politics of archiving are applicable to other fields, there is in this respect something specific or even singular about a *cultural studies* open access archive. For in its concern for anti- and interdisciplinarity, its emphasis on "practical" politics, its self-reflexive relation to culture, the everyday, and the other—be it seen in terms of sexuality or gender, race or ethnicity, and tradition of engaging with the new, the different, the marginal, and the excluded—cultural studies is arguably in the process of replacing literary studies and philosophy as the means by which the university thinks about itself.[9] Cultural studies therefore seems to me to provide a privileged site of, and mode of access to, questions of ethics, politics, and of academic legitimacy in a way that, say, physics and the cognitive sciences, and even literary studies and philosophy, do not. And yet, if cultural studies is to be seriously engaged in "thinking the university otherwise," it needs a "Weberian supplement," precisely because the kind of "deconstructive" analysis Weber provides tends to be kept within specific limits by cultural studies. Drawing on the work of Weber thus allows us to shift cultural studies beyond some of the limits it has set to its own ongoing reconceptualization of politics, ethics, and the university.[10]

A New Code of the Digital?

As anyone who has spent even a small amount of time online will be able to confirm, it is often hard to tell, when surfing the web, what can be classified as legitimate knowledge and what cannot. This is because electronic publications do not have the same aura or authority as professionally produced paper texts. As long as they possess a basic level of technological know-how, anyone can publish on the web and make their publication look reasonably impressive in a way one cannot with a self-published print-on-paper text, as the latter will tend to lack the quality of paper, typography, illustrations and general all-round "glossiness" of a professionally produced title. Most academic online journals have attempted to address this issue by imitating their paper counterparts: in their "page" layouts; their publication of material in the form of "papers" written in a linear, sequential form; their size and length; their reliance on international editorial boards of established academics who have already proven themselves in the "paper" world, and especially in their peer-reviewing and certification processes.[11] They have complied with these protocols in order to reassure the university that they are providing recognizable forms of quality control with respect to this new medium, and hence editorial legitimacy. The problem with the attempt to maintain academic authority in this manner *after* the transition to the digital medium is that it assumes, even as we move from an epoch of print-on-paper reproduction to one which operates increasingly in terms of bits, pixels and computer files, that academic texts will more or less maintain their traditional form, as derived from the attributes of writing, marking or tracing on paper, even when these texts are reproduced digitally; that these texts will therefore continue to be recognizable as "proper," legitimate, pieces of work as these terms are defined in and by the code or language of paper; and that digital academic texts can, and indeed should, therefore be judged according to systems and mechanisms (complete with their social, cultural, and economic hierarchies and filters, standards and values, rules and procedures) that have their basis, if not their origins, in the print-on-paper world.

Such papercentrism is not confined to the production of online academic journals. A similar set of assumptions underpins many of the better-known open access archiving models. In his influential account of how self-archiving can "free" the research literature, Stevan Harnad argues that the way to "distinguish self-publishing (vanity press) from self-archiving (of published, refereed research)," and thus establish the latter's authority and legitimacy, is precisely by means of peer review. He writes:

> The essential difference between unrefereed research and refereed research is quality-control (peer review) and its certification (by an established peer-reviewed journal of known quality). Although researchers have always wished to give away their refereed research findings, they still wish them to be refereed, and certified as having met established quality standards. Hence the self-archiving of refereed research should in no way be confused with self-publishing, for it includes as its most important component, the online self-archiving, free for all, of refereed, *published* research papers.[12]

It is the publisher and referees of the prestige journal that control quality, then; the archive itself is seen as merely providing access to the already certified data. Harnad's parenthetical remarks regarding quality control highlight the fact that online-only academic journals are still too new and unfamiliar to have gained the level of institutional recognition that would allow academics to see them as "established" and "of known quality." Even the relative few that have acquired such a status have almost invariably been able to do so only by reiterating the protocols of their traditional printed-paper counterparts, especially and above all their peer-review processes. In this context, for the "established peer-reviewed journal" Harnad talks about, we can really read established peer-reviewed paper, or at least papercentric, journal. What Harnad's emphasis on accreditation by established peer-review journals of quality means, in effect, is that the authority and legitimacy of a digitally self-archived academic text is derived from, and has its basis in, the world of hard-copy, print-on-paper publishing. What is more, this is the case regardless of whether this process of certification happens directly, by means of the peer-review service provided by an actual paper journal, or indirectly, via that of an online-only journal "of known quality." Although the medium of the latter may be digital, its quality-control procedure (and hence the online journal itself) is necessarily dependent for its legitimacy on a system of peer review that has its "origins" in the "paper" world, and that is in turn dependent on that world for its own authority and legitimacy.

All of this has significant consequences for the way in which a proper, legitimate piece of digitally reproduced academic writing and research is conceived, defined, and understood; and thus for how we might decide what to welcome into a physics or—to return to my own "experiential" example—cultural studies open access archive and what to cast out; what is deemed important and valuable, and what irrelevant and worthless. And it is at this point that questions of ethics come to impose themselves, although they were never really absent. (I am using "ethics" here not according to traditional moral philosophy with its predefined codes and norms, but rather in the sense Jacques Derrida gives to the term, based on his reading of Emmanuel Levinas. Following Levinas, Derrida defines ethics as an infinite and aporetic responsibility to an "unconditional hospitality.")[13] For in both the models of electronic publishing we have looked at so far in which peer review is used as a means of maintaining academic authority—that of open access journal publishing (what is called the "golden road" to open access) and open access self-archiving (the "green road")—we can see that a papercentric, if not indeed the literal print-on-paper form, is clearly being imposed on the writers of scholarly texts.[14] In order to be recognized as legitimate and gain accreditation, electronic academic texts operate on the principle of "limited hospitality": they are in effect being limited and restricted to a papercentric, if not indeed the literal print-on-paper, form. Yet must we *really* insist that digital cultural studies texts conform to the standards and hierarchies of the paper world so that we can understand and judge them, and hence possibly include them in a cultural studies archive? Is this not to take too little account of ways in which electronic writing and publishing may differ from that of print-on-paper; and thus to risk restricting the production, publication, and even understanding of electronic texts to that which is merely a repetition of the same, or at least the very similar?

What happens, for example, if and when writers and researchers stop attempting to transfer print-based conventions and aesthetics into the electronic medium and produce texts that are specific to the digital mode of publication; texts that are not restricted to the book or essay format, but that are "born digital" and are therefore perhaps not even recognizable as texts in the print-on-paper sense? (There are various examples one could provide here: not just hypertext, but also codework and the database— regarded by Lev Manovich as a symbolic form for the digital age—as well as blogs and texts such as those produced using wikis that, inspired by open source and similar models, are written by large groups of often anonymous people using free content and open editing principles.)[15] Or what happens when the very concept of "text" becomes, as Andy Miah has argued, "increasingly uninteresting or useless" as writers utilize new software, such as Macromedia's Flash, which has the effect of rendering the "text" more as "image than text, ungraspable and flat, layered with a virtual and invisible hyperness . . . [and] the sub-level of hyperness, which is really what is of interest when discussing hypertext, derives from the nature of the browser, rather than some new characteristic of text"?[16] One does not even have to resort to such apparently "avant-garde" examples to draw attention to this issue. The same problematic is a feature of the most conventional digitally reproduced academic publication, as the very weblike structure of the web often makes it difficult to determine where texts end—or begin, for that matter. All the cutting and pasting, grafting and transplanting involved means that the boundaries between the text and its surroundings, its material support, are blurred and can become almost impossible to determine online—as indeed can those separating authors, editors, programmers, producers, consumers, users, and commentators/critics:

> All this may sound fine and largely innocuous but scholars and researchers stake their career on well-defined products, that is to say objects endowed with stability relative to time and place. Print, through physically tying text to paper and multiplying the result hundreds of times, managed to harden words. In going digital, texts lose this physical stability, this guarantee of permanence. Again, this may look somewhat inconsequential until we stop and think that the whole idea of the author depends on it.[17]

How then are such digital texts to be judged and assessed? Are the established ("papercentric") standards and criteria for judging, reviewing, and certifying academic work sufficient for responding responsibly to digitally reproduced texts? Or does the (potentially) radically different nature of electronic publishing (its ability to incorporate audio, images both moving and still, animation, CD-ROM, websites, blogs and so forth) require the invention of new standards and new criteria for the maintenance of "quality control"? Perhaps we need a new knowledge, a new grammar, a new language and literacy, a new (visual/aural/linguistic) code of the digital that is capable of responding to the specificity and indeed singularity of such texts with an answering singularity and inventiveness?

The Parasite and the Guest

This is not to suggest that all judgment and decision making be done away with, but to raise the following question: what constitutes a proper piece of digital cultural studies writing or research? How are we to distinguish the "guest" from the "parasite," the welcome contribution to the cultural studies field (but we can pose similar questions in relation to literary studies, philosophy and indeed the humanities and knowledge in general) from the unwanted, the illegitimate, the unworthy, that which is without quality or merit? With what authority, according to what legitimacy, can we make such decisions? On what criteria are they to be ultimately based?

Traditional moral philosophy teaches us that we can only make such ethical decisions if we have a law, a rule, or a set of procedures that enact a limiting jurisdiction, that allow us to judge, to discriminate, to determine value and worth, and consequently to reject, eject, or exclude. Indeed, when it comes to questions of disciplinarity, institutionalization, and archiving, it is still necessary to judge and to make decisions: to elect, filter, and select what is to be contained in such an archive and what is not. A certain exercise of power, and with it a certain injustice, thus takes place as soon as the archive is founded. In fact the responsibility of making a decision I am referring to is inescapable. This responsibility certainly cannot be eluded by refusing to decide. Such a refusal would still be a decision—only a poor one, since it would not consciously be assuming the responsibility of deciding. But if responsibility cannot be eluded simply by refusing to judge or to decide, neither can we rid ourselves of the responsibility of making a decision by deciding once and for all what the rules and values governing our judgments and decisions are: that they are going to be those of the system currently used with regard to print-on-paper publishing (peer review and so forth), and that these rules and values are going to apply to everything for the foreseeable future, in all imaginable circumstances. As Jacques Derrida says in a text that, like this one, is very much concerned with the pragmatics of deconstruction, "if you give up the infinitude of responsibility, there is no responsibility."[18]

Judgment and decision making, then, cannot be abandoned or done away with. The problem is rather with the authority of any such decision and its mode of performance. The rules, procedures, standards, and criteria by which judgments, interpretations, selections, and decisions are made in the paper world regarding certification and accreditation cannot be simply and unquestioningly extended and applied to electronic texts. That is why it is insufficient to respond to the problem of the decline in academic monograph publishing by calling, as some have done, for all research to be put on the Internet, and for equal value and status to be then attached to online publications. Digital publishing cannot be automatically assumed to be merely a prosthetic extension of print-on-paper publishing. That would be to take too little account of the potential difference and specificity of the electronic medium, its material form and properties, as represented by the hardware, software, operating system, browser, programming code, graphical interface, icons, frames, hyperlinks, location-sensitive pull-down tables, multiwindowed screens and the ability to add, copy, delete, refresh, and reformat content, to provide just a few of the most obvious examples. In fact, it could be argued that no judgment or decision would be made here at all, that that would also be a refusal of responsibility. For if one already presumes to know the rules, laws, values, and procedures by which something is to be decided and assessed, if one imagines that one already knows in advance that which is to be judged—in this case cultural studies, what it is, what form it takes, how it is to be recognized, and thus what is worth including in a cultural studies archive—then there is no judgment or decision. Its place is taken by the mere application of a rule, law, or program. In order for there to be a decision, the identity of a discipline, of cultural studies, cannot be known or decided in advance. As Derrida puts it, "if there is a decision, it presupposes that the subject of the decision does not yet exist and neither does the object. . . . Every time I decide, if a decision is possible, I invent the who, and I decide who decides what."[19] I would even take this so far as to insist that this injunction applies not just to "new" cultural studies texts, those that have yet to be published or receive academic accreditation, but to the "whole" of the cultural studies corpus or canon: to the history of what is thought or understood to be cultural studies. In short, we must not be content with placing digitized versions of, say, Raymond Williams's *Culture and Society* or Stuart Hall et al.'s *Policing the Crisis* in the archive, confident in the knowledge that the authority and legitimacy of these texts as classic works of cultural studies is already assured: by history, the field, the "discipline." This would be merely to apply a pre-given rule or program. (Which is not to say such "classic" texts would *not* be included, just that this decision should not be made automatically, in advance.)

Still, if judgment cannot be avoided, neither can the question of the status and legitimacy of digital academic work be resolved, as one might initially be tempted to think, through the development of decision-making systems, peer-reviewing procedures, and rules for the provision of certification and accreditation catering specifically to texts that are born digital. It is not merely a matter of electronic publishing being different from paper publishing (in a manner similar to the way in which, as many people have pointed out, to teach online one needs to do more than simply put course materials on the web). The problem goes deeper than that—to the extent that the electronic mode of reproduction raises fundamental questions for what scholarly publishing (and teaching) actually is; and in doing so not only poses a threat to the traditional academic hierarchies, but also tells us something about the practices of academic authority, legit-imation, judgment, accreditation, and institution in general. In fact, echo-ing a critique of the structure of the sign that was first produced by Derrida some years ago and which has recently been replayed by Bernard Stiegler,[20] I want to risk the following proposition or hypothesis: that aca-demic authority is already "digitized"; that it is in a sense always already in a similar condition to that which is brought about by the process of digitization.

The University Lives On/Online

We can thus see that nowhere are the implications of Weber's analysis of the institution and of the process of instituting perhaps more apparent than with respect to the question of the maintenance of academic quality control and certification. Who now qualifies as a bona fide peer reviewer, referee, grant-application assessor, RAE panelist, or tenure-committee member? And with what legitimacy are they able to make the decision as to what to privilege and what to denigrate or exclude from a given institu-tion, discipline, journal, or indeed archive? On the basis of their member-ship of the profession? Their publication record? Their position in a recognized university department? Their completion of a certified course of training? As Geoffrey Bennington has noted when commenting on the manner in which "the legislator is always, undecidably, also a charlatan," "[t]he radically performative laying down of the law by the legislator must create the very context according to which that law could be judged to be just: the founding moment, the *pre-*, is always already inhabited by the *post-*."[21]

To argue that at the origins of the academic institution lies an aporia of authority does not amount to a naïve attempt to destroy this authority. This "deconstructive pragmatics of institutions," to adopt Weber's termi-nology, is not a *destruction* in that sense. Weber himself emphasizes the need to consider what he calls "the conditions of *imposability*," by which he means the "conditions under which arguments, categories, and values impose and maintain a certain authority, even where traditional authority itself is meant to be subverted" (19). If we acknowledge that violence is intrinsic to authority, we must—to follow both Weber and Derrida—resort to rules, conventions, and stabilizations of power. This is precisely the moment of the emergence of politics. Deconstruction, for Derrida, is a way of showing that, "since convention, institutions and consensus are stabilizations," they must be seen as fixing in place something intrinsically unstable and chaotic. "Thus, it becomes necessary to stabilize precisely because stability is not natural; it is because there is instability that stabilization becomes necessary; it is because there is chaos that there is need for stability."[22] Derrida perceives this chaos and instability as a threat *and* a promise; it is the condition of both the possibility and impossibility of ethics and politics, as well as of the decision. The aporia of disciplinary legitimacy and institutional authority thus entails an opportunity—which is always also a risk—to rethink or think otherwise, and hence to *change*, the manner in which the academic institution *lives on*. The transition to the digital mode of reproduction and publication opens up, via its exposition of the instituting process, precisely such an opportunity.

The ethical problem I am describing here (of infinite responsibility to an unconditional hospitality to the other and the necessity of responding, of making a decision) is by no means new. It certainly did not originate with the invention of IT. As Weber has shown, a delimitable space such as a discipline cannot be constituted without also remaining open to that which lies outside it—that which is not that discipline, but also that which is "not knowledge." A discipline has to have a certain relation to others—of both inclusion and exclusion—in order to be a discipline. Disciplines have always been structured in this way, even when they were conceived as autonomous and self-contained. Moreover, it is not only disciplines that have been suspended over this aporia of authority: all the institutions and practices associated with the formation of knowledge—the university, the scholar, the author, the reader, the text, the book, and so on—have *always* existed in what could be described as a "digital condition." This condition has been intensified and made more transparent by what is conventionally referred to as "the digital age." However, as Adrian Johns reminds us in *The Nature of the Book*, up until the middle of the eighteenth century the book was an unstable object, with Shakespeare's first folio, for example, including not only more than six hundred typefaces but also numerous discrepancies and inconsistencies regarding its spelling, punctuation, divisions, and page configurations. As a result, readers had to make critical decisions regarding particular manuscripts, their identity, consistency, dependability, and trustworthiness, on the basis of "assessments of the people involved in the making, distribution, and reception of books."[23] Already early in the history of the book, then, readers were involved in making judgments around questions of authority and legitimacy: concerning what a book is and what it means to be an author, a reader, a publisher, and a distributor. The development of the concepts of the author, standardized reproduction, mass-printing techniques, copyright, established publishing houses, editors, and so forth all meant that many of these ideas subsequently began to appear "fixed." As a consequence, readers were no longer required to make decisions regarding questions of authority and legitimacy. Such issues were forgotten (much as we have seen throughout this chapter, they were also forgotten around questions of academic and disciplinary authority). However, the digital mode of reproduction promises to place us in a position where readers are again called on to respond and to make such judgments and decisions about the nature and authority of (digitized) texts and of the disciplines, fields of knowledge and registers these texts are supposed to belong to (or not), precisely through its loosening of much of this "fixity."

This is another way of interpreting my earlier claim that academic authority is already digitized, that it always already exists in a similar condition to that which is brought about by the process of digitization. What *is* new (and what is thus historically specific to this particular moment in time) is the extent to which digital reproductive technology makes it possible to multiply, to a perhaps unprecedented extent, the permeability of this border, this frontier control, and thus bring the problem of what, in this case, can and cannot be legitimately included in cultural studies *as cultural studies* to attention and thematize it. For while disciplines have always attempted to police their borders, digital publishing, not least because of its speed, the number of texts that can be produced, published, archived, preserved, and stored, the geographic range over which those texts can be distributed and disseminated, and the relative ease and low cost of all this, together with the lack of stability, fixity, and permanence of digital texts themselves, has the effect of highlighting the irreducibly violent and aporetic nature of any such authority, making it much more visible. Indeed, what is interesting about digitization is precisely the extent to which it radically brings into question "the existing definition and delimitation of knowledge," as Weber puts it, "as well as the conditions of its practice: in short, the *discipline* and the *university*" (49).

"*it*" Again

Let me conclude by exploring in a little more detail how we might take advantage of the current changes within higher education—and especially the emphasis that is being placed on the importance of IT to the "knowledge economy." So far we have seen how digitization provides us with an opportunity to think the institution of cultural studies, and with it the institution of the university, differently, and thus to alter the manner in which they both *live on*. Assuming that we *do* want to make the most of this opportunity, how *are* we to decide what to welcome into the cultural studies archive? How *are* we to make a responsible ethical judgment over cultural studies in a situation that, as we have seen, is marked by an irreducible ambivalence of disciplinary delimitation and an aporia of institutional authority? For help in addressing these questions I want to return to the work of Weber. I want to begin by drawing, not on what in the circumstances might appear to be his most obviously relevant texts, *Institution and Interpretation, Mass Mediauras*, or even his more recent essays on the future of the university, but on a lesser-known early essay in which he discusses another form of IT. This is iterability, a concept Weber repeats after Derrida, and to which he ascribes the nickname "*it*."

In "Signature, Event, Context" Derrida shows how, if communication is to function as writing, it must be "repeatable—iterable"—legible, in the absence not only of its "original" meaning, context, referent and of "every determined addressee," but also in the "absence of a determined signified or current intention of signification."[24] Replicating Derrida's account of iterability in "It," Weber focuses on the way in which the process of cognition (also) always involves repetition; the way in which, in order to be able to *cognize* something, we already have to be able to *re-cognize* it, that is, *re-peat* it, see or take it *again*.[25] To know and understand an object (for instance, a piece of "original" digitally reproduced cultural studies research), to perceive, conceptualize, interpret, judge, or assess it, to determine what it is, and just as important what it is not, we therefore need to be able to compare and assimilate this "new" object to that which is already known and understood. Iterability is thus necessary when it comes to thinking about the production of knowledge for Weber, since it is only through such repetition that the object in question can be measured against an earlier already-known and familiar instance, and by means of that comparison established and recognized as the same or at least similar.

The question of iterability also lies at the heart of the transition from paper to electronic publishing (from it to IT), I want to argue. In a further repetition of his analysis of iterability, this time in the context of a discussion of "the future of the humanities" and, indeed, the university, Weber acknowledges that wherever it is a question of repetition, technology and telecommunication are never far away. Why? Because, as Benjamin was perhaps one of the first to clearly state, the mode of being of modern technology is *repetitive* and *reproductive*. The "work of art," so Benjamin, must henceforth be discussed with respect to its intrinsic "reproducibility." And such reproducibility involves inscription: the tracing of traits: photography, cinematography and now, we might say, videography.[26]

Yet viewing cognition in terms of a process of repetition and comparison with an earlier instance constituted as the selfsame constitutes only one aspect of the process of knowledge acquisition. Any act of intellection also has another dimension, one that, although it can never be entirely absent or removed from the scene, is often excluded, repressed, or ignored. For if cognition entails a reduction of what is unknown to what is familiar, it also involves remaining open to what cannot be assimilated, but instead transforms the familiar into something that is decidedly less so. To put it another way, while the act of intellection denies the object in question its newness, its difference, its heterogeneity, this very act must also establish contact with something that is new, different, foreign, other. Otherwise, how are we able to distinguish between knowledge and mere misunderstanding, projection, hallucination, or illusion? In fact heterogeneity, difference, alterity, otherness are introduced into the act of intellection by the very process of repetition and comparison out of which recognition, and hence the acquisition of knowledge, emerges. The "alterity" presupposed by all repetition can never be entirely absorbed into the identification of the same; there will always be something left over, some excess or remainder.[27]

Any attempt to know and understand an object through perception, conception, interpretation, judgment, or assessment must by necessity proceed by means of these two "distinct, if interdependent operations" (2): the one involving a certain closure; the other involving an openness to what in its very newness, difference, and heterogeneity requires an alteration and transformation of these systems in order for it to be capable of being understood. The question that remains to be answered is: How are we to do both at the same time? This "problem and its implications have constituted one of the major occupations and preoccupations of Western thought" (3), according to Weber. As in the case of disciplinary identity (but really we are talking about the same thing, this "tension between openness and closure [also characterizing] the university both in its social function and its epistemic practice"),[28] in order to be able to know and identify something we cannot place limits on the process of cognition; yet at the same time we have to place limits on it. We do not know where to stop or call a halt to this process; but if we want to *know*, we have to arrest it somewhere. Given that, as far as cognition is concerned, the operation of re-cognition, assimilation, and reduction of the unknown to that which is similar and familiar cannot be avoided—any more than it is possible to think of a "'text' without limitation . . . [o]f writing without some sort of closure"—the issue here becomes not "*whether*" such limitations are to be imposed on this process "but *how?*"

Weber insists that it is not so much the existence and survival of closure as such that needs to be explored, "but rather the manner in which [closure] lives on; not whether or not such an assumption must be made, but rather how it is performed and with what consequences."[29] Even if iterability enables recognition and understanding, it makes them possible only as forms of misrecognition or misunderstanding, "since the object recognized or understood will never be fully present to consciousness, nor entirely identical to itself."[30] For Weber, "misunderstanding" does not constitute the opposite or other of understanding but rather an intrinsic part of it. Misunderstanding cannot therefore be removed from the process of cognition in order to make the act of perception, conception, interpretation, judgment, or assessment more legitimate and authoritative, and thus help to establish the identity and difference of a particular discipline as a legitimate and accredited field of knowledge. Rather, misunderstanding is part of what makes the process of cognition possible. This immediately raises questions for those ideas concerning the legitimacy and authority of academic scholarship addressed in this chapter. What now is the status of that knowledge by which the other is to be understood if misrecognition, error, projection, hallucination, and illusion cannot be denied or excluded from the analysis, but are all terms for that which makes it possible in the first place—"'the structure of iterability,' in short" (9)? This question becomes even more pertinent to the case in hand (that is, the digital reproduction, publication, and archiving of the cultural studies research literature) when one considers that the problem of authority is something that electronic media, with their opening up of the academic institution's space of authority and legitimation to intrusion, transformation, and reconfiguration, make increasingly apparent. As Weber argues in another essay concerned with both repetition and the future of the university:

> The very notion of scholarship tends to take for granted the enabling exclusions and limits through which any field of knowledge is constituted as a

closed and self-contained area. In a world of increasing virtualization, taking such exclusions for granted is less and less effective, and perhaps less
and less efficient. It is not a mere accident that the vocabulary imposed by
the computerization of information is one that stresses dynamic relations,
rather than static fields. The Internet consists of web sites, of links and
networks, not of self-contained realms or fields. And the economic value of
commodities, as is well known, is not inherent in their physical makeup nor
accessible in their immediate manifestation, but rather a function of complex relations. Both economic and technological factors thus contribute to
a virtualization of reality which can no longer be effectively articulated by
traditional notions of knowledge, based on a criterion of truth as the adequation of thought to its object. In the face of virtualization there is a tendency which by no means is unmitigated to reconstrue the relation of
knowledge to the unknown. Hitherto, one could say, the unknown was
regarded, from the point of view of academic scholarship, primarily as the
other or negative side of knowledge: as the not-yet-known. But in the light
of virtualization, the unknown becomes as it were the element or medium
of knowledge, not merely its negative other.[31]

Again, the legislator is always, undecidably, also a charlatan, it seems.
Is this a "proper" analysis? Have I really built such an open access archive?
Am I only joking? Are you sure? Can you tell?

The Exception

Weber's argument in "It" proceeds by way of a discussion of a certain
"closure" in the strategy of deconstruction (13), through to a connection
between iterability, apprehension and anxiety, Freud, and from there, in
later texts, to an analysis of Kierkegaard, "experimenting," the university
in a "virtual world" and, indeed, the very future of the humanities. Weber's analysis of apprehension and anxiety in "It" can certainly be connected to his account of the emergence of professionalism as an "effort to
establish a measure of self-control . . . on the part of . . . a group, seeking
to define and to maintain a certain identity in the face of an extremely
dynamic, unsettling, and powerful reorganization and transformation of
society," as he puts it in *Institution and Interpretation*.[32] Such anxiety is
particularly apparent in much of today's academia over the possible effects
of digital reproduction on scholarship. This raises the question whether
the institution's desire to ultimately locate the legitimacy of electronic
texts in the paper world may not be read as an attempt to "establish and

to institutionalize" a "system of defense,"[33] and thus as a response to this anxiety over the shift from print-on-paper to digital publishing, and in particular the fear that academic texts reproduced using IT may not be so easy to understand or judge. In other words, is this desire on the institution's part not simply a means of coping with, and establishing a measure of control over, a prospective crisis in academic authority that is being brought about (to a certain extent at least) by the rise of the "knowledge economy"? But since I have to stop the chain or network of links and connections somewhere, I will end here for now and bring things to a close with some final remarks on the implications of Weber's analysis for the institution of a cultural studies open access archive.

To sum up, then, what Weber's work on "it" demonstrates is that knowledge, understanding, and judgment involve "the aporetic possibility of remaining open to the trace of the other in repetition even while confronting the same. This possibility is aporetic insofar as this opening to the other can never be free of a degree of closure, of assimilation and appropriation."[34] What this means for cultural studies is that, in order to understand itself after the invention of the Internet (but not just *after* the Internet, since iterability is an intrinsic feature of all judgment and understanding), for it to be able to judge and decide on the status of texts that are "born digital," cultural studies must consist of a nondialectical, or not simply dialectical, aporetic "opening *of* and *toward*" that which is different, new, foreign. In the context of the cultural studies archive, this suggests an opening toward not just those "legitimate" forms of knowledge which are traditionally included in cultural studies' interdisciplinary repertoire (that is, those encompassed by disciplines such as sociology, philosophy, art history, literary theory, and so forth; more marginalized knowledges, such as those associated with differences of gender, sexuality, race, or ethnicity; as well as, increasingly, those found in formations of cultural studies outside the Anglo-American/Australian nexus—in places like Poland, Finland, Turkey, South Africa, Brazil, Taiwan, Japan, Singapore, South Korea), but also those "legitimate" knowledges ascribed to disciplines which have either been marginalized or excluded from cultural studies. (The more commercially "profitable" areas of study—science, technology, electronic and computing engineering, hospitality, sport, tourism, leisure studies, and so on—which are privileged by the contemporary university for meeting the needs of industry and society in the new global economy, but that are often found wanting when judged according to cultural studies' more cultural or politically committed criteria, could all be included in this category. So, too, could the likes of sociology, political economy, social policy, and anthropology, albeit to varying degrees and extents, depending on the particular situation and circumstances.)

Rather less obviously, Weber's work on "it" suggests an aporetic opening toward forms of "knowledge" that are not, or not yet, regarded as "legitimate," including those associated with IT which are not recognizable as legitimate if judged by the rules and conventions of the "paper" world (emails, email lists, databases, blogs, wikis, wikified texts); as well as what might be called "non-knowledge"—the apparently useless, unimportant, irrelevant, worthless, trivial, or mistaken (hypnosis, for example, or projection, hallucination, illusion, transference, naffness, spectrality, phantomism). More radically still, it suggests an opening toward that which refuses to fit into cultural studies; that which is not cultural studies" other, but is *"other than the other itself,"*[35] and which rather resists cultural studies as new, different, foreign, heterogeneous, innovative, or exceptional and, resisting it, pushes cultural studies into adopting new forms and inhabiting new spaces in which it may no longer recognize itself *as cultural studies.* In other words (and to reiterate Weber once again), cultural studies must be rethought from the point of view of the "exception; which is to say, from the perspective of what refuses to fit in, what resists assimilation, but what, in so doing, reveals the enabling limits of all system, synthesis and self-containment."[36] For there is a paradox or contradiction or, indeed, *aporia* in the relation to the "other" or the "outside" of knowledge. Identifying and naming these "non-knowledges" (even as misunderstanding, misrecognition, error, or illusion) is what makes this relation possible. It is only by identifying and naming them that we can have any such relation to these non-knowledges. At the same time it is also that which renders this relation impossible, because this relation is in effect only being extended to that which *can* be named and identified; whereas the difference between non-knowledge and the other of knowledge is that the latter cannot be named or identified—it is rather that which knowledge cannot or does not know, and which is therefore indeed the other of knowledge. The aporetic relation to non-knowledge thus involves a break with knowledge, with what can be known. It requires that we open knowledge up, not only to that which can be named and identified as the other of knowledge (as non-knowledge, or *not yet* knowledge or knowledge-to-come), but also to that which cannot. In the context of an open access archive, it requires that we open ourselves to the unknown, anonymous other; that we be prepared to give a place to this other, to let it in, to receive it without necessarily asking it to respond reciprocally, by identifying or naming itself, not just as legitimate or not-yet-legitimate, but even as non-knowledge or the unknown.

Granted, there is a risk (which is also of course a chance), that as a result the contents of any such cultural studies "open" archive will not look too much like cultural studies, or "legitimate" academic scholarship, or knowledge even, at least as these are currently commonly conceived and most easily recognized (and especially as they are understood according to the conventions of print-on-paper publishing). Yet at the same time this questioning of cultural studies is also "perhaps" the most "responsible" thing for cultural studies to do, at least in Derrida's sense of the term, since there can be no responsibility, and no ethics, no politics, and indeed no cultural studies, I would argue, without the experience of the undecidable; without, in this case, the constant (re)taking of the decision of what cultural studies is.

Will a cultural studies open access archive really make it possible for us to do this? Obviously we cannot be sure. If a transformation in the material supports of knowledge, from paper and analogue to digital is underway at the moment, the development of the cultural studies open access archive I am involved with can certainly be seen as a (small) part of this process, experimenting with how this transfiguration in support is going to change the very content and nature of knowledge. And yet at the same time, any such archive undoubtedly risks failing, visibly if not indeed spectacularly— perhaps precisely because of the questions it encourages us to address. Still, this risk—of paralysis, of chaos, of the archive being more or less unused or unusable—is just that of the situation, of trying to do something different, something interesting, something ethical. At the very least CSeARCH provides an opportunity for cultural studies to take on, rather than merely act out, the effects of the ambivalence Weber explores in his work. It thus demonstrates that it is possible to envisage at least one alternative form of institutionalization of the kind Weber looks toward at the end of *Institution and Interpretation*, when he writes about conceiving "institutionalized practices of a 'discipline' that would assume the ambivalent demarcations that make it, and them, possible."[37]

CHAPTER 6

Ambivalence: Media, Technics, Gender

Marc Redfield

> No faith, therefore, nor future without everything technical,
> automatic, machine-like supposed by iterability. In this sense, the
> technical is the possibility of faith, indeed its very chance. . . . This
> double value, is it not, for example, that signified by a phallus in its
> differentiality, or rather by the phallic, *the effect of the phallus*, which is
> not necessarily the property of man? Is it not the phenomenon, the
> *phainesthai*, the day of the *phallus*?—but also, by virtue of the law of
> iterability or of duplication that can *detach* it from its pure and proper
> presence, is it not also its *phantasma*, in Greek, its ghost, its specter,
> its double or its fetish? . . . Matrix, once again, of a cult or of a culture
> of the generalized fetish, of an unlimited fetishism, of a fetishizing
> adoration of the Thing itself. . . . And this would perhaps be the place
> to enquire why, in the most lethal explosions of a violence that is
> inevitably ethnico-religious—why, on all sides, women in particular
> are singled out as victims (not "only" of murders, but also of the rapes
> and mutilations that precede and accompany them).
>
> —JACQUES DERRIDA, "Faith and Knowledge," trans. Samuel Weber

Just as it has become increasingly clear that the "return of religion" cannot
be understood simply as an archaism within modernity's deterritorializing
dynamic, so it has also become clear—at least to those who worry about
such things—that the "aestheticization of the political" cannot be understood simply as a historical phenomenon, consignable to the mass politics
of the early twentieth century, or to the print-based bourgeois cultures
of an even more bygone era. The analogy is not an arbitrary one. If, as
Jacques Derrida has argued, a profound connection exists between mediatization and Christianity because of the latter's emphasis on "the incarnation, the mediation, the *hoc est meum corpus*, the Eucharist: God become
visible," this is to say that Christianity embraces its own mediatization
or televisuality precisely to the extent that it affirms itself as an *aesthetic*
religion—the religion that discovers transcendence in and through the
phenomenality of body and sign.[1] And if, as Derrida goes on to assert,
"mediatic manifestations of religion, Christian or other, are always tied,
in their production and their organization, to *national* phenomena" (61),

this is once again to testify to the continuing power of the aesthetic, which has always been inseparable from Western-style nationalism, even as nationalism has been inseparable from the emergence and efflorescence of media and transport technologies.[2] In all cases these relations or intersections are characterized by ambivalence. What we call "media" is perhaps in the end another name for the enactment of the aesthetic as a self-divided, self-displacing technique of manifestation. Or perhaps we might wish to say that modern aesthetics emerges as part of—in a sense, another name for—what Heidegger understands as modern technics. "Interpreted in a Heideggerian perspective," Samuel Weber remarks, "television can be described as the culmination . . . of the metaphysical tradition of representation," precisely because it both exaggerates the wish to dissolve representation into presence, and also thereby heightens the "internal ambivalences" of this tradition.[3] Distance seems to be overcome by television, yet "the points of reference that allow us to determine what is near and what is far" are confounded (122); the difference between seeing-there and being-there is rendered invisible, but with the result that we can never know whether or to what extent we are seeing it "live." "In the uncanniness of such confusion," Weber suggests, "what Derrida has called the irreducible 'iterability' of the mark—that repeatability that both allows a trait to constitute its identity while splitting it at the same time—manifests itself in the only way open to it (since it is not of the order of manifestation), namely, as the *undecidable being of the televised images we see*" (121, Weber's emphasis). The ancient question of language, of the iterability of the mark and the phenomenality of the sign, returns to us as the question concerning technology. And that question is always also one of the aesthetic: of the sensuous apprehension of meaning, and the difference and displacement that makes all presentation possible.

Of the critics whose thought has made a difference in this area, arguably no one has tracked the filiations among aesthetics, technics, and politics as patiently and effectively as Samuel Weber. Inhabiting a recognizable tradition of critical thought marked out by names such as Derrida and de Man, Weber's texts provide a powerful refutation of the idea that deconstructive criticism has ignored politics and history. From *Unwrapping Balzac* (1979)—an unwrapping of Balzac that is also, among other things, a sustained reading of Marx's *Capital*, attentive at every turn to the role of commodification, circulation, exploitation, and administrative control in Balzac's text—to the more recent essays on wartime, media, and the university, Weber's work has consistently examined "institution and interpretation": the instituting force of interpretations; the interpretative directives of institutions; the interference between instituting act and meaning instituted. If there is a leitmotif to be traced in his work over the last thirty years, it is that of *ambivalence*. The word itself—as the quotations provided above already begin to suggest—appears at important junctures in his work since his earliest publications, denoting the tension and instability of an aporia or double bind, and serving as something like Weber's version of Derridean *différance*. To my knowledge Weber never comments directly on the etymology of this word; but since of all critics writing today he is arguably the most sensitive to word-origins and translation-effects, it is worth noting that *ambivalence* combines doubleness (*ambi*) with a word, *valence*, that derives from the Latin *valentia* (strength, capacity) and is now used in chemistry to denote an atom's synthetic power. Ambivalence is double synthesis, too much synthesis; and Weber's fondness for this term goes along with his sustained and rigorous attention to the power, the effects, of aporia. In his important 1997 essay "Wartime" he proposes that "ambivalence marks the ineffaceable intrusion of the foreign, the alien, the other into the constitution of the self and same," and "names the constitutive violence against which the constitution of the subject and the self retains the status of a persona, in the etymological sense of a mask."[4] In this text he goes on to argue that this "constitutive ambivalence" characterizes "the medium 'television' no less than the Freudian drives" (101); and that powerfully synthetic move is typical of Weber's criticism, which mimes as it interrogates the excessive syntheses of ambivalence, as *Mass Mediauras* shows:

> The reality of television thus no longer follows the traditional logic and criteria of reality. It is no longer a function of identity or of its derived form: opposition. Far and near are no longer mutually exclusive but rather converge and overlap. Such convergence brings a different aspect of reality to the fore—the reality of *ambivalence*. (125, Weber's emphasis)

Thus Weber has always moved easily—yet always carefully and rigorously—back and forth between questions of interpretation and questions of institution. The task of reading is always a matter of tracking the "ambivalence of demarcation" that grounds (by failing to ground) our experience of aesthetico-cultural institutions and mass media as well as of literary texts.[5] The politics of aesthetics unfolds in and as such ambivalence.

In one respect, however, Weber's attention to ambivalence seems to become, if not itself ambivalent, curiously indirect or discreet, even teasing. In the Western tradition, the question concerning technology has always tangled into questions of gender and sexual difference. Restricting

ourselves for the moment to the pleasures of etymology, we may note that
the legendarily complex Greek word *techne* connects, via its root *teko*, to
tikto, itself also a word of some intricacy: it means to give birth, and can
refer to either male or female roles (of the mother, to bear; of the father,
to beget); to breed, hatch, lay eggs, bear or produce fruit; and, generally
and metaphorically, to give birth, bring about, or produce. Thus, within
the field of *techne*, the apparent binary opposition between *techne* and *physis*
redoubles and knots—as does the apparent binary opposition between the
sexes. Behind the more stable association with the maternal body called
up by the Latin *natura* (from *natus*, born) lies an ambivalence, a region of
techne indistinguishable in Aristotelian terms from *physis*, since the principle of production seems, here, inherent. Yet what is that principle? Is a
mother a generatrix or—as Aeschylus had Apollo proclaim at the end of
the *Eumenides*, and as Aristotle was to argue a century later—is she a mere
vessel or incubator, a technical supplement? What is a father? What is
reproduction, and what is sexuality in its more-than-reproductive excess?
As we shall see, even in an era of DNA and genome-mapping, versions of
these ancient questions remain in play, insofar as they are and have always
been rhetorical and political rather than simply scientific questions, bound
up with issues of production, perception, mediation, media; with the politics of gender and technics. Indeed, as the border between the technical
and the natural has become more uncertain, figures and fantasies of sexual
and gender difference have arguably become more loaded and persistent,
if also correspondingly volatile. How might such figures play out during
moments, or scenes, in which the "constitutive ambivalence" of media is
making itself legible?

Weber is certainly well aware of such questions, and it would be wrong
to say that he evades them. It is rather that he not infrequently calls them
up only to leave them hanging at crucial moments in his essays. Two examples may suffice. In the powerful title essay of *Mass Mediauras*, Weber
weaves together readings of Heidegger's "The Age of the World Picture"
and Benjamin's "The Work of Art in the Age of Mechanical Reproducibility" in order to delineate how "the subject-securing function of the world-
picture"—the objectification of the world as an image for a subject, which
is how Heidegger characterizes the basic impulse of modernity—"raises
the question of what might be called the kinetic or 'cinematic' structure
of that picture" (81).[6] Weber's close reading of Benjamin's text uncovers a
link between, on the one hand, mechanical reproducibility, and, on the
other, the masses—the masses in movement, nomadic and displaced. Mass
movements "are the result, or rather, the corollary, of that movement of

detachment, *ablösen*, that marks the decline of the aura" (85). Yet it turns out that an "irreducible element of taking-leave" already inhabits the work of art's aura: there is, as it were, a certain mass movement at the origin, a distancing and separating; and this "can help to explain something that Benjamin himself at times seems to have had difficulties coming to terms with: the fact that the aura, despite all its withering away, never fully disappears" (87). Weber's deconstructive reading thus powerfully reimagines the aura as bound up with the displacements effected by technics itself. And it is at this point that, following Benjamin's "On Some Motifs in Baudelaire," he evokes a figure: the feminine figure of the *passante* in Baudelaire's "A une passante," as glossed by Benjamin.[7] It may be helpful here to recall the poem:

> La rue assourdissante autour de moi hurlait.
> Longue, mince, en grand deuil, douleur majestueuse,
> Une femme passa, d'une main fastueuse
> Soulevant, balançant le feston et 1'ourlet.
> Agile et noble, avec sa jambe de statue.
> Moi, je buvais, crispé comme un extravagant,
> Dans son oeil, ciel livide où germe l'ouragan,
> La douceur qui fascine et le plaisir qui tue.
> Un éclair . . . puis la nuit!—Fugitive beauté
> Dont le regard m'a fait soudainement renaître,
> Ne te verrai-je plus que dans l'éternité?
> Ailleurs, bien loin d'ici! Trop tard! *Jamais* peut-être!
> Car j'ignore où tu fuis, tu ne sais où je vais,
> O toi que j'eusse aimée, ô toi qui le savais![8]

Weber never really provides a reading of this poem—that is not the purpose of his essay—but like Benjamin he leans on it, allowing the *passante* to embody "*the singular leave-taking of the singular*, whose singularity is no longer that of an original moment but of its posthumous aftershock—'*Un éclair . . . puis la nuit!*'" (104–5, Weber's italics). And—again like Benjamin—he never really comments on the gender of this *passante* (or, for that matter, on that of the voyeur who narrates the poem). His text hints that the "flash" suspended by the "three dots that mark the passing of the *passante*" may indeed have something to do with the luminous *Schein* of fetishism, since the ellipses simultaneously mark a rupture and "allow [the *passante*'s] Medusa-like gaze to hold out the promise of a resurrection" (95).[9] But the reference to Medusa remains, as it were, a solitary lightning-flash, as do other glancing references to the gender of this "abysmally ambivalent apparition" (95). Weber's interests lie elsewhere:

The "mass" here, invisible and nameless, is precisely that ambivalent, di-
vergent *movement* that carries the *passante* even as she appears to emerge
out of it. The movement of the mass is ambivalent because it entails stasis
no less than mobility, suspension no less than progression. . . . The law of
dispersion and collection that governs the ambivalent movement of the
allegorical mass can therefore be designated by the term: *coming-to-pass*.
The mass qua crowd appears as what it is in withdrawing before what seems
to be an individual, feminine figure, that of the *passante*. But the ostensible
individuality of this passerby is anything but individual: she comes to be
only in passing by. And in so doing, she reveals herself to be the allegorical
emblem of the mass, its coming-to-be in and as the other, in and as the
singularity of an ephemeral apparition. The mass movement—the mass in/
as movement—produces itself as this apparition, which provides an alternative to the formed and mobilized masses of the political movements of the
Thirties. (96–97)

From Baudelaire to Benjamin to Weber—and, inevitably, to the present
essay as well—there passes a certain fetishistic interest in this *passante*: she
occasions, for the critic as for the protagonist of the poem, a moment or
movement of *eclaircissement*, while also remaining something of a mystery.
She "reveals herself to be the allegorical emblem of the mass" and allows
Weber to bring into sharp focus his reading of the Benjaminian shock
experience (I shall say more about that reading a little later)—but only to
the extent that she also remains a *fugitive beauté*, passing by. Her appari-
tional quality, which is of course precisely what interests Weber, is no
doubt a literary effect that any reading of this text, or chain of texts, will
have to repeat; but it seems fair to ask how such apparitionality or "coming-to-pass" might relate to gender and gender difference.

Consider one other example of this sort of theater of reading in Weber's work, in which an insight passes to the critic—to Weber, and to
us—via a reading, and repetition, of a first-person character's illuminating
encounter with a feminine figure. In his short, dense essay "Religion, Repetition, Media" (2001), Weber elaborates a notion of medium as "space
itself being beside itself" through an interpretation of a scene from
Kierkegaard's *Repetition*.[10] Weber contrasts the "uncanninness" of "'media,'
whether performances in the Königstädter Theater or the electronic
media of our time," with a second aspect of media, one that "serves to
frame and contain the uncanniness"; and he discerns the appearance of
this second aspect in the apparition of a "figure" to which the narrator of
Kierkegaard's text, Constantin Constantinus, draws attention while seated

in the theater, watching his favorite actor Beckmann perform a farce. Here is Kierkegaard's text:

> Then in the wilderness surrounding me I saw a figure that cheered me more than Friday cheered Robinson Crusoe. In the third row of a box directly across from me I saw a young girl, half-hidden by an older gentleman and lady sitting in the first row. The young girl had hardly come to the theater to be seen. . . . When I had watched Beckmann and let myself be convulsed with laughter . . . my eyes sought her and the sight of her refreshed my whole being with its friendly gentleness. Or when in the farce itself a feeling of greater pathos burst forth, I looked at her, and her presence helped me to yield to it, for she sat composed in the middle of it all, quietly smiling in childlike wonder.[11]

Weber mimes and glosses Constantin's gesture, suggesting that "this image of a young girl . . . calms and reassures [Constantin], gives him a point of reference and orientation. . . . [He] sees in it the constancy he fails to find in or as repetition" (52). In the final movement of his essay he offers a daring interpretation:

> In conclusion, without being able to argue it at length, I will simply assert, as a hypothesis for investigation, that the yearning and repose Constantin identifies with the figure of the young girl marks the point where the experience of the modern media converges with a certain "return" of the religious, if not with religions. Like all technology, the development of the electronic media follows the ambivalent law, or graphics, of prosthetic supplementarity: an "extension" of human capacities, it simultaneously distances and undermines what it extends, exacerbating the vulnerabilities of the finitude it seeks to alleviate and protect. Long before the actual emergence of specifically *electronic* media, its advent was prepared by a notion of theatrical writing: of writing as theater and theater as inscription . . . in which performance ceases to be primarily representation and becomes linked with transport, passage, and partition. In this movement, the place of the spectator, the audience, takes on a constitutive significance. The address to the other links writing and theater to what we call "religion." (52–53)

Weber's career-long interest in the theme, topic, and event of theatricality lies behind this analysis of the relation between media and religion. What makes a representation theatrical is its address to an other, a "third one"; and it is precisely here that Weber discovers the passage to religion— religion as an "address to the other." But when we ask why this "figure" of the return of religion should be a feminine figure—what sort of compensatory fantasies or symbolic economies might be involved there—Weber's text remains silent. The young girl is a rather different character from the woman (who is presumably a widow—she is in "grand deuil") in Baudelaire's poem; but the two play a curiously similar dramatic role in their respective texts, and it would be interesting to know why.

I shall return to the *passante* and the young girl, but first want to look at a few other texts, starting with some older work of Samuel Weber's. His apparent reluctance to attend to gender and its ambiguities in his recent writings on media might seem all the more surprising given his career-long interest in certain aspects, at least, of psychoanalysis, and his important early work on Freud and Lacan. And in fact, if we go back to his earliest written, if not quite first published, book, *Unwrapping Balzac*, we discover a text that attends scrupulously to the deployment and ideological employment of gendered difference.[12] With Balzac, to be sure, as with much nineteenth-century writing, it might be thought that one can only with some difficulty avoid discussing sexuality and gender; but the world is well-stocked with studies of Balzac that manage to say little enough, particularly in comparison with Weber's philosophically and psychoanalytically informed reading. From the courtesans, whom the protagonist meets at the press banquet and who "incarnate devouring desire" (55), to the glittering figure of Foedora, who personifies "the fetishistic vision par excellence" (95), to the *figure blanche* of Pauline at the end of the novel, who "is, or seems, the fulfillment of a dream, the image of a maternal presence defending against all danger" (159), Weber tracks the ways in which feminine figures evoke and ward off the instabilities of desire, identity, and modern life. "Foedora," he observes—and this observation sums up much of what one might want to say about the ideological role of misogynistic figuration in discussions of modernity—"has no 'heart,' her eccentricity is irreducible, and yet her 'heart' is precisely her 'heartlessness,' her center 'is' her eccentricity. She transforms a determinate absence—as such she is never to be 'had'—into the sign and veil of a transcendent presence" (103). For she works her ambivalent magic at the crosshairs of the fetish, and "fetishism—of money, of the phallus, and of the imaginary as such—defines the innermost origin and end of a subject-producing-its-Self" (86). Under such circumstances, a reading of institution and interpretation is always also a reading of gender and its troubles.

It is possible that Weber's suspicion that "the Lacanian interpretation of castration" entails "a certain experience of *perception*" (166) played a role in the recession of gender as a critical category in the work he did subsequent to the Balzac dissertation. Indeed, the books on Lacan and Freud that Weber wrote in the mid-1970s and published in German more or less at the same time that *Unwrapping Balzac* appeared in North America can seem surprisingly, even strategically, uninterested in gender and sexuality. For eventually one comes to suspect that Weber has an un-announced goal in these books: the detaching of psychoanalysis from its addiction to or fetishization of sexual difference. *Return to Freud (Rückkehr zu Freud* [1978]) remains one of the finest "introductions" to Lacan ever written precisely because it pursues so confidently a very particular inter-pretation—it would be no exaggeration to say, a forceful displacement or *Entstellung*—of Lacan. Without pausing to criticize, Weber simply rereads Lacan along poststructuralist lines, emphasizing the role of language as "the articulation of non-identity" in Lacanian theory, and, as noted, pay-ing relatively little attention to the drama of gender so central to Lacanian and all other forms of psychoanalysis.[13] When the topic of gender eventu-ally arises—as of course it must, given that "castration" is "the hinge upon which Freudian psychoanalysis turns" (140)—Weber's constant point of emphasis is *difference*. We are to link "the conflictual aspect of difference to sexual difference, where 'bisexuality,' far from naming the reconcilia-tion of this difference, indicates its ineradicable character" (79). The La-canian phallus "represents, but only by effacing," the "differential relation of the sexes" (145). One senses that Weber, in his charting of these much-sailed seas, would be glad to let the phallus go, have it wander off to the point of getting lost—or at least *entstellt* (distorted, disfigured, displaced). This is in some sense what happens in *The Legend of Freud (Freud-Legende* [1979]), where over the course of Weber's deconstructive reading of Freud the phallus lisps into the "thallus" (which, technically, is part of a mush-room: "A vegetable structure without vascular tissue," according to the OED entry cited by Weber, "in which there is no differentiation into stem and leaves, and from which true roots are absent"). The thallus, a queering of phallus into fungus, marks the pressure of "error" as "constitutive of the very gesture of denomination itself."[14] Sexual and gender difference are articulations of that error. And in its final section, *The Legend of Freud* stages a certain "return" to gender, cannily repeating, with a difference, the trajectory of *Beyond the Pleasure Principle* toward the stories of sexual difference and desire told in Plato's *Symposium*. Freud recalls Aristopha-nes' myth of the origin of sexual difference so as to tell a story about the unifying drive of Eros; Weber draws attention to some of that myth's sub-tle peculiarities. "Like Freud and most other commentators of this text,

Aristophanes seems to state unequivocally that human beings were originally whole" (153); however, not only is Aristophanes' account framed by
various performative complications, his myth of double-beings and their
splitting hints at a certain doubleness and dubiousness at the origin (they
had a single head; what happened, Weber asks in an Aristophanic spirit,
to the head when the double-body was split? [155]). Ambiguity, then—an
excessive synthesis—at the origin. And, once split by Zeus, the wounded
bodies require supplemental medical care, so Apollo intervenes, armed
with technologies of repair:

> [Apollo] therefore turned the face around, pulled the skin from all sides up
> over what today we call the belly, and just as one pulls together the strings
> of a purse, he drew the ends together and tied them in the middle of the
> belly in what today we call the navel. The resulting wrinkles he smoothed
> out for the most part, and moulded the chest with the aid of a tool like that
> used by shoemakers to smoothe out creases in the leather, except for a few
> wrinkles that he left around the belly and navel to serve as a reminder of
> the ancient accident. (190e–191a)[15]

Scarred by lack, the sundered bodies yearn for their other halves so absolutely that, intertwined, "they died from hunger and other neglect, for
they would not do anything apart" (191b). So, in a subsequent passage
that Freud does not quote, Aristophanes, as Weber puts it in *The Legend
of Freud*, "tells of a second, repeated intervention, designed to save the
moribund bodies from themselves, from their deadly desire to be reunified
and whole—to be, in short, a self" (159):

> Thereupon Zeus took pity and placed another means at their disposal, by
> shifting [*metatithesin*] their private parts to the front, instead of on the side
> where they were before, since previously they had reproduced not in one
> another but in the earth, like crickets. Now, however, he shifted them [*met-
> etheke*] to the front and thus allowed them to reproduce in one another.
> (191b–c)

Weber remarks that "this second intervention does not merely repeat the
first; it adds a new direction: instead of dividing, cutting, and separating,
it shifts, dislocates, and rearranges the reproductive organs, bringing repetition, as it were, to the fore" (159). And we in turn may read Weber's
reading here as his text's closing account of sexual difference as "dislocation," as "a certain *Entstellung*" (160): a disfiguration or difference without
binary symmetry or unitary origin. (Indeed, the Greek verb rendered as
"to shift" in this passage, *metatithemi*, with its distancing prefix and slightly
violent sense of substitution or transfer, evokes *Entstellung* rather nicely.)

One might wish to say that what matters for Weber in these and subsequent texts is "difference itself," rather than the registers of sex and gender in or for themselves; yet since he is always careful to point out that "difference itself" is different, as it were, from itself—is rather a returning of difference to the narcissistic grip of the *Begriff*—he is always reading specific articulations of difference. Sexual difference remains prominently marked, therefore, in these scenes of interpretation, but by virtue of being marked, is also always caught up in difference and self-difference, in the iterability and fungibility that makes all marking possible. There results, in Weber's texts, that particular reserve or hesitation, teasing half-motion or indirection that we noted above. Yet I would also suggest that gender and sexual difference are radically if implicitly queried, queered and destabilized in these scenes, precisely as a result of Weber's reserve: a refusal to comment that is always *also* an ongoing marking and remarking of gender difference. His reserve, in this sense, may be read as functioning performatively as a reading—a reading of the rhetoricity of gender difference; of a radical queerness that cannot speak its name. Such *Entstellung* is always also self-concealing. The *passante* and the young girl whom we encountered earlier surface in Weber's text, as they do in Baudelaire's, Benjamin's, or Kierkegaard's, as seemingly stable entities from the point of view of gender. Such, we may hypothesize, is one of the functions of these highly feminine figures—to serve as fixed points in a mobile context. Weber says as much, though without saying anything about gender per se ("this image of a young girl . . . calms and reassures [Constantin], gives him a point of reference and orientation"). Yet this apotropaic function is also hollowed out by the differential movement ("the mass in/as movement") that underwrites it.

We still need to bring into sharper focus the link between what we may call the ambivalence of gender, on the one hand, and on the other hand the predicament of "coming-to-pass" that is at once unveiled and concealed by modern technics and the media—"a mass movement of collection and dispersion, of banding together and of disbanding," as Weber puts it in *Mass Mediauras* (106). As a way of broadening our frame of reference and sharpening our focus on issues of media and technics in relation to gender, let me turn to a text that at one time had considerable influence on these kinds of discussions, and is today perhaps somewhat undeservedly forgotten: Marshall McLuhan's *The Mechanical Bride* (1951). Preceding by a decade *The Gutenberg Galaxy* (1962) and *Understanding Media* (1964), this early study of McLuhan's announces many of his signature themes:

the politics of media images; the passivity of consumers; the power of technology to make and mold human bodies and subjectivities. Decades before its *floriat* in the American academy, McLuhan is doing "cultural studies" in this intermittently cranky and brilliant book, each short chapter or section of which analyzes an ad or some other image drawn from the orbit of what McLuhan calls "industrial folklore."[16] The chapters have funkily laconic descriptive titles ("Front Page," "Li'l Abner," and so forth) and are organized according to no obvious plan; though the sections occasionally reference each other, overall the book is a collage or kaleidoscope, miming in its format and typography the media onslaught it analyzes. A little past the center of the collection, however, is a section titled "The Mechanical Bride," preceded by "Love-Goddess Assembly Line"; and as one might expect, given the book's title, these sections orient and epitomize the analytic-descriptive project. We may glance first, though, at an earlier section, "Co-Education," which is one of the chapters of this book that can seem particularly idiosyncratic and dated. Originally driven, McLuhan tells us, by pioneer privation, the American experiment in coeducation now reflects the tyranny of technology:

> Education in a technological world of replaceable and expendable parts is neuter. Technology needs not people or minds but "hands." Unobservant of the automatic leveling process exercised by applied science, we have let it carry us along to the point where the same curriculum and the same room serve to prepare boys and girls alike for the neuter and impersonal routines of production and distribution. (53)

The metonymy "hands" with its lurking suggestion of bodily fragmentation or mutilation lends an extra anthropomorphic twist to the repeated word "neuter." Technology neuters; it dulls the difference between the sexes, a predicament McLuhan eagerly associates with homosexuality ("After fifty years of co-education, what about that sag in the heterosexuality quotient?"). A felt anxiety about masculinity runs through the text ("One effect of World War II in putting millions of men in military uniform was to restore to them a large degree of masculine confidence and certitude" [70], etc.), and peaks in the "Love-Goddess Assembly Line" section, which examines "feminine glamour ads" that "insist on their relation to the machine" (94).

McLuhan writes here in part as a shrewd analyst of "one of the most peculiar features of our world—the interfusion of sex and technology." The fantasized transformation of women into replaceable parts that he observes in midcentury American consumer society both horrifies and fascinates him; and he offers an analysis that in part, or in one of its moods, has affinities with that of Weber reading Benjamin or Kierkegaard. The assembly-line goddess gives a reassuring body to modernity. Her curves are the curves of statistical analysis, phenomenalized as erotic figure: "it is out of the extreme discontinuity of modern existence," McLuhan hypothesizes, that "there is being born today the vision of a rich and complex harmony. . . . [I]t is only natural that this way of seeing should be put to the service of discovering the proportions and cleavages within one's immediate time and society" (97). Yet this keen analysis never gets underway except as a repetition of the ideological phenomenon being analyzed. McLuhan's sly gendering of "time and society" as a body with "proportions and cleavages" shades rapidly into a less ironically controlled fantasy of reading:

> The reader has to be a second Ulysses in order to reveal the siren onslaught. Or, to vary the image, the uncritical reader of this collective novel [of the ad agencies and Hollywood] is like the person who looked directly at the face of Medusa without the mirror of conscious reflection. He stands in danger of being frozen into a helpless robot. (97)

Consumer society itself becomes here a woman (a "siren onslaught," "the face of Medusa") to be resisted by the technically cunning male reader, Ulysses or Perseus, who knows how to hear and see without being turned into a robot. Manipulating the ropes and mirrors of "conscious reflection," this superreader will use technology without becoming technologized—the fantasy of power that McLuhan's text *also* relentlessly demystifies by insisting on the prosthetic claim of technics. We encounter here the fundamental contradiction driving this book. On the one hand, all technology, as an extension of "man," modifies its user. This theme, already prominent in *The Mechanical Bride*, provides McLuhan with some of his most dramatic rhetorical flourishes in his subsequent books on media (for example: "By continuously embracing technologies, we relate ourselves to them as servomechanisms. That is why we must, to use them at all, serve these objects, these extensions of ourselves, as gods or minor religions").[17] On the other hand, McLuhan's texts dream, at these moments, of a reflective, critical process that would be nontechnical, above the technical. Like Benjamin, McLuhan sketches a scenario in which the shock experience is parried by consciousness; but unlike Benjamin, he shies away from the possibility that consciousness itself might be entangled in a certain technicity. Yet at the same time, his text constantly and often quite self-consciously undermines this dream of a purely external technics by suggesting that the critical stance itself necessarily mimes or repeats the object it analyzes. Here, for instance, by referring to mythic male figures of technical control (Odysseus tied to the mast; Perseus wielding mirror, helmet, sandals, sword), McLuhan registers the technicity of reflection even as he fantasizes for himself and the reader a story of consciousness's victory over and mastery of the technical.[18] The double bind of the prosthesis eventuates in a personification and gendering of modernity as a feminine monstrosity.[19]

This symbolic economy is particularly visible in the eponymous "Mechanical Bride" chapter, where the virgin-dynamo theme culminates in an excited image, or mininarrative, of McLuhan's own making:

> To the mind of the modern girl, legs, like busts, are power points which she has been taught to tailor, but as parts of the success kit rather than erotically or sensuously. She swings her legs from the hip with masculine drive and confidence. She knows that "a long-legged gal can go places." As such, her legs are not intimately associated with her taste or with her unique self but are merely display objects like the grill work on a car. They are date-baited power levers for the management of the male audience. (98)

The modern girl has been "taught" to "tailor" her "power points"—as befits a cyborg, she has been made, not born. It is as a result of that teaching or shaping that she possesses "power levers" with which, Circe-like, she transforms men into emasculated consumers. And consequently, though the impersonal forces of consumer culture motivate the passive voice of her construction ("she has been taught"), the modern girl appropriates these forces to the point of becoming the privileged figure of their manifestation—the "mechanical bride" of McLuhan's title. Thus consumer culture once again resolves—luridly, if ambiguously—into a problem of gender identity. As in the "Co-Education" chapter, gender difference threatens to erode under technology's impact: "The switchover from competitive display to personal affection is not easy for the girl. Her mannequin past is in the way." Meanwhile, men spiral into an oedipal whirlpool: "The display of current feminine sex power seems to many males to demand an impossible virility of assertion" (99). The woman is phallic both in her fragmentation into fetishized body parts and in her power to fragment or castrate men: "surrounded by legs on pedestals, [men] feel not won but slugged" (99). She embodies and channels the shock experience—the experience of "being-slugged"—and thus to some extent mitigates it, transforming it into the threat of "castration"—a dramatizable, eroticizable threat that spurs fantasies of an unfragmented body and subjectivity that would have existed *prior* to castration.[20] As Weber summarizes in *Unwrapping Balzac,* "castration" serves to designate a last-ditch effort to retain an image of the Other (the maternal phallus), and with it, an image of the Self. For if the Self is to be whole, then the object of his desire cannot be any less so: the mother must have the phallus, or at least she must have had it (and *be* it). In this perspective, "castration" implies the desire to keep the image whole through an image of the hole. (167)

Yet, Weber adds, "castration" is also "a *story*," one that "inevitably exceeds whatever it can tell" (ibid.). It transforms a radical ambiguity, an uncertainty of reading (am I seeing this? am "I" seeing?) into an image (of loss or lack: the maternal phallus) and a seemingly determinate trope (the fetish, substituting for the imaginary and always already missing maternal phallus). Difference thus becomes something that can be *seen*. Yet the original ambiguity endlessly haunts the fetish and the castration-narrative: hence the slippage of agency in scenarios like McLuhan's, and the ongoing display of aggression directed at the "mechanical bride." The figural logic of prosthesis, which underpins the discourse on technics at least since Plato's *Phaedrus*, always potentially mobilizes gendered tropes because the figure of prosthesis twines into the figure of the body—the putatively natural, but supplemented, potentially mutilated body. (Why would it need supplementation if it were not always already incomplete, marked out, maimed?) McLuhan's understanding of technology as the "extensions of man" is thus an ongoing and intermittently excited appreciation of "man's" mutilation. As one of the more mythically overstuffed sentences in *Understanding Media* puts it, the subject drugged by the new media "ignores the nature of the medium, of any and all media, in the true Narcissus style of one hypnotized by the amputation and extension of his own being in a new technical form" (26). Though prosthesis is "autoamputation", it also arrives from outside, from the technical other; and the name of that other is the feminine as threat to the stability of gender difference. Thus, finally, like the enigma of Foedora in *La peau de chagrin*, "the mystery of the mechanical bride," as McLuhan describes it in his book of that title, must proclaim itself as precisely that, a mystery (101), inaccessible to critique, because the critique constantly reveals itself to be caught up in the fragmenting discourse of the prosthesis. Inevitably, as one might expect given the données of the castration story, and given the anxieties about production and reproduction conjured up by the subject of technics, the feminine as (phallic) other becomes the feminine as (phallic) mother. Mothers, McLuhan tells us—mothers who dream of successful technocareers for their sons—exacerbate the problems of the modern world; and in a revealing turn of phrase, he suggests that such mothers embody mediation itself: "The objectives of a commercial society, when filtered through the *medium* of maternal idealism, acquire a lethal intensity" (76, my italics). The medium is the maternal.

Legible at such moments is an ideological economy akin to what Mark Seltzer calls the "logic of naturalism," whereby "a threatening female productivity" is managed by rendering the mother, in updated Aristotelian fashion, "merely a *medium* . . . of the force of generation."[21] That "force of generation" then easily becomes the threat of a devouring feminine desire. "Donnez-moi des millions, je les mangerai; je ne voudrais pas garder un centime pour l'année prochaine," Euphrasie tells a shocked Raphael in *La peau de chagrin* (cited in Weber, *Unwrapping Balzac*, 55). McLuhan segues from meditating on the mechanical bride—the cyborg as "modern girl"—to quoting and summarizing a Fritz Leiber story, "The Girl with the Hungry Eyes," in which

> an ad photographer gives a job to a not too promising model. Soon, however, she is "plastered all over the country" because she has the hungriest eyes in the world. "Nothing vulgar, but just the same they're looking at you with a hunger that's all sex and something more than sex." Something similar may be said of the legs on a pedestal. Abstracted from the body that gives them their ordinary meaning, they become "something more than sex," a metaphysical enticement, a cerebral itch, an abstract torment. Mr. Leiber's girl hypnotizes the country with her hungry eyes and finally accepts the attentions of the photographer who barely escapes with his life. In this vampire, not of the blood but of spirit, he finds "the horror behind the bright billboard. . . . She's the eyes that lead you on and on and then show you death." She says to him: "I want you. I want your high spots. I want everything that's made you happy and everything that's hurt you bad. I want your first girl. . . . I want that licking. . . . I want Betty's legs. . . . I want your mother's death. . . . I want your wanting me. I want your life. Feed me, baby, feed me." (101)

The infinite, impersonal hunger of capitalism for profit thus becomes the threat of a feminine desire so overwhelming, so much "more than sex," as to be indistinguishable from a quasi-maternal threat of inundation or incorporation—another version of McLuhan's "siren onslaught," which only a hermeneutic Ulysses can survive. And that gendered drama relays the excitement and danger of mediation, which is to say: mechanical reproducibility, coming-to-pass. For, despite the differences of tone and circumstance, we are not too far here from the kind of phenomenon that

draws Weber's and Benjamin's attention when they note that the Baude-
lairean poet "succumbs to the fascination of 'eyes that do not see': '*les yeux
fixes/Des Satyresses ou des Nixes*'" (Weber, *Mass Mediauras*, 100, quoting
"Über einige Motive," 649/"On Some Motifs," 190). The fixed eye of the
femme fatale is "the hungriest eye in the world" precisely because it is
also, in this lurid fantasy, the eye of a camera, which is capable of endless,
impersonal apprehension, and which, Benjamin writes, "imparts to the
instant [*Augenblick*] an as it were posthumous shock" ("Über einige Motive," 630/"On Some Motifs," 175). If, as Weber writes, "what Benjamin
refers to as 'shock' . . . is invariably ambivalent: it designates *both* the trau-
matic incursion and its defensive warding-off" (98), the figure of the
woman here functions, in Elissa Marder's fine phrase, as a "shock ab-
sorber." As Marder notes of "A une passante," the eponymous *passante* is
"only called a 'femme' (woman) in her absence, *after* she has passed away."
It is thus, she concludes, that "the poem attempts to arrest, photographi-
cally, the impossible temporal disjunction evoked by her passage" (83). By
fixing the *passante* as a woman, the text gives a body—a potentially maternal, reproductive body—to mediation-as-masses-in-movement. And legible in the interstices of such scenarios is an uneasy figural economy
whereby the uncanny dislocations and replications of mediation are embodied and gendered, so that a would-be reflective subject may anxiously
imagine itself amputated and masterful—amputated because masterful,
masterful because amputated.

The subject imagines itself, that is, the subject of and for technology—an ambivalent role for all sorts of reasons, but perhaps above all
because this subject can never be sure it has really been able to choose to
be itself. No interpreter of such a predicament can remain safely outside
this text—which is also to say that no interpreter can entirely avoid reproducing its gestures of technical and theatrical mastery. As Weber has
taught us, we begin to assess the violence with which ambivalence works
to conceal itself only by dwelling with ambivalence as the enabling condition of critical reading. Because of their exemplary patience with ambivalence, Weber's cannily reserved texts help us take a step toward answering
the grim question with which Derrida leaves us in the paragraph I posted
as this essay's epigraph—"why on all sides women in particular are singled
out as victims" of "ethno-religious" violence.[22] They are singled out because no act of faith can fail to imply "everything technical, automatic,
machine-like supposed by iterability"—because no intention, presence, or
identity can seal itself off from a more fundamental coming-to-pass of

technics. Women are associated with the uncontrollable within technics so as to facilitate fantasies of technical control. The arbitrariness of that association renders those fantasies uncertain, and hence violent: a violence that becomes literal when, as so often in our technically saturated world, the wages of faith are being paid.

CHAPTER 7

Modernism and the Medium: On Greenberg and Weber

Andrew McNamara

For all the talk about feeling, pleasure, and beauty, the aesthetic remains at its root a proposition, and a "disturbing" one at that. Admittedly, what is disturbing also has a strong allure; and it is this allure, this critical provocation, that proves most disturbing. Yet when Kant proposed considering the aesthetic as an *idea*, he did not aim to limit it to a cognitive proposition. Instead, he highlighted how the aesthetic poses a more general consideration: How does one come to terms with the aesthetic? While Kant argues that the aesthetic can legitimately be considered an idea, he complicates it by questioning the adequacy of any approach to it: according to the *Critique of Judgment*, an aesthetic idea amounts to "a presentation of the imagination which prompts much thought, but to which no determinate thought whatsoever, i.e., no [determinate] *concept*, can be adequate, so that no language can express it completely and allow us to grasp it."[1] Kant makes clear that the aesthetic does possess discursive significance even though it cannot be adequately grasped by language or concepts. To be sure, an entire armory of intricate elaborations is erected to keep its critical momentum afloat, yet it holds a distinctive position insofar as this idea eludes thought.

The subtle, but precarious delineation of the aesthetic idea came to a head later with the advent of modernist abstraction in the twentieth century. At once, the fine line between modern abstract art and design patterns or ornamentation appeared to have become frayed—meaning that the fine line between autonomous, purposeless art and purposeful design was not always readily apparent. At such moments, the recourse to Kantian formulations became quite pronounced in criticism, even though Kantian philosophy was rarely examined in any detail. A crucial moment is that of mid-twentieth-century American formalist criticism. In a general survey of art of the 1960s, Thomas Crow asserts that the vital issue for formalist accounts of art was the assumption that abstract painting—in contrast to design or ornamentation—constitutes an "expressive communication" between an artist and a "contemplative spectator."[2] Because he does not feel particularly compelled to defend the formalism he is discussing, Crow merely mentions this pivotal distinction in passing, as though it represented an unimpeachable founding proposition that did not require any further elaboration.

This enigmatic formulation is pivotal to other considerations equally central to the modernist visual arts, such as the medium, representation, identification, and self-referentiality. Although it does not emerge from an art history or visual arts background, Samuel Weber's work focuses upon the same considerations as well as the riddle of the Kantian aesthetic legacy. One claim sets Weber's analysis apart from art-historical analyses of modernism, and that is his assertion that "self-referentiality" is "perhaps the distinctively modern form of reference."[3] This is significant because it collides with Clement Greenberg's enduring definition of modernist art practice as self-critical or self-referential. Toward the end of his essay "Upsetting the Setup," Weber explicitly implicates modern art within this mode of reference: "Whether in economic practice or modern art, objects are de-objectified by becoming increasingly subject to the calculations of a subjective will struggling to realize its representations and thereby to place itself in security [*sich sicher zustellen*]."[4] Weber suggests that modernist self-referentiality is the predominant way of grasping knowledge and of understanding our orientation to the world. It is not a recent development, nor an avant-garde innovation. In fact, the modernist avant-garde stance may simply constitute a late phase in this ongoing process, not its radical threat.

This chapter maintains an oddly nuanced ambition in regard to Weber's argument about "self-referentiality." On the one hand, it welcomes the challenge the latter poses to familiar conceptions of modern art. In addition, it asserts that Weber's incisive examination of issues such as the medium, representation and identification, as well as the Kantian aesthetic legacy, allows a better recognition of the apprehensive aspects of aesthetic inquiry, which many otherwise extremely robust art-historical analyses tend to downplay. On the other hand, it will also be asserted that Weber's analyses can assist in a critical reevaluation of the scope and ambition of modernist visual-art practices, which may even prove capable of counteracting his conclusion that such practices remain part and parcel of the modernist urge to "self-referentiality." This is not to say that modern art simply escapes this dominating form of reference. Instead, the point of the detailed analysis that follows is both to highlight the continuing struggle with this mode of referencing within the visual arts and to offer a new way of critically evaluating the modernist legacy by gauging the effort to evade "self-referentiality" as a self-enclosed system.

Reading Opacity

What is interesting about this conjunction of issues—the medium, representation, and aesthetic idea—is that it comes to a head over debates concerning how to best interpret visual images. Surprisingly, this concern frequently assumes sociopolitical overtones. Certain versions of cultural studies, for instance, emphasize an integrative and connective approach, whereas that of the avant-garde by contrast might be characterized as dissenting. Lindsay Barrett's study of the purchase of Jackson Pollock's *Blue Poles* by the National Gallery of Australia in 1973 presents a case in point. For Barrett, the work's significance lies in its capacity to illuminate the social and political circumstances of its purchase, which amplified tensions surrounding the reformist program of the then Whitlam Labor government.[5] As such, the book, while extremely engaging, has very little to say about the actual painting, *Blue Poles*. Instead, the work acts like a cipher for an analysis of this specific social and political context. In this sense, Barrett's study provides an exemplary case of a particular type of visual culture or cultural studies approach, which reads outward from an image to elucidate a broader context.

This is no accident; Barrett approvingly cites Wendy Kozol's reading of *Life* magazine because it helps illuminate another context, "American 'family values' in the 1950s." More importantly, Kozol's key contention for Barrett is that *Life* magazine's audiences "did not, nor were they meant to, read isolated photo-essays; they read them along with other photo-essays and advertisements and related them to other cultural discourses." Barrett not only cites the quote, but extends it: "These texts speak directly in fact, in the political language of the time, to the constituents of the new global society, informing them as to what was happening in 'their' world, letting them know what was going on, what was of relevance to 'them'" (76–77). This approach provides the basis for Barrett's analysis of the 1959 *Life* magazine article on five abstract expressionist painters, "Baffling U.S. Art: What is it About?" When Barrett refers to avant-garde rhetoric of that general period, a remarkably different consideration is evident. As an example, he cites Mark Rothko's 1947 statement that the "familiar identity of things had to be pulverized in order to destroy the finite associations with which our society increasingly enshrouds every aspect of our environment."[6] While Barrett notes that such a dense and cryptic remark did little to help explain abstract art at a time when it was being denounced as Communist, he pays scant attention to it other than to equate its stance with Cold War rhetoric about "freedom."[7] Thus, Rothko's comment is subsumed within the determining context of the Cold War and McCarthyism, and thus a mere reflex of American free-enterprise ideology. Ironically, the inference is that this is appropriate for *Life* magazine, but a compromise for an artist.

This is not to say that such co-option could not occur regardless of the critical intent of Rothko's remark. It is just that in terms of the politics of "reading," it is the interpretation that determines the meaning of a work of art, or aesthetic inquiry, completely in terms of a sociopolitical context that is assumed to constitute the more socially aware, politically attuned reading. Counterintuitive as it may sound, this is precisely the presumption that modernist artists and critics challenged. When Rothko raised the prospect of pulverizing "finite associations" as well as the "familiar identity of things," he was aiming to emphasize how abstract, nonmimetic paintings possess a genuinely critical, if recondite, value. Such work, he felt, stood in antithesis to narrowly instrumental demands characteristic of modernity. In his 1940 essay "Towards a Newer Laocoon," Clement Greenberg aimed to clarify this impetus further by giving it a very specific focus. He underscored the role of the medium in visual art and effectively reversed a traditional priority: "To restore the identity of an art the opacity of its medium must be emphasized."[8] Writing against the pressure of right- and left-wing totalitarianism, as well as against the commercially blunt demands of commodity capitalism, Greenberg sought to convey how ambitious art became opaque when read against its social context, which is where its dissenting political ambition could be located.

The emphasis upon opacity primarily serves to undermine the presumption that visual texts "speak directly." Greenberg reverses the general assumption that regards the medium as transparent and then turns it around by insisting that this emphasis (upon opacity rather than transparency) furthers the critical scope of Western culture. In other words, he introduces a broad social-cultural explanation of this tendency at the very point where art, due to its drift toward highly abstract-formalist outcomes, might appear to have eliminated the connection. While the avant-garde grapples with the opacity of its medium, Greenberg perceives a contrary momentum building that diminishes critical-cultural scope: "really important issues are left untouched because they involve controversy . . . creative activity dwindles to virtuosity in the small details of form, all larger questions being decided by the precedent of the masters."[9] He calls this a "motionless Alexandrianism." It attests to the shying away from difficult issues and propositions, such as the intense and often seemingly fruitless struggle with opacity waged by the avant-garde. This winding-down of critical scope testifies to the rise of "kitsch."

According to Greenberg's explanation, kitsch cannot be equated solely, or even exclusively, with a high-low cultural distinction. For him the term relates once again to how visual images are read. "Kitsch," and the multitude of forms it designates, signals an assuring sense of continuity between the visual image and life. "Kitsch" yields identifications, Greenberg retorts disparagingly in "Avant-garde and Kitsch," that "are self-evident immediately and without any effort on the part of the spectator—that is miraculous" (16). Its appeal, in other words, rests on the assumption of the directness of the visual image and the transparency of its medium— and thus upon an indivisible union between what is communicated and its viewers or listeners.[10] Kitsch, he complains, is mechanical, formulaic; it does not even demand time. But it sure is seductive! For Greenberg, its "irresistible attractiveness" relates to its seductive identificatory power, which Weber labels "identificatory simplification." Such identification, Weber asserts, stems from the presumption that visual representations are "immediately sensual" and thus "a privileged and direct access to reality."[11] Greenberg argues something remarkably similar, though this is confused by the use of the term "kitsch," which burdens the emphasis toward class and educational distinctions. It is also hampered by his use of the haphazard art-historical example of the Russian artist Ilya Repin, whose accessibility is contrasted negatively with Picasso's approach. "In Repin's picture the peasant recognizes and sees things in the way in which he sees things outside of pictures—there is no discontinuity between art and life." Compared to this enticement of instant identification premised upon a sense of a direct link between life and representation, Greenberg laments that the avant-garde appears "so austere and barren."[12]

No matter what one thinks of his examples, Greenberg's critical ambition is clear. He highlights opacity in order to counteract the appeal that treats the visual image as straightforwardly direct. Hence, he regards the avant-garde emphasis upon the opacity of the medium as capable of disrupting identification by underlining the discontinuity between art and life. Greenberg insists his position is not, however, theoretical. He does not prescribe, but merely describes what had already manifested itself within the trajectory of avant-garde modernism. Tracing this trajectory is far from straightforward. The focus upon "austere and barren" opacity, for example, enables cultural momentum. Like a futurist, Greenberg opts for movement and motion over the inert repetition of tradition—and thus, Alexandrianism. Yet, at the same time, Greenberg's ambition is to explain how the modernist avant-garde *perpetuates* the tradition of painting, albeit in new ways, thus revealing it to be a viable, enduring, and still critically alert activity. Against standard explanations of the avant-garde, Greenberg argues that its experimentation does not signal rupture—at least, not in any straightforward manner—but instead it strives to find a way of emulating the summits of past achievement under quite different conditions of possibility.

There are further surprises and fluctuations in Greenberg's intriguing analysis. If kitsch presents a simple, but irresistible, form of seduction by promising directness and the immediacy of the unmediated, then Greenberg envisages a not-too-dissimilar achievement for the avant-garde—it is just that Greenberg privileges the promise of "art" speaking directly to a contemplative viewer rather than the generic visual images of commercial culture speaking directly of their socio-political context. According to Greenberg's account, the avant-garde pursues "purity" by focusing upon medium opacity. It leaves nothing to identify with except art exploring its own processes:[13] "Painting and sculpture can become more completely nothing but what they do; like functional architecture and the machine, they *look* what they *do*. The picture or statue exhausts itself in the visual sensation it produces. There is nothing to identify, connect or think about" (34).

There is nothing to identify with, Greenberg qualifies, but "everything to feel"! Unencumbered by distracting identifications, only feeling remains and this means engaging with purity—a pure aesthetic engagement—valid only on its own terms. The avant-garde artist, Greenberg contends, imitates God "by creating something valid solely in its own terms." This assertion of absolute sovereignty is immediately qualified. By pursuing absolute autonomy, the artist comes up against the formidable constraint of the medium. Before the medium the artist is never masterful, never proves transcendental, but always remains inhibited. It "cannot be arbitrary and accidental," Greenberg expounds, that the pursuit of absolute values must "stem from obedience to some worthy constraint or original."[14] When particular traditional forms and accepted notions diminish in potential, art pursues *absolute* values, and thus abstract or nonobjective art results. Investigating the constraint of the medium becomes the priority of each form of art and the affirmation of particular identities—whether national, regional, class, ethnic, religious, or otherwise—falls away as a concern and diminishes. Each discipline in art, according to Greenberg, must strive for purity by separating itself from its neighboring art form thereby securing the identity of the art form in its medium-specificity.

Rosalind Krauss has complained that it is difficult to raise the term "medium" in the visual arts without mentioning the name "Greenberg." The name has come to stand for a treatment of the medium, she continued, that reduces it to a "mere physical object," thus revealing both "its reductiveness and drive toward reification." While Greenberg's approach to the medium was clearly reductive, Krauss's dismissal presents an ironic outcome, if true, because his initial ambition was to counteract any "drive toward reification." The subsequent difficulty for any critical inquiry into the medium within the visual arts is that the dictum concerning the specificity of the medium is directly equated with modernism (so much so that the term, modernism, is regarded as directly identifiable with the aspiration to medium specificity in a manner that parallels Greenberg's assessment of kitsch). Yet pivotal to the enduring critical claims of the modernist legacy—that is, its critical legacy for contemporary practice—is its questioning of straightforward presumptions about representation, identification and the medium. By questioning such propositions of directness, modernist art counters the temptation to read through the work, to presume the medium to be transparent, and thus to privilege the immediacy of the unmediated. In short, it amounts to a vital critical interruption. Thus, while Krauss decries the fact that medium-specificity, according to the overly influential Greenbergian schema, usually means "being reduced to nothing but its manifest physical properties," she also concedes that it is "nonetheless intrinsic to any discussion of how the conventions layered into a medium might function." It is necessary, Krauss continues, that "a recursive structure" be able to specify itself ("at least in part")—even if a self-differing specificity.[15]

Even this qualification about specifying itself "at least in part" remains firmly indebted to Greenberg's definition. According to this view, the modernist critical challenge is crucial because it involves specifying itself at the expense of the compelling urge for identificatory investments, which (as we have seen in the case of Greenberg) it seeks to reclaim by other (more "elevated" aesthetic) means. The claim to specificity is, as just mentioned, intrinsically aligned to key aspects of its critical ambition by emphasizing the opacity of the medium and in challenging representation. In an earlier study, Krauss argued that modern art asserts itself by its "will to silence, its hostility to literature, to narrative, to discourse."[16] This defiance pinpoints the oblique radicalism of the modernist visual arts throughout the twentieth century. Hence Thierry de Duve's assertion—not an overly controversial one, by the way—that "although the issue of specificity has presented itself to every practice during Modernity, nowhere has it been more acute than in the practice of painting." The reason for this audaciousness, he insists, is that "it was in painting that the self-referential striving for purity became both the exclusive object of esthetic theory and the all-encompassing subject matter of practice."[17] Despite this claim for radicalism, the modernist ambition is defined in such a way that it also accords perfectly with Weber's depiction of the ubiquitous critical priority of modernity: that is, the striving to ensure a certainty of knowledge and of practice within circumscribed limits, which fence off and ground its condition of possibility, by excluding everything presumed to be foreign. Thus, there is a strong tendency within the visual arts to domesticate the challenges of treating the medium as opaque by seeking to ensure that its implications remain readily graspable. This is achieved by limiting its province to certain "immanent" parameters and then recruiting its exploratory potential to the cause of purity and sensuous immediacy.

From Immediacy to Lack to an "Indeterminate Other" and Back Again

It is therefore barely surprising that an odd ambivalence runs through these ruminations. Formulations regarded as inimical to the avant-garde are identified, rebuked, and then dispatched as kitsch, only then to reappear in a new guise within the avant-garde or modernist framework. By exalting the critical constraint of the medium, the avant-garde promotes engagement with a recondite alterity that it never subdues. Furthermore, the radical gambit of Rothko and Greenberg is to risk the most culturally sustaining assumption dedicated to the visual image: its power to elicit identification. Yet Greenberg (and he is far from alone) seeks to snatch this power straight back again. Avant-garde art may undercut, even "pulverize," finite mimetic associations, but the pulverizing allows the aesthetic experience to be felt more or less directly once all arbitrary practices and nefarious presumptions are dispensed with. Being autonomous, modernist works "*look* what they *do*" and hence acquire the allure of self-adequate presentations. This is of course a proposition that Kant sought to question in relation to the aesthetic. The question this discussion raises, however, does not simply concern what proposition, idea, or presentation can be adequate to the aesthetic, but also is there any alternative to striving to secure self-adequate presentations?

Analysis of Weber's work suggests there is, but it involves reexamining some basic propositions. The antithesis of "identificatory simplification," for Weber, is "reading," which is regarded as "more derived, abstract, and 'intellectual.'" While identification seems infinitely preferable because less painful, it also elicits a "kind of paranoiac response," which Weber argues sustains "the suspicion that what one is being shown is not necessarily what is really going on: 'The truth is out there,' but 'trust no one' to help you get at it." Thus, the realist and the paranoiac response work "in tandem." If there is to be an alternative "mediation" upon the visual medium, then Weber opts for one that begins with an analysis of what is not immediate in producing this sense of "immediacy"—an analysis which examines the way in which this sense of "immediacy" is "apprehended, experienced, interpreted, and manipulated."[18] In short, it will entail scrutiny of the specifics of the medium, and thus we are returned to a primary preoccupation of modern avant-gardism.

Weber differs from Greenberg precisely because he scrutinizes what is least immediate in conveying "immediacy" and avoids the urge for a higher form of immediacy. With the more familiar household example of television, Weber delves not into the content of television but into its medium, and thus what appears a deceptively direct process of transmission. The "unity of television as a medium of presentation" relies upon a sense of simultaneity—an instantaneous sense of immediate presence. Of course, this apparent unity of perception relies upon, as Weber suggests, "a *split* or a *separation* that camouflages itself by taking the form of a visible *image*."[19] The televisual image has no one place, being here and there. It instead takes place at a sequence of places: at the site of production, of reception and of transmission. Television overcomes spatial distance with a sense of simultaneity that remains ambivalent. "Television takes place in taking the place of the body." "It overcomes spatial distance only by splitting the unity of place and with it the unity of everything that defines its identity with respect to place: events, bodies, subjects" (117). This splitting is therefore essential to creating this sense of simultaneity that overcomes distance—everything is presented directly, right *here, there before our eyes* screening distance and its fracture.[20]

Even though he identifies the radical trajectory of modernist painting with a "self-referential striving for purity," Thierry de Duve is rare among readers of Greenberg in seeking to locate a similar disjunctive questioning of the medium firmly within the latter's critical ambition. Reading "between the lines" of his text, de Duve insists that for Greenberg the medium constitutes the other, or "the other is the medium." As a consequence of his reformulation, de Duve treats "kitsch" in a very specific way as a term designating "a narcissistic round-trip that confirms the other's suppression in the object." "Kitsch," de Duve continues, "holds up a mirror without resistance to self-love. Because there is no confrontation, this self-love regresses toward primary narcissism; therefore it is not love at all, but pleasure gleaned from the disappearance of otherness."[21]

Because the avant-garde acknowledges the obdurate physicality of the medium, it must recognize that its desire will never be fulfilled narcissistically. This realization proves highly unsettling, however, and attempts at compensation come from the most unlikely sources and in various guises. De Duve's example is T. J. Clark's Marxist redemption of Greenberg, which diminishes the focus upon negation and absence—thus, the discontinuity between art and life—by recuperating it in terms of representation and the notion of an absent addressee. Put simply, formal negations or "lacks"—"the black square, the infinitely flimsy skein of spectral color"— act to "fill in" gaps, or social absences. Negation, for Clark, virtually stands for the avant-garde's depiction of its own quandary: whom does it address with its oblique formulations? These "lacks" spell the failure of the bourgeoisie and "the lack of an adequate ruling class to address." De Duve contests Clark's posing of a question along the lines, "what do these works 'stand for?'" precisely because it is this urge for representational retrieval (as replacement or deputation) that modernism seeks to unsettle and disqualify.[22] De Duve, in contrast, asserts that Greenberg advocates *surrender* before the medium as a central aesthetic principle, and this has the advantage of suggesting "a duel between the artist and his medium, a struggle as much in the nature of love as of war, and which results in a capitulation, an abandonment, or an acquiescence. Whether in the register of war or love, the artist finds himself in the position of the conquered and not the conqueror; the least one can say is that these are not the connotations most frequently attached to the word 'avant-garde'" (52–53).

For de Duve, this less familiar understanding of the "avant-garde" can be attributed to Greenberg's twin emphasis upon a "discontinuity between art and life" and surrender in confrontation with a medium. De Duve, in turn, translates this unfamiliar understanding of the modernist avant-garde into a consideration of "convention" understood in terms of what holds as a pact around the "name of art." For de Duve, this pact stands as the collective address that replaces Clark's social absences as lacks. In this way, de Duve recasts elements of Greenberg's "doctrine," but only "on the condition, of course, of understanding that to accept a convention doesn't mean to submit to it but to consider that art is born from constraint; on the condition that artistic constraint be identified with the necessity for a pact to be sealed around the name of art; and on the condition that everything spring from the demand for a pact, that is, from the address to an indeterminate other" (86).

Understood this way, Greenberg's focus upon the opacity of the medium amounts to a crucial recognition of constraint as a basic requisite of ambitious art practice. De Duve views the singular *force* of the avant-garde as emerging from this struggle with constraint: "the force of such works is to draw a redefinition of the entire medium in their wake" (68).[23] Such inventive force dramatically redefines what is expected of a medium. Accordingly, it has the potential to unsettle the very terms of its acceptance. It is this instability, which even if momentary, exposes the apprehensive dimensions of the aesthetic, and this instability and apprehensiveness provokes efforts, even within the most "radical" or audacious quarters, to find something that can "stand in" for this potential void of address and to offer instead some form of certainty or fulfillment.

Performing Modernism

De Duve offers an inventive reexamination of the doctrine that he associates with Greenberg's criticism. This is extremely important given that the term "modernism" in the visual arts still remains strongly associated with the very specific and limited definition that Greenberg gave it.[24] The strength of de Duve's reading is that it reveals Greenberg's thinking on modernism to be far more complex and rich than it has often been given credit for. The difficulty is readily apparent too: the critical insights that de Duve finds most challenging tend to be domesticated or curtailed at the point of their maximum critical momentum; and they are curtailed in a manner that decidedly concurs with Weber's outline of the limiting condition of modernist self-referentiality.

Weber views "self-reference" as a type of performance because it "distinguishes itself from all others, above all from the objects of its representations." As Weber typifies this self-referencing movement, it works to divest itself of:

> all "content" in order thereby to demarcate its own self-identity, henceforth to be determined in nothing but *the process of representing as such*, which is to say, in the process of "doubting" as opposed to the determination of that which is doubted. As its name suggests, "doubting" is duplicitous. It doubles and splits itself off from what it doubts and, in doing so, establishes a purely formal relation to its own "performance." The grounding force of the Cartesian cogito, by which it attains *certitude*, resides in precisely this doubling, splitting and demarcating movement, which produces a kind of pure performativity.[25]

The "doctrine" of modern art, as de Duve outlines it, clearly adheres to this paradigm. It wishes to maintain and assert its identity in a splendid self-certainty by separating itself from what it presumes to be external to it—thus, according to this particular definition of modernism, the fine arts distinguish themselves from the decorative or utilitarian arts; the visual arts from literature (but also, though with less certainty, from film, photography and pop culture); painting from sculpture. It thereby readily accords with one of most conservative trajectories of our culture— "conservative," that is, in terms of *conserving* itself in self-reference. Anything external must be amalgamated to a purely self-referential internal criterion; otherwise it must be excluded. Weber seeks to emphasize how pronounced and pervasive this process has become. Is it correct, then, to assert that modernist avant-gardism is simply another manifestation of a wider phenomenon that increasingly encompasses everything from the instrumental approach to technology and the medical sciences, to more recent configurations such as the corporate university, and the highly circumscribed, but simultaneously ubiquitous rhetoric about accountability and excellence?

Greenberg's portrait of modernism initially appears to diverge from Weber's explication of modern self-reference as that form of identification based upon vehement processes of exclusion. Ultimately, however, it conforms to it. In the 1940s, when developing his "doctrine," Greenberg argued that the avant-garde confrontation with the medium—in both love and war—dismantles identification: "there is nothing to identify, connect or think about." Yet, this dismantling leads to a significant qualification: lacking anything to identify with, a viewer realizes that there is "everything to feel."[26] Whereas de Duve emphasizes force, Greenberg mitigates it. The surrender to the resistance of the medium turns out to yield something more spontaneous and immediate than that associated with kitsch identifications—the modernist avant-garde strips away identifications to the point where one engages with "immediately sensuous art." Abstract art is abstract because "it is almost nothing else except sensuous." In the visual arts, as Krauss observes, one confronts the medium as a sheer physical presence; the plastic arts of painting and sculpture, as Greenberg tells it, "affect the spectator physically." Modernism yields a superior historical consciousness because it strips back conventions to direct physical immediacy and this secures the vantage point of self-realization: the "arts lie safe now, each within its 'legitimate' boundaries."[27]

Possessing secure boundaries enables distinctive judgments—this is the crux of the issue underlying this version of modernist self-reference. Modernism may not constitute a break with the past; instead, it may be considered to have grasped it more truly and thoroughly than ever before. The posing of "legitimate boundaries" is vital to the safety of the arts and to the possibility of gaining a superior historical vantage point.[28] Greenberg even proclaims that there has been "a fairly constant distinction between those values only to be found in art and the values which can be found elsewhere." Yet, going by his early diagnosis, one might suppose that kitsch's viral-like, corrosive power, if true, would have undermined any of those "constant distinctions" or values. Indeed, Greenberg remarked that kitsch, "by virtue of a rationalized technique that draws on science and industry," erases any such distinction in practice.[29] Greenberg's thought is prone to such broad, sweeping and ultimately limiting categories so that inevitably self-criticism becomes heavily tied to demarcations and defensive delimitations.

De Duve contests Greenberg's doctrine when it comes to this assumption of a "fairly constant distinction." To agree with Greenberg about this "constant distinction" means concurring with "the sterile tautology decreeing that art is what the institution names art." For de Duve, this aspect of Greenberg's doctrine requires urgent contestation because it diminishes the decisive impact of the avant-garde heritage, which throws open the "regulative idea of painting upon its name" to everyone's critical attention and judgment. It is therefore crucial to contest Greenberg's tautological conflation regarding art and history, de Duve urges, "before another tautology decrees that life is what the institution calls life."[30] To accept "a fairly constant distinction" within art is to diminish the jolting impact of any forceful redefinitions of medium and, in addition, it means accepting the kind of settled demarcations as well as the muteness of continuity with regard to legacies that Greenberg earlier associated only with Alexandrianism. It is as if Greenberg, finding the "barren and austere" avant-garde disruption of identification too unwieldy and uncomfortable, felt that it required compensation—hence, Clark is not alone in seeking it; and while this compensation admittedly produced a more tenuous social position for art, it also acquired a more secure identity for art. De Duve, in other words, departs from Greenberg precisely where he mitigates *force* and conjoins it to a vision of modernist painting that seems suspiciously close to Alexandrianism.

Love and Judgment: A Bruising Performance

As a critic, however, Greenberg is a loving judge who practices an infectious "aesthetic positivism." This is where Duve seeks to retrieve Greenberg's critical reputation as well as to revive the critical-aesthetic inquiry into modernism: in the arena of love and confrontation, opacity and desire, judgment and redemption. De Duve wants the criterion for evaluating Greenberg firmly fixed upon considerations of feeling and judgment and audacity. Greenberg's redeeming feature is that he is not truly a theorist, even when "launching theoretical readings." Instead, his "aesthetic positivism" stands boldly before the evidence of the work, following the rule of "consulting only one's feeling before the work, but then saying nothing about it; of speaking only of what one sees; of rendering one's verdict" (34).

De Duve warmly admires Greenberg's strong value judgments: never in Greenberg do we find "those falsely modest provisos such as 'in my opinion,' 'I believe that'—or even worse, pusillanimous pedantries 'in the eyes of the present writer.'" Instead, with Greenberg, one finds only strength of conviction and the clear, precise rendering of a verdict. Such a buoyant example exposes the paucity of present-day comparisons: "It's a long time since I've read anything similar (or wrote anything similar, I admit) in contemporary criticism." Why is de Duve so limp, so circum-scribed, so "slow to judge," as is everyone else nowadays, and why is Greenberg such a beacon of critical strength? Today, de Duve laments, people refuse to judge (35).

Greenberg is cavalier with theory, especially with Kant—in "Modernist Painting" (1960), he abruptly asserts, "Kantian self-criticism . . . has found its fullest expression in science."[31] Yet theory will weigh heavily upon the generations that follow. In order to examine Pollock, de Duve confesses—much like St. Augustine confessing a unsavory past—he would have relied upon a prefab critical armory: then it would become a question of theory by numbers because de Duve was, after all, a "young professor overflowing with more or less well-digested theory, with 'critiques of the dominant ideology,' and 'the deconstruction of representation.'" Applying these blindly and automatically, de Duve would have proceeded like a theory robot: "I'd have reproached Pollock for his Jungian analyst, when a Lacanian would have done so much better." As if to dramatize this crippling circumspection and to show how it leaves him so indecisive, de Duve breaks off, "I don't disavow all that, there's still some truth in it, but nonetheless. . . ."[32] Theory, it turns out, is "kitsch-like" too—being mechanical and formulaic, bloodless and loveless—its redundancy virtually parallels that of contemporary art since the 1960s in its desperate efforts to remain "avant-garde," which means contriving ways to be ever more startling and innovative. In Greenberg's terms, this is the double redundancy of our time.[33] De Duve is limp because the "glory days" have gone both in art and in criticism and when kitsch reigns virility goes out the window.[34]

If the cultural environment is pervaded by kitsch, what does it mean to judge aesthetically? Rosalind Krauss offers an intriguing indication within an environment described by Frederic Jameson as one of a global "image permeation," which sounds suspiciously reminiscent of the concerns of both Rothko and Greenberg. Krauss aims to revisit the question of the medium within the visual arts by examining the approach of Marcel Broodthaers, who, like Rothko, rejects the flattening of everything to finite associations. The Belgian artist had a term for this propensity, "monomania." Like Weber, he felt this "monomania" was equally operative within the arts manifested by trends such as Minimalism—and, perhaps by (Krauss's) implication, Greenberg's focus on the physicality of the support as the basis of medium-specificity. Broodthaers's contrary strategy involves embarking on a "fictional" double-take that "allows us to grasp reality and at the same time what it hides."[35] This corrosive layering,

Krauss argues, aims to expose what can "stand for, or allegorize, the self-differential condition of mediums themselves." The strategy is twofold: it seeks out the "redemptive possibilities encoded at the birth of a given technical support," but also lingers, as Krauss explains, in the wake of "high orders of technology," just where they render "older techniques outmoded," thereby allowing us "to grasp the inner complexity of the mediums those techniques support" (46).

Such a strategy probes the medium and the technical apparatuses it supports, but without enclosing it within an identity defined in terms of its physicality or instrumentality. For Krauss, this attentiveness to a "differential specificity" within the "total saturation of cultural space by the image" (in Jameson words, a "complete image-permeation of social and daily life") constitutes a zone of great critical possibility today. To discern this critical possibility, in a case of déjà vu for the visual arts, means to discern what fails to designate "differential specificity" and what fails in this respect once more acquires kitsch-like characteristics. For Krauss, the requisite culprits are "the international fashion of installation and intermedia work." These approaches display complicity "with a globalization of the image in the service of capital." Only artists such as James Coleman or William Kentridge escape this fate because they embrace "the idea of differential specificity," meaning that they embrace their medium as one that they need "to reinvent or rearticulate" (56).

Krauss's conclusion reiterates de Duve's assertion that the force of modernist singularity redefines the possibilities of the medium. Her evocative account of Broodthaers's layering of the fictional within the medium reveals that the much-heralded contemplative viewer must do a double take when approaching such work. All critical possibility lies with this capacity to discern the real as fictional and the fictional as real. Yet the question that nags away behind this redrafting of the critical approach to medium is, how does one command such a towering position from which to judge all installation and intermedia work as condemned from the outset?[36] The presumption recalls Greenberg's position on history and thus also the summit derived from assuming "a fairly constant distinction," except in this case it involves a fairly constant distinction between differing treatments of the medium.

In fact, if there is any constant factor here, it is the circularity of these arguments that derive from Greenberg's scrutiny of the medium in the visual arts. There is no dispute that this emphasis pinpoints Greenberg's enduring critical contribution to art history. The difficulty is that all ensuing engagements with his legacy wind up heralding judgment as a sovereign operation: judging demarcates thoroughly and exclusively; it establishes what is more immediate than the sham immediacy of kitsch; in confrontations it will deliver love rather than war. For Greenberg, wherever demarcations collapse, kitsch is bolstered. Rather than explore whether art might effectively operate within these perpetually faltering boundaries, the "avant-garde" is instead defined conservatively and defensively as if it were a fossil to be shut away and preserved from further withering. Rather than consider the errant destiny of art, the shift of focus from an "avant-garde" speculation to one concerning the fate of "modernist painting" consolidates critical attention upon a preoccupation with "legitimate boundaries," safety in identity and a devotion to border patrols. This drift from the "avant-garde" moment to that of "modernism," so defined, is one to be resisted, and Krauss depicts Broodthaers as an artist who actively refuses the drift toward the insularity of this "monomania."

Two further objections can be raised to this particular Greenbergian way of defining modernism. The first is art-historical. In the period immediately following World War II, Greenberg's art-historical markers remained decisively tied to the parameters established by the School of Paris, essentially in the years preceding World War I.[37] In contrast Broodthaers recapitulates a strategy predominant in the interwar period, but subsequently almost submerged until the 1960s: the exploration of the possibilities of art within nonimmanent boundaries, which is largely interdisciplinary and inquisitive about the relations and impact of different media upon one another. Clearly this is the issue at stake for a range of avant-garde strategies dating back to cubist collage, Dada, various forms of constructivism, and the Bauhaus, as well as van Doesburg and Rietveld in all their different ways. This is not to say that we require terms such as the "postmodern" or the "postmedium" to pinpoint what is at stake. It means insisting instead, along with Broodthaers, on a theoretical objection to this whole way of conceiving modernism and the medium in the visual arts. Hence, my second objection is theoretical rather than historical. De Duve's preferred method of redeeming Greenberg fails to provide convincing evidence that such an approach will ultimately prove conducive to upholding what he finds most compelling in modernism—its contesting of regulative ideas and its attempt to evoke a form of self-referentiality that is not defined defensively or tied to narcissistic identifications.

Singularity, Desire, and the Politics of Sociability

De Duve makes aesthetic judgment the key to redeeming Greenberg's insights on the alterity of the medium. That being the case, neither theory nor empiricism can be regarded as the pivotal considerations. Aesthetic judgments are not theoretical; they are not cognitive, and, as Kant bluntly asserts, they do not involve a "logical universal validity governed by concepts."[38] At the same time, the sense of singularity implied here is not simply empirical. "There can be an empirical history of taste," Weber suggests, "but its theoretical value would be nil. And what is worse, such a history would have to miss the distinctive singularity that makes an aesthetic judgment aesthetic."[39] That singularity rests with the fact that, lacking adequate concepts, there is nothing to arrest or subsume the particular case. This implies, as Weber teases out its consequences, that the particular case "requires a reorganization and reworking of those concepts. If such a reworking is what constitutes the a priori principle of judgment, then its product, whether it is cognitive or aesthetic, will always entail an element of change, of transformation" (142). If one tries to determine the object, then the judgment will prove determinate, whereas the aesthetic inquiry involves a move—and only a move—toward subsuming the particular. True to this dictum, Greenberg always protested that he did not prescribe art; he did not attempt to determine its course.[40] If art were science, it would be sufficient to uncover its underpinning laws and perhaps predict its future direction. Yet, Greenberg, like many powerful (read quasi-determinate) critics, found himself resistant to the course of most contemporary art from the 1960s.

Aesthetic judgment, however, occurs in the movement to arrest without fully arresting, to grasp without adequately grasping. Thus the consequences of this movement are played out as the consequences of representing in the broadest sense—not representing the things we are talking about but, as Weber puts it, in our very "ability to represent: the other, the different, the heterogeneous, the unknown, the unnameable."[41] Representing and judging are the crucial features of the avant-garde heritage, particularly because, as de Duve asserts, it challenges one to judge freely: "That it should be everybody's and anybody's business to judge art is precisely the epistemological—and political—heritage of the Modernist culture. . . . The self-application, since the Indépendants, of the regulative idea of painting upon its name was indeed to be the historical content of Modernism: the duty to judge freely, in matters of art and culture, and, symbolically, in matters of ethics and politics as well."[42]

The epistemological-political "heritage of the Modernist culture" is to contest regulative ideas (again this is the crucial issue in contesting Greenberg's "tautological" conflation of art and history). If this means contesting an equally significant tautology decreeing "that life is what the institution calls life," as de Duve would have it, then by implication the challenge extends to contesting what the institution decrees to be "knowledge," to be "excellence," or even "health," and so on.

The reflecting judgment that fascinates Weber needs to perform a double take in representing—virtually equivalent to the avant-garde scrutiny of representing as well as its questioning of what adheres seemingly matter-of-factly as a set of secure practices and conventions under a "name"—although for Weber this double take occurs because it is reflective insofar as "it reflects its own desire, rather than the object it ostensibly judges."[43] Desire, as de Duve attests in his reading of Greenberg, is often connected to the image of judging within aesthetic inquiry. What de Duve fails to consider adequately is that the narcissistic round-trip of kitsch plays an equally pertinent role with judgment—it remains in fact its most favored aspiration. Pleasure and desire are frequently valorized in aesthetics, particularly in considerations of aesthetic judgment, yet in comparison to topics such as the medium and representation they are treated rather simplistically—or more accurately euphorically. If we are talking love, as de Duve does, then the object of our love, as Freud tells us, is often regarded "in the same way as our own ego, so that when we are in love a considerable amount of narcissistic libido overflows on to the object." By a process of gradual elevation, the object becomes more sublime and ineffable until the object takes the place of the ego ideal.[44] In the wake of the avant-garde heritage with its disruptions of traditional conventions and expectations, this process is ambivalent; the ideal passes between the object and judging itself in an unresolved roundabout.

To accept a convention, to repeat de Duve, does not mean simply submitting to it, for it equally means that one is confronted or propelled as much as it means judging freely. There is constraint; the artist is as much conquered as conqueror. Only in the movement of judgment, ironically, does one find true spontaneity and a love without confrontation, a supreme ideal demarcating and establishing self-reference. The crucial flaw in Greenberg's important portrayal of the modernist avant-garde is that love and judgment are always sovereign; any confrontation with an unremitting other falls away in a depiction of a love that only seeks fulfillment in self-presentation and hence culminates—no matter the nuances—in that narcissistic round-trip identified by that forever-expanding term, "kitsch." Everyone wishes to be sovereign: to command a position, to hold forth with stability and to assert something for which there is due return, but it is even better if desire or love are satisfied. Love means being confirmed in one's position, which for all the talk of love is not very romantic. All that can be said for theory is that it does not produce this rendezvous; it is more like the "barren and austere" formulations that Greenberg links originally with the avant-garde. Nevertheless, as Greenberg implies, there is an allure in this austerity that does not rendezvous, an allure in which the medium remains opaque in the aftermath of what one does not grasp and consume, and which for all that effort remains there yet again to be reached. This is what proves enduring about Greenberg's focus upon the question of the medium in modern art. It is just that Greenberg possesses no means to explain this allure other than as an aberration—and this presents an ongoing issue for the definition of modernism and adducing its legacy within contemporary art.

It is ironic that the most frequently espoused model of aesthetic pleasure and desire is one best captured by Greenberg's definition of kitsch as promising a narcissistic round-trip of direct and immediate identification. One reason for this constant recourse to such an aspiration is that it draws upon an aesthetic-artistic understanding of singularity as sovereign. The epitome of a successful artwork is one that is viewed as uniquely sovereign—it is indeed a highly inflated ego ideal—and this cherished achievement is transferred to aesthetic judgment as its ultimate ideal (of course, it is regularly idealized in other spheres, such as politics). It is a depiction that lacks any constraint or impediment even though faced with them all around. In section 60 of the *Critique of Judgment*, Kant explicates what he regards as the basic communicative aspirations of art, which complicates this presumption of achievement as a sheer elevated surge. The greatest capacity of fine art, indeed the "highest degree of its perfection," Kant asserts, is the cultivation of our mental powers by "what we call *humaniora* (the humanities)." Humanity in turn involves a twofold capacity: on the one hand, "the universal *feeling of sympathy*" and, on the other, "the ability to engage universally in very intimate *communication*" (Kant's emphases). It is a twofold process because having a great idea is insufficient. It is equally crucial to be able to impart it to others in a convincing manner. When combined, these capacities testify to the "sociability" of human beings; it is the expression and mode of our humanity.[45] Quite simply, humanity refers not only to the capacity to develop ideas, but also the effort to convey them, to communicate them to others.

Weber presents an intriguing reading of this passage from Kant by characterizing the twofold process as a "partial imparting." Weber emphasizes the partial or "part" aspect of the German terms that Kant uses in this passage referring to "participation." Weber thereby translates the passage from Kant to emphasize that the humanities or humanity signify at once "the universal feeling of *taking-part* [*Teilnehmungsgefühl*]" and the power "to *impart oneself* [*mitteilen*]." Weber's literalness aims to underline the fact that "sociability" [*Geselligkeit*] involves taking part and imparting oneself—that is, it involves "imparting of the particular, the partisan and the partial."[46] The particular or specific, however, can never stand alone for it must be conveyed by a universalizing momentum, referring to what we call sociability or humanity. Yet if fine art and the humanities in general constitute the area of human activity devoted to examining the particular, then it can never quite succeed in its basic task because its very effort of imparting necessarily involves a subsuming act. The universalizing momentum communicates by generalizing and it cannot therefore proceed without eradicating what is particular or specific to its own particular inquiry. As Weber puts it, this process is ambivalent: "the particular concern with the particular, the unpredictable, the unexpected, defines itself through a heterogeneity from which it can never entirely eradicate itself" (138).

The dilemma lies with attempting to contextualize a particularity or, alternatively, quantifying the qualitative. Weber explains the dynamic that Kant wishes to convey—and that he in turn wishes to accentuate by the example of looking up words in a dictionary—an apt choice for this discussion given the focus upon naming and conventions. If we take the example of language and dictionaries, we start off referring back from a new language to our mother tongue and then we proceed with increasing proficiency to the use of intralanguage dictionaries. Weber's point is that we soon reach a stage—"either disconcerting or exhilarating"—where it becomes difficult to ascertain the most appropriate meaning and "we are constrained to choose between meanings without being certain of which criteria we should use" (145). Beyond questions of high-level language proficiency, Weber suggests that there is a more basic operation at play that "is intrinsically endless, and yet in order for it to function at all we must *arrest* it" (145). This arresting is necessary, but it highlights the essential, but conflictual, aspect of sociability (imparting the particular as well as taking part) and thus highlighting its "ambivalent character." The particular must be imparted, though it can "never be entirely transcended," and yet it can never simply persist by itself, as an isolated fragment, in "its isolated particularity."[47]

The dual process of partaking and imparting requires a certain self-effacement, though this is never entirely successful. Because it is conflictual, then, like Freudian repression, this effacement leaves traces (144). So to succeed at all in imparting the particular, a process of arresting occurs and it forms the basis of our organized view of the world. To be organized, we arrest, Weber proclaims, to the extent that we "must 'forget' this irreducibly undefinable vestige, this set of exclusions that is neither entirely indeterminate nor fully determinable" (145). This suggests the limits of identity politics insofar as it is based upon imparting a coherent, fully communicable identity as the basis of authentic action in social life. On the other hand, Weber's discussion also suggests that the communicative bridge that Kant cherishes necessarily subsumes particularity in communicating, so that communication is possible only by accentuating its effacement (of the particular, the heterogeneous, the indefinable vestige).

This focus upon the twofold, ambivalent structure of sociability shows that Weber's emphasis does not rest with the accentuation of sheer alterity, the spiral of endless deferral in the face of the priority of the other that is so often associated with deconstruction. This is clear in his treatment of singularity, which he seeks to distinguish "from the individual that often contains and absorbs it."[48] This is because, as Weber explicates it, "Singularity, which is perhaps the other face of the other, is not what takes place first of all, once and for all, an entirely unique event, but, paradoxically, what emerges in and through repetition, as what is left over and doesn't fit in. The singular is (the) odd. In place of the undivided origin or of the original individual, the singular emerges when something doesn't quite *fit*—which means, fit *in*."[49]

The singular is what remains in the aftermath of the best efforts of determination; it is not that which precedes critical determination and every effort of contextualization, unique and separate from the outset. One of the least observed, but most important achievements of Weber's engagement with aesthetic inquiry is his refashioning of "singularity." It is this quite different conception of singularity that preserves the most critically insightful aspects of the investigation into the "opacity" of the medium.[50]

Could it be that in the self-denigrating portrayal of his performance as a critic-theoretician that de Duve comes closest to the challenges posed by the apprehensive dimensions of the aesthetic idea? For the desire

elicited by the aesthetic idea proves evocative in disappointing self-posses-
sion—it is all the more desirable for being both elusive and touching.
Lacking as it does an adequate presentation to align with, it still confronts
one in proximity, as an irresistible movement to be arrested, though never
fully subsumed. If passion, as Cixous characterizes it, is "always of the
order of a summit," then it is "as if the vibrations of one being were produced in the cadence and rhythm of the other." The event of this desire
is experienced "as a tearing of the thick flesh of resistance, as a happy
wound but as a wound nonetheless."[51] If one were to translate this passage
into the different register of judgment with, say, Greenberg, the reverberations of the aesthetic play a central role, but without even a happy
wound—or, at least, one that will always need to be mitigated.

Is this because an entire tradition tends to translate aesthetic inquiry as
the experience of the ineffable (and thus akin to Freud's depiction of the
inflated love object), when in fact as Kant proposed, and Weber highlights
this original proposition of Kant's, the aesthetic idea is rather "unnameable" (*unnennbar*) (151)? Naming things properly, and demarcating things
as specific, allows them "to be seized, grasped, means comprehending
them once and for all"—that is, according to the assumption that we define them properly, if we get the definitions right![52] What proves assuring
is that proper nouns designate and gather in things and concepts, and
thus gathers our way of grasping things and operating within the world.
Grasping things, by accounting for them, secures knowledge. Apprehension is usually understood in this sense as a grasping that is reassuring
insofar as it renders "the unknown knowable . . . universally replicable,"
while the future is "brought under control and alterity made assimilable."
Knowledge, so conceived, amounts to the "formal movement of self-iden-
tification through self-reference," everything is gathered up and the virtual situation contained and made assimilable to reference (68). Kant
instead left the aesthetic inquiry with a proposition: an apprehensive
apprehension.

Such an apprehensive inquiry also involves, as Weber notes, both a *sujet
supposé savoir* and a *sujet supposé aimer* (always fondly transcribed as a rite
of passage in the arts). The auratic quality of this event has the tenor
of suggesting that something has happened, and taken place, but as the
encounter with singularity that risks and resists the judging desire of the
ego ideal.[53] The reverberations of such an inquiry persist as a genuinely
apprehensive challenge to reflecting and representing where much is
risked, including many egos, and where compensation is sought all the
time, yet still the process of imparting the particular and coming to terms

with the aesthetic continues unabated. This critical vestige persists against the constant effort to *name*—that is, to seek to grasp and secure— conventions, institutions, and regulative ideas on our behalf. In one sense, this is an inescapable compulsion, but our critical struggle is to allow other ideas and understandings to persist. Modern art is one name for such a struggle; it stands for a most conservative effort of self-referentiality, but it also designates one key space for rehearsing and giving name to other possibilities.

CHAPTER 8

It Walks: The Ambulatory Uncanny

Susan Bernstein

Samuel Weber's work has a remarkable range. He has written on Freud and Lacan, Nietzsche and Heidegger, Balzac and Hoffmann. His work addresses all the crucial issues of critical theory, from questions of hermeneutics and deconstruction to problems of professionalism and the structure of the university. Weber is one of the most timely writers in the field on literary studies, able to articulate issues of tradition with contemporary cultural and critical polemics. He is tremendously active in the professional community; he has lectured in France, Germany, Holland, Australia, Singapore, and of course the United States. He has taught in Berlin and Frankfurt, Paris and Strasbourg, as well as at Northwestern, Johns Hopkins, and other American universities. This list is not meant to invoke authority; rather, Weber's facility of motion reflects his commitment to a practice of translation and interpretation with a social and political dimension. His careful and lucid readings, whether of "the uncanny," the political, or media technology and aesthetics, always keep critical topics alive, refusing the tendency toward reification or programmatic phrases. His work continues to open questions and is, as he has suggested, *"criticism underway."*[1] Insofar as his critical engagement is timely, one might also say, invoking Nietzsche, that it is untimely as well, in its ability to sidestep the unfortunately common hunger for novelty, and to remain instead committed to repetitions and rehearsals that continue to translate and transmit, to open discourse and make it available for fresh readerships. I would like here to follow in his footsteps a bit and take this book reflecting upon his work as an opportunity to revisit the topic of the uncanny.

Weber's essay "The Sideshow, or: Remarks on a Canny Moment," first published in 1973 and reprinted in the expanded edition of *The Legend of Freud* in 2000, is now a classic in the literature of the uncanny. Reading Freud's essay "Das Unheimliche," along with Hoffmann's "Sandman" and Villier de l'Isle-Adam's novel *l'Eve future*, Weber makes an important intervention in arguing against the many prior approaches to this topic which had tended to understand it solely as an "emotive phenomenon" identified with feelings of fear, anxiety, weirdness, and the like. "Such a position," he writes, "misconstrues the peculiar structure of the uncanny, or more precisely, ignores the fact that the uncanny has a particular structure, which, however intimately bound up with subjective feelings—above all anxiety—is nonetheless determined by a series of 'objective' factors that in turn stand in a certain relation to literary discourse" (208).[2] He thus joins in the discussion that begins to understand Freud's text as itself a case of the uncanny,[3] and indeed of the literary uncanny. Weber points to Freud's failure to define the uncanny in a final or complete way, suggesting that this is not an error on Freud's part, but rather tells us something about the uncanny itself. At the same time, Weber steers clear of defining the uncanny as an "object." Rather, what characterizes the uncanny is precisely the impossibility of looking it "straight in the eyes, as it were . . . peeling and paring away its external layers to get at the 'conceptual kernel' within and yet unable to ever eliminate the (growing) shadow of doubt— all this indicates that even if the uncanny is not conceived as an irreducibly subjective sentiment, its objective structure cannot be determined solely in thematic terms" (1115). The uncanny calls not for a definition, a collection of thematic terms, but rather, as a " 'formal,' textual structure," it demands *reading*. This insistence on reading, foregrounding the textuality of the uncanny, points to the ways in which the uncanny functions as a critique of identity. "The *reading* that I now propose to undertake," Weber writes, "seeks . . . to avoid the impasse of interpretations which— like Freud's *Musterung*—conceive and organize their own activity, consciously or unconsciously, in terms derived from a notion of perception ('vision') which in turn is based upon ontological presuppositions that the problematic of castration precisely and decisively dislocates: namely, upon the presence and identity of the 'object' in question" (1115).

Since Weber's article was published, several other lively texts on the topic[4] have helped "the Uncanny" became a fetish concept whose descriptive potential has tended to overshadow the fact that the uncanny puts in question the possibility of definition itself.[5] Weber's work on the uncanny, in contrast, focuses on reading and textuality, rather than on conceptual results. His reading of the uncanny continues in the essay "Uncanny Thinking" (1999), also added to the new edition of *The Legend of Freud*. Interestingly, the two pieces on the uncanny are both supplements to the original book and thus destabilize the identity boundaries of *The Legend of Freud*.

Weber's discussion in the earlier essay, while giving due importance to the problem of castration in the uncanny, reads this in the Lacanian tradition as a problem of the unreliability of vision, the strange crossing from sense perception to the symbolic order, and the emergence of anxiety around the creeping conviction of the subject's incompletion, lack of wholeness and fallibility. That is, he does not reduce it to the castration scenario, as Freud does in his (mis)reading of the "The Sandman":

> For what the child "discovers"—that is, interprets—as "castration" is neither nothing nor simply something, at least in the sense in which the child expects and desires it to be: what is "discovered" is the absence of the maternal phallus, a kind of negative perception, whose object or referent—perceptum—is ultimately nothing but a difference, although no simple one, since it does not refer to anything, least of all to itself, but instead refers itself indefinitely. . . . Castration thus structures the future identity and experience of the subject, by confronting it with its unconscious desire as a violent and yet constitutive difference, preventing the subject from ever being fully present to itself, or fully self-conscious. (215–16).

This castration anxiety, then, is not literally about the boy's fear of losing his penis, but surrounds what Weber describes as a "restructuring of experience, including the relation of perception, desire and consciousness, in which the narcissistic categories of identity and presence are riven by a difference they can no longer subdue or command" (216–17).

The differences between presence and absence, and sameness and difference, self and other, are of course particularly at stake here. All of these pairs are troubled by the destabilization of binary opposition that Freud formulates as one of the fundamental features of the uncanny, that is, between the *heimlich* and the *unheimlich*, the "homey" and the "foreign," the familiar and the strange. While the uncanny is often discussed in terms of these pairs, most importantly, the opposition itself is untenable. Freud points out: "Aus diesem langen Zitat ist für uns am interessantesten, dass das Wörtchen heimlich unter den mehrfachen Nuancen seiner Bedeutung auch eine zeigt, in der es mit seinem Gegensatz unheimlich zusammenfallt" ("What interests us most in this long extract is to find that among its different shades of meaning the word 'heimlich' exhibits one which is identical with its opposite, 'unheimlich'").[6] One might even read *unheimlich* here as an adverb, for the coincidence of a term with its opposite is itself uncanny. Uncanny is the word always falling away from itself into its opposite, yet affirming itself in doing so. The uncanny comes into being as a violation of the law of noncontradiction. Like a ghost, it "is" and "is not."

The opposition between subject and object also falls away with the erosion of the structure of identity; subject and predicate can no longer keep their boundaries intact. The uncanny is not a stable concept (subject) to which the predicate of a clear definition can be attached. Likewise, there can be no reliable identification of a text or event as uncanny, no stable thing to which the qualities of the uncanny can be predicated. The propositional structure of adequation collapses in uncanny writing, for the model of adequation requires that each member stay on its own side of the copula. Weber remarks: "the alert reader will hardly remain insensitive to the peculiar merging of subject matter and discourse in Freud's essay. Yet this merging does not simply fulfill the exigencies of theoretical discourse, the adequatio intellectus et rei, since here the 'adequacy' of discourse and object rends as much to dislocate the discourse as to locate the subject" (209). However, this does not mean that the uncanny is some ineffable quality about which nothing can be said. In fact, the naming of the uncanny is constitutive of it, helps to bring it about, and partakes in it; this relationship is one that can be further examined.

Speaking of the uncanny thus calls for some caution, or perhaps, it makes explicit the caution required when trying to define anything at all. Martin Heidegger discusses the pitfalls of definition in his essay "Zur Seinsfrage," "On the Question of Being," which, incidentally, entails some mention of the uncanny. Heidegger takes issue with Ernst Jünger's efforts to find a "good definition" of nihilism. He clearly criticizes the definitional procedure that takes the object of inquiry to be a stable and separate entity waiting to be defined by propositions. Instead, Heidegger allows questions to "turn towards" what they ask about, hoping thus to dislodge the oppositional relationship separating and desiccating both the subject and object poles. This is how he asks about the essence, the *Wesen*, of a thing:

Woher kommt dieses Wesen? Wo haben wir es zu suchen? Welches ist der Ort des Nichts? Wir fragen nicht unbedacht zuviel, wenn wir nach dem Ort sauchen and das Wesen der Linie erörtern. Doch ist dies etwas anderes als der Versuch, das zu leisten, was Sie [Jünger] verlangen: 'eine gute Definition des Nihilismus'? Es sieht so aus, als werde das Denken wie in einem magischen Kreis fortgesetzt um das Selbe herumgefördert oder gar herumgenarrt, ohne sich doch je diesem Selben nähern zu können. Aber vielleicht ist der Kreis eine verborgene Spirale. Vielleicht hat sich diese inszwischen verengt. Dies bedeutet: die Art und die Weise, nach denen wir und dem Wesen des Nihilismus nähern, wandeln sich. Die Güte der rechtmäßig verlangten 'guten Definition' findet ihre Bewahrung darin, dass wir das Definierenwollen aufgeben, insofern diese sich auf Aussagessätze festlegen muß, in denen das Denken abstirbt.[7]

From where does this essence come? Where must we seek it? What is the locale of the nothing? We shall not be asking too much in an unthinking manner if we search for the locale and in our discussion locate the essence of the line. Yet is this something other than the attempt to provide what you demand: "a good definition of nihilism"? It looks as though thinking is continually led around or even chased around the Same as though in a magical circle, yet without ever being able to approach this Same. But perhaps the circle is a concealed spiral. Perhaps this spiral has in the meantime become more constricted. This means: the manner and way in which we are approaching the essence of nihilism are being transformed. Whatever is good in the "good definition" that you rightfully demand will prove its worth in our giving up the desire to define, to the extent that this desire must become fixed in propositional statements in which thinking dies out.[8]

The occurrence of the "magical circle" recalls the "circle of fire" Nathanael repeatedly invokes in Hoffmann's "Sandmann" as he goes mad. Weber recalls this phrase in his analysis of "Uncanny Thinking" in the essay added to the new edition of *The Legend of Freud*. Paraphrasing Heidegger, Weber describes how "in leaving what he knows for the unknown, man seeks to impose his order on all areas of life. But although he succeeds in developing great skill in organizing and opening realms of being, he finds himself thrown back again and again onto the paths he has already traversed. In short, like Nathanael in 'The Sandman,' man here is caught in a circle. In it, 'he turns around and about in his own circle' (Heidegger 121/157), caught in the rut of the all too familiar and however agile and ingenious he may be in discovering all sorts of paths, there is no way out" (26). Finally, Weber argues that for Heidegger, the uncanny happening or event disrupts this circle, breaks it apart, and creates the possibility of an openness towards something other, something strange and alien. Just as in the passage directed towards Jünger and nihilism, Heidegger expands the magical circle of his questioning into a spiral that might change the path of thinking. Weber's reading of Heidegger in this essay focuses on the uncanny as the possibility of an opening, of change, of repetition with a difference.

What kind of difference does uncanny thinking make? If we return to "Zur Seinsfrage," the difference destroys the technological relationship between a dominating subjective force and its "*Bestand*," what stands at its disposal, by establishing instead an inclination, a turning towards, that is a genuine relation. The turning towards would actually partake in Being (*Sein*) which could no longer be understood as an object separate from the process of turning towards. To indicate this new status of *Sein*, Heidegger recommends that it be written crossed out. "Die kreuzweise Durchstreichung," he explains, "wehrt zunächst nur ab, nähmlich die fast unausrottbare Gewöhnung, 'das Sein' wie ein für sich stehendes und dann auf den Menschen erst bisweilen zu kommendes Gegenüber vorzustellen" (405) ("The crossing out of this word initially has only a preventative role, namely, that of preventing the almost ineradicable habit of representing 'being' as something standing somewhere on its own that then on occasion first comes face-to-face with human beings" [310]).

This revision of the materiality of writing reshapes what it names and, at least if Heidegger is right, presents a relation between human inquiry and Being which is not that of subject and object. Because this relation no longer obtains, one cannot properly say that Being "is" as one would say of an object. In fact, *Sein* presents itself precisely as the *Sein des Seienden*, that is, the being of that which is and thus is not itself something that "is" or appears. Since Being "is" not, or is that "was ganz und gar kein Seinendes ist," it can present itself "im Gesichtskreis des wissenshaftlichen Vorstellens . . . nur als Nichts . . . [darbieten]" (412) ("within the perspective of scientific representation . . . that which is not in any way a being (namely, being) can present itself only as nothing" [316]). Coinciding at the point which is not, *Sein* and *Nichts* become interchangeable. Opposition no longer holds. Importantly, this "nothing" is not itself nothing, but also cannot be said to be anything: "Dieses Nichts, das nicht das Seiende ist und das es gleichwohl gibt, ist nichts Nichtiges. Es gehört zum Anwesen. Sein und Nichts gibt es nicht nebeneinander. Eines verwendet sich für das Andere in einer Verwandtschaft, deren Wesensfülle wir noch kaum bedacht haben" (413) ("This nothing, which is not being and which is nevertheless *given*, is nothing negative. It belongs to presencing. Being and nothing are not given alongside one another. The one employs itself for the other in a kinship whose essential fullness we have as yet scarcely pondered" [317]).

The relation Heidegger establishes here between *Sein* and *Nichts* thus resembles the coexistence of the *heimlich* and the *unheimlich* in Freud's essay. Heidegger's "es gibt" points to the way in which this point of confusion and coexistence of opposites can be named without a proper subject position; neither Being nor nothing can properly bear the copula "is." We might say the same thing about the uncanny which has no essential core, but certainly does come to us in a variety of literary and theoretical texts. Heidegger himself invokes the uncanny in "Zur Seinsfrage" to describe the operation of the term *Sein* crossed out, indicated here as *Sein(x)*: "Als die unbedingte Versammlung solchen Stellens schwindet das Sein(x) nicht hin. Es bricht in einer einzigen Unheimlichkeit auf" (408) ("As the unconditioned gathering of such setting in place, being(x) does not disappear. It irrupts in a singular uncanniness" [313]). The turning and shifting of *Sein* and *Nichts* is indicated where the ability of *Sein(x)* to signify is interrupted by its own motion, by its own signifying, and is prevented from becoming a concept or stable signified. The graphics of the crossing out interrupts meaning, in a peculiar uncanniness, which also allows *Sein* to irrupt, to open up, or to get underway. The uncanny i(nte)rrupts.

In addressing Jünger, Heidegger joins his examination of nihilism in considering the current state of things. He agrees that a proper understanding of nihilism is still wanting. Citing Nietzsche, Heidegger describes this misunderstood or forgotten nihilism as an uncanny guest:

> Der Mangel trübt das Urteil über den Blick bei der Beurteilung unserer Lage. Er macht das Urteil über den Nihilismus leichtfertig und das Auge blind für das Gegenwart 'dieses unheimlichsten aller Gäste' (Nietzsche). Er heißt das 'unheimlichste,' weil er als der unbedingte Wille zum Willen die Heimatlosigkeit als solche will. Darum hilft es nichts, ihm die Tür zu weisen, weil er überall schon längst und unsichtbar in Haus umgeht. Es gilt, diesen Gast zu erblicken und zu durchschauen. (381)

> This lack dims our view in assessing our situation. It makes a judgment concerning nihilism ready and easy and blinds us to the presence of "this most uncanny of all guests" (Nietzsche, *Will to Power*; Outline. *Werke*, vol. XV, 141). It is called the "most uncanny" because, as the unconditional will to will, it wills homelessness as such. This is why it is of no avail to show it the door, because it has long since been roaming around invisibly inside the house. The task is to catch sight of and see through this guest. (292)

The uncanny guest, a figure for nihilism, understands *Nichts* to mean simply nothing rather than the peculiar something/nothing of the pair *Sein* and *Nichts* and thus supposes that there is no ground or transcendent opening to being—that there is only *Seiendes*, appearance and no essence, nothing behind it. The will to homelessness means just this: the emphatic belief that there is nothing but the ontic, no opening, no other than ourselves.

The first appearance of the uncanny in "Zur Seinsfrage," then, comes in the figure of a guest, a figure both familiar, as one invited or welcomed in, and an alien invader. We might translate Heidegger's "es gibt," in this case, as "it walks." The uncanny walks around the house invisibly, before being known or recognized. It walks to announce itself before being present; its walking interrupts our understanding to show its temporal and spatial distention, the absorption of a content or concept in the narrative spasms that allow the uncanny to come forth, over time, never whole. To reiterate, the uncanny cannot be properly understood, since it signifies the disruption of the proper and the instability of understanding. Weber reminds us:

> Nevertheless, the shunting aside of the uncanny by most "scholarly" discourse and research doesn't succeed in putting it to rest. Rather, like the Sandman, the uncanny crops up again and again, with surprising resilience, where it is least expected: as a figure of speech, an atmosphere of a story, an allegorical instance. Announced by the sound of approaching steps, of heavy breathing, wheezing or coughing, or other semi-articulate sounds, uncanny figures and situations return to remind us of the difficulty of distinguishing clearly between language and reality, between feelings and situations, between what we know and what we ignore. Defiguring of the figure, the Sandman [the uncanny guest] marks the spot where what is (there) and what is not, presence and absence, coming and going, can no longer be clearly distinguished. (19–20)

Weber's passage and the spasmodic appearances of the uncanny in Heidegger's essay point to its syncopated structure which makes it impossible to define the uncanny. We find the same problem in the oft-cited lines from Schelling:

> Der reine Himmel . . . nachdem die dunkle and verdunkelde Gewalt jenes unheimlichen Princips (unheimlich nennt man alles, was im Geheimniß, in Verborgenen, in der Latenz bleiben sollte und hervorgetreten ist)—jener Aether . . . konnte erst sich ausspannen, nachdem de Gewalt jenes unheimlichen Princips, das in den frügeren Religionen herrschte, in dem Mysterium niedergeschlagen war . . .[9]

The pure heaven . . . after the dark and darkening violence of that uncanny principle (we can uncanny everything which should have remained se-creted, in the concealed, in latency, but has come forth)—that ether could only spread itself out after the violence of that principle that had ruled in earlier religions was struck down into the mystery.

The quality of *unheimlich* results from the movement of the ground or principle; that is, the principle is not itself uncanny until it has violated its own nature by stepping forth into actuality, into the ontic. The uncanny principle, then, really describes a dynamic structure of coming forth un-bidden and being covered over again. What remains is a "Mystery," a word like *Sein* that creates a void behind it, a negative ground.[10] If the Mystery is like a scab, it points both to *Seinsvergessenheit*—the empty signi-fier, the forgetting of being—and to *Verborgenheit*, concealedness—the condition of not-being-revealed that allows for something to creep into view.[11] For Schelling, the world of Greek mythology is constructed pre-cisely on this kind of ambiguous ground or unground: "Die homerische Gotterwelt schließt schweigend ein Mysterium in sich, und ist über einem Mysterium, über einem Abgrund gleichsam errichtet, den sie wie mit Blu-men zudeckt" (649) ("The world of the Homeric gods encloses a mystery silently within itself and is erected over a mystery, over an abyss, which it covers over as if with flowers").

The uncanny opens as the flowers strewn over the abyss, the covering over its own hollow. The flowers of Greece repress the abyss below them; the uncanny guest, in contrast, reminds us of the absence he presents.

The walking of the uncanny guests leads us into the textuality of the uncanny. For it spreads itself out, suggests approach or arrival, yet only to draw back the suggestion of meaning that comes forth in its perambula-tions. Freud's famous wanderings through the red light district of a small Italian village partake in this ambulatory uncanny. The anecdote serves as an example of the uncanny brought about by the repetition of the same that invokes an uncanny feeling, Freud says, when accompanied by "cer-tain circumstances." Freud finds himself in a neighborhood, "über deren Charakter ich nicht lange in Zweifel bleiben konnte"[12] (249) ("of whose character I could not long remain in doubt" [237]). Hurrying away, pre-sumably from the token of his own lust, Freud finds himself in the same street again, now beginning to attract attention. Interestingly, Freud does not actually mention any repressed or emerging desires; but the attention he draws suggests that his body, helpless and "*führerlos*," is becoming a meaningful sign for others. Upon his unlikely third return to the same street, we begin to believe that his repressed desire has come forth. Yet what he says is: "Dann erfaßste mich ein Gefühl, das ich nur als unheimlich bezeichnen kann" (249) ("Now, however, a feeling overcame me which I can only describe as uncanny" [237]). The naming of the uncanny here recognizes that the seemingly meaningless motion of the body, in coinciding with itself in the street of painted women, turns into a meaningful sign. That it, what ought to have remained hidden, has come forth. The uncanniness, though, remains attached to the repeated movement; its explanation by way of repressed desire does not do away with the uncanny effect brought about through walking.

The working of the uncanny obscures the effort to understand it and thus refers us back to a nonunderstanding that is its real sense (what Weber describes as "backing out"). Of the uncanny it might be said, as of "a certain German book" in Poe's "Man of the Crowd, "er [sic] lässt sich nicht lesen"[13]—"it does not suffer itself to be read." This story shares in the uncanny of repetition of the same. As the ambulatory uncanny, it privileges the walking body, the signifying process, over any interior or meaning that might characterize it as a whole or replace it as its end. In walking, the excesses of time and space, of the materiality of writing, of the process of signification, have priority over any signified sense, any subjective interior, any invisible cause or ground.[14] The convalescent narrator, I recall, is seated in a London coffeehouse. "With a cigar in my mouth and a newspaper in my lap, I had been amusing myself for the greater part of the afternoon, now in poring over advertisements, now in observing the promiscuous company in the room, and now in peering through the smoky panes into the street" (475). He amuses himself by establishing abstract generalizations within which he subsumes the characters who pass by. The categories are "obvious" (clerks); "The division of the upper clerks . . . it was not possible to mistake." . . . "There were many individuals of dashing appearance, whom I easily understood as belonging to the race of swell pick-pockets." . . . "The gamblers . . . were still more easily recognizable." The moving bodies are read and replaced with a stable conceptual content that states their essence or meaning: "although the rapidity with which the world of light flitted before the window presented me from casting more than a glance upon each visage, still it seemed that, in my then peculiar mental state, I could frequently read, even in that brief interval of a glance, the history of long years" (478). The diachrony of life is revealed in a synchronous image as its content, process replaced by result. This cognitive procedure is interrupted by the appearance of a particular figure whose nature cannot be revealed. The narrator takes a turn toward him:

"I felt singularly aroused, startled, fascinated" (all qualities, by the way, which might be associated with the uncanny). " 'How wild a history,' I said to myself, 'is written within that bosom!' Then came a craving desire to keep the man in view—to know more of him." As his desire overcomes him, the cool analytic position is abandoned. "Hurriedly putting on an overcoat, and seizing my hat and cane, I made my way into the street. . . . With some little difficulty I at length came within sight of him, approached, and followed him closely, yet cautiously, so as not to attract his attention" (479). With these sudden, jerky and compulsive bodily movements, the reader is dislocated and leaves his seat in the coffeehouse to follow his man. He has entered into the circulation of signifiers and thus has actually already fallen into the uncanny, for the track he lays out in pursuit becomes the first in a repeated series.

The narrator suggests that the meaning of the man will be revealed if he is pursued, that his walking will reveal a meaning as his destination. Yet the more adamant the search, the less plausible the signs become. The reader of the text also follows closely, expecting each detail to be a clue. "Here a change in his demeanor followed." We wait to hear what, in fact, is going on. "He walked more and more slowly and with less object than before—more hesitatingly." Are we approaching the goal? "He crossed and re-crossed the way repeatedly, without apparent aim"—but surely the aim will soon be made clear? But repetition begins to disappoint us; its condensing points appear, yet lead nowhere. "A second turn brought us into a square, brilliantly lighted and overflowing with life. The old manner of the stranger reappeared. . . . I was surprised, however, to find, upon his having made the circuit of the square, that he turned and retraced his steps. Still more was I astonished to see him repeat the same walk several times" (479). Even as he becomes familiar, his strangeness increases: "A few minutes brought us to a large and busy bazaar, with the localities of which the stranger appeared well acquainted, and where his original demeanor again became apparent, as he forced his way to and fro. . . . His head again fell on his breast; he appeared as I had seen him at first. . . . As he proceeded . . . his old uneasiness and vacillation were resumed" (480). As in Heidegger's phrase, it is useless to try to show him the door. In or out, this man doesn't settle. Inside the gin bar nothing is different: "With a half shriek of joy the old man forced a passage within, resumed at once his original bearing, and stalked backward and forward, without apparent object, among the throng." As the story draws to a close, the circumambulations of the city continue in an unending cycle, revealing nothing. "Yet he did not hesitate in his career, but, with a mad energy, retrace his steps at once, to the heart of the mighty London. . . . But as usual, he walked to and fro, and during the day did not pass from out the turmoil of that street" (481).

The ambulatory uncanny remains impervious to efforts to stop it, to gather it, to decipher it. The narrator concludes: "This old man is the type and the genius of deep crime. He refuses to be alone. He is the man of the crowd. It will be in vain to follow; for I shall learn no more of him, nor of his deeds . . . and perhaps it is but one of the great mercies of God that 'er lässt sich nicht lesen'" (481). The old man is deeply improper; he never goes home, he never turns in, he never reveals an interior. But in fact he does reveal the lack of an interior, the presence of an absence, the fact of illegibility. This figure breaks off in a "singular uncanniness," pursuing its wild circle of fire interrupted by the repetition of the words: "Er lässt sich nicht lesen." This quality of the German book of the first paragraph is now transferred to the text in which it finds itself: "The Man of the Crowd." (The book is indicated by the pronouns *er*, a masculine third-person that could easily refer to "man," rather than by the neuter *es*, which would replace the German word *Buch*.) In failing to read, we read; in reading, we fail to read. The process of reading overshadows its inter-pretive result—a lack of insight or understanding. This result, which is none, displays the strange cohabitation of opposites of the uncanny, the violation of the law of noncontradiction. It also plays with the distinction between diachrony and synchrony, or the experience of the uncanny over time (walking, reading) and the conclusion or characterization we attribute to it after the process has ended (understanding). While the text does stop, we might say it doesn't really quite "end." It functions as the uncanny happening Weber outlines in "Uncanny Thinking." The uncanny hap-pening, as for Heidegger, disrupts the narrative of the empirical in the relation to death. "It should be noted," Weber writes:

> that when it comes time to formulate just why and how the uncanny is "nothing special," . . . and that it has nothing to do with dying considered as an actual event, Heidegger resorts to the present participle of the verb "to happen" (*geschehend*) in order to designate the temporality that distin-guishes the uncanny as happening from death as an empirical event. This is of particular interest given his preceding remarks on the circularity of the paths that mark one's history and on their tendency to revolve around themselves. "Circle of fire . . ." The circle of familiarity, of the home, tends to turn into the less virtuous solipsism, tautology, and even death, from which one can easily yearn to escape, to break out in search of adventure

and the unknown. But such yearning supposes that one can find the beginning of the beginning, the circumference of the circle of the familiar and
the family. Otherwise, how can one hope to escape? (26)

Focusing on the present participle as marker of a "temporality of disjunction," Weber argues that, for Heidegger, the uncanny opens a "breach"
in this circularity in breaking with one narrative level—the empirical—and
opening another. The point of disruption would at least suggest a point of
possibility: "In being thus overwhelmed as breach, human being is forced
to open itself to alteration, transformation, deformation. For it is only in
this forced and violent opening, which can also entail violence and even
disintegration, that there is space for something else to happen." In Poe's
text, this breach or disruption is glimpsed in the scission of self-citation,
in the subsumption of "The Man of the Crowd" under the man of the
crowd, or the vertiginous experience of reading the unreadable, a de facto
experience that has no logical meaning. The narrator's conclusion renders
the repetitive motions something "other than simply the return of the
same" (28), yet also does not erase them. The phrase "es lässt sich nicht
lesen" functions like Heidegger's crossing out of *Sein*.

Over this phrase, or the crossing out, reading stumbles. This stumbling
is itself the experience of the uncanny. In his well-known text on *The Fantastic*, Tzvetan Todorov's main purpose can be understood to be the stabilization of the distinction of discursive levels that will keep the critic's
position outside of the uncanny. Todorov allies the critical position with
the synchronic view of the text. As his subtitle indicates, "A Structural
Approach to a Literary Genre," the critic is interested in general rules, not
in the idiosyncrasies of singular experiences. He writes: "'The Fantastic' is
a name given to a kind of literature, to a literary genre. When we examine
works of literature from the perspective of genre, we engage in a very
particular enterprise: we discover a principle operative in a number of
texts, rather than what is specific about each of them."[15] This literary theorist's knowledge is oriented toward a general principle, an intellectual con-
struct that can subsume many cases within it. He thus establishes a
hierarchy, in which a stable general principle, an object of knowledge,
stands above the many and variable particular cases, the empirical texts,
that the concept includes.

In rising above the variability of singular cases to a general principle,
Todorov also shifts attention away from emotional responses of a particular reader to the safer stance of intellectual certainty. He rejects the emotional response as unscientific:

We are told that it is pointless to speak of genres . . . for the work of art is essentially unique, valuable because of what is original about it that distinguishes it from all other works, and not because of whatever in it may resemble them. . . . This response implies a romantic attitude with regard to the material under observation. Such a position is not, strictly speaking, false; it is simply extraneous. We may certainly like a work for one reason or another; this is not what defines it as an object of study. (5)

This passage displays the duality of the subject of enunciation: the voice of Todorov, the unmarked voice of the theorist who enunciates general principles; and that of an "I" or a "we," an embodied subject sitting around reading who has this or that response to the book he or she is holding in his/her hands. Todorov presents his theoretical conclusions about the fantastic, the uncanny and the marvelous, from the higher perspective of the scientist who has purified and rejected whatever may have come from the realm of the unchartable senses of taste, emotion, and the like. Thus two hierarchies are in place: that privileging the concept of the genre over the particular case; and the pure and objective theoretical voice over the bodily bound reader, occupied with a material text in time and space: that is, reading.

Todorov defines the fantastic as the realm of ambiguity between reality and dream, truth and illusion. The fantastic emerges at the conjunction between two narrative levels framed by differing assumptions about what is real. "The fantastic occupies the duration of this uncertainty. Once we choose one answer or the other, we leave the fantastic for a neighboring genre, the uncanny or the marvelous. The fantastic is that hesitation experienced by a person who knows only the laws of nature, confronting an apparently supernatural event" (25). Todorov goes on to specify: "The fantastic, we have seen, lasts only as long as a certain hesitation. At the story's end, the reader makes a decision even if the character does not; he opts for one solution or the other, and thereby emerges from the fantastic. If he decides that the laws of reality remain intact and permit an explanation of the phenomena described, we say that the work belongs to another genre: the uncanny. If, on the contrary, he decides that new laws of nature must be entertained to account for the phenomena, we enter the genre of the marvelous" (41).

The process of reading remains imbricated in the ambiguities and uncertainties of a particular subject position. The theorist, in contrast, decides about undecidability and establishes certainty about uncertainty, thus mastering the confusion between reality and illusion characterizing the process of reading. The decision placing a text safely within the bounds of a genre comes "after" we have finished reading, after we have torn our eyes away from the marks on the page, sit back and reflect, and consider the text as a whole.

While Todorov attempts to hold these two levels apart in a stable hierarchy, the uncanny inevitably brings about their collapse. Todorov describes the process as follows: "There is an *uncanny phenomenon* [my emphasis—"il y a un phénomène étrange"] which we can explain in two fashions, by types of natural causes and supernatural causes. The possibility of a hesitation between the two creates the fantastic effect."[16] If the terms uncanny, fantastic and marvelous can only apply to the work as a whole, after the completion of reading, then how can one account for this "uncanny phenomenon" experienced "while" reading? The theoretical voice is itself syncopated and cannot name its own experience without passing through a narrative time loop. The uncanny is already there before it arrives; and Todorov's definite classifications can only postdate an example or case of the uncanny that must occur before the uncanny can be defined. The particular uncanny phenomenon thus predates and conditions the possibility of discovering a principle or rule of the uncanny, much as Todorov will then try to establish the independence of the rules he sets up. What takes place here is a certain overturning of a logical hierarchy. Generational difference collapses: the son precedes the father, and the theorist unwittingly falls back into the position of an ordinary reader, who must read without yet knowing what he reads, whom the text prepares for the effects to come.

The covert preparation for the uncanny is of course the preamble of the uncanny itself. The repetition producing uncanny effects has been carefully laid in to the text in ways which a first reading cannot possibly identify. The uncanny does not repeat a certain X; rather, it emerges in the recognition of repetition, through the connection of disparate and distant moments stretched over the temporal and spatial expanse of the text. When we notice repetition, the uncanny will have occurred; it can have no beginning, for we can never see the first element of a repetitive structure until it has already been repeated.[17] In dealing with the uncanny, we will always remain subject to the passive and ignorant position of the first instance which we can never grasp directly. In the recognition of an uncanny effect, at best, we can become aware of the way we have been manipulated by the text, how it leaves its mark on us before we can notice it; and perhaps our reading, too, is programmed and controlled in ways we cannot master. In our "first reading," where the uncanny will have had its effect before we have been able to conceptualize it, we must momentarily have forgotten ourselves.

If critic and reader cannot be definitively divided and held separate in a stable manner, we lose Todorov's certainty about uncertainty, and are ourselves dragged into the confusion between reality and illusion that is in question. The experience of dislocation, loss of control, the sense of the origin of the "I" in an other or elsewhere, the experience of self-forgetfulness: these lapses of consciousness are frequently thematized in uncanny texts. Hoffmann describes the resulting anxiety in a passage referring to the uncanniness of an incident of magnetic hypnosis:

> Vielleicht deutet gerade das auf die Macht frender psychischer Einflüsse, denen wir uns willkürlos hingeben müssen. So wie die Somnambule sich durchaus nicht ihres somnamulen Zustandes erinnern und dessen, was sich in demselben mit ihr begeben, so kann vielleicht jene grauenhafte Angst, deren Ursache uns verborgen bleibt, der Nachhall irgendeines gewaltigen Zaubers sein, der uns uns selbst entrückt. (3:801–2)

> Perhaps this indicates precisely the power of strange and alien psychic influences to which we are compelled to surrender ourselves. Just as the somnambulist can not remember her somnambulic at all and what happened to her during it—perhaps in the same way, that horrifying anxiety whose cause remains obscure may perhaps be the distant echo of some violent magical force which has entranced us and torn us away from ourselves.

This horrible anxiety, a certain loss and nonpresence of self, is associated with a passive and feminine, a displaced, nonoriginal or aboriginal position. It also invokes a kind of pleasure, which is perhaps why we enjoy uncanny stories, intermingled with anxiety. This anxiety is meant to ward off the seduction of the position described: one which is "improper" and inappropriate. The thinker does not want to be a sleepwalking reader controlled by the alien powers of another, the text and author before us, in our hands. It is not surprising that Goethe, the "father" of German literature, writing of Hoffmann, would speak of "sick aberrations, the spasmodic utterances of a being tortured nearly to death," against which he issues the following command: "We must renounce and tear ourselves away from these ravings if we do not want to become mad ourselves."[18] Goethe's remarks betray the fear of mimetic contamination: the fear that "I," this subject, am nothing but a copy of one that came before me, that my reading and thinking are compelled to repeat something before, and beyond, me and my control. The fear that I am a double, a copy, an imitation, and not a self-originating essence.[19]

In Hoffmann's writing, the uncanny accumulates around the narrative contact between self and other, presence and absence. The magnetic scene, as suggested earlier, frequently thematizes the spectacle of the self dislocated from itself. Hoffmann is inventive in describing this self-dislocation (*entrückt*). The uncanny is distinguished from other types of horror precisely as the experience of something unrecognizable. Hoffmann writes: "'I imagine I could certainly endure the sudden fright caused by some horrible apparition; but the uncanny workings of an invisible being affecting me would surely drive me mad. It is the feeling of the most utterly helpless impotence and unconsciousness which must certainly crush the spirit'" ("Ich kann es mir denken, dass ich den plötzlichen Schreck irgendeiner grauenhafte Erscheinung wohl ertragen könnte, das unheimliche, den äußern Sinn in Anspruch nehmende Treiben eines unsichtbaren Wesens, würde mich dagegen unfehlbar wahnsinnig machen. Es ist das Gefühl der gänzlichen hülflosesten Ohnmacht, das den Geist zermalmen müßte") ("Die Automate," 2:432).

The uncanny characterizes the vision of the invisible, the autonomous "effect" whose ground is simultaneously asserted and withdrawn. The "unsichtbares Wesen," like the Being of beings, does not appear, "is" not; yet it is also fundamentally related to, linked to, in action in, what it makes possible. Insofar as it is named here, one cannot simply say that it "is not" at all. What Hoffmann describes as helpless unconsciousness is, perhaps, the turning towards another kind of thinking that is not based on opposition and conceptual hierarchies. It is the experience of the unconsciousness, the mind which is no mind. Importantly, this remains an *event*, an *experience*, of limitation itself. It is not a "consciousness" of anything nor the appearance of a delimitable "unconscious." The uncanny destroys the hierarchy of essence and appearance and the logic of adequation and manifestation it supports.

The opening to the tale "der Unheimliche Gast" is filled with several anecdotes describing the horror and uncanniness that surround phenomena with hidden causes. From the title of the story, we would expect that the personage it names would reveal something essential about the uncanny. Yet he does so only in the way of the uncanny—indirectly, *entrückt*. The story is lodged within Hoffmann's collection, *Die Serapionsbrüder*, which follows the literary meetings of four friends: Ottmar, Cyprian, Theodor, and Lothar. These characters meet to read their compositions out loud and comment on them. Many of the stories were composed earlier or separately; critics have often dismissed the frame of the Serapion Society as a mere conventional device that does not contribute anything to the texts. Ottmar presents the text, "der Unheimliche Gast," composed, he says, "in Cyprians Manier." The plot is rather complicated. The story opens on a stormy night in the parlor of the Colonel's home. His wife, his daughter Angelika, and her French companion Marguerite are receiving for tea the two friends, Dagobert and Moritz. Inspired by the frightful weather and the coziness (*heimlichkeit*) of the domestic shelter, the friends pass the time telling horror stories, each one increasing the general uncanny feeling thus provoked. Despite the objections of the Colonel's wife to these tales, they nevertheless continue as if in an inevitable chain. This chain is abruptly interrupted by the unexpected entrance of Count S—I, the uncanny guest. He seems to have been invited, but no one recognizes him. When the Colonel arrives home, he acknowledges him as a dear friend, to whom he owes everything: honor, money and even his life (the reason for this debt is never clarified).

Dagobert and Angelika are secretly in love. The Count, however, has come to ask for her hand, for he became enamored of a portrait of her that the Colonel had shown him. But the suit of the Count, the same age as the Colonel, is rejected by the daughter Angelika, and her bond with Dagobert is settled. In the meantime, war breaks out again. When Dagobert and the Colonel are called into battle, the Colonel's family is left in the care of the foreign Count, for whom they begin to develop an increasing affection. After the news arrives of Dagobert's death, the Count gains an unexpected control over Angelika, who agrees to marry him despite her mother's suspicious misgivings. At the moment of the wedding, Dagobert reappears; Angelika falls into a magnetic stupor; and the Count is struck dead.

It turns out that the Count is a magnetizer and has used his occult powers to devise Dagobert's disappearance, falsely reported as death, and Angelika's submission. Yet the powers of good prevail and the spell is broken. The story ends with a repeat of the hearth-scene in Dagobert and Angelika's home; they recall with bemusement the wretched night of the uncanny guest's arrival and the temporary disaster's caused by him—disasters now resolved in the reconstitution of the domestic scene.

In the opening to the story, Dagobert tells of the horrible tone; Angelika speaks of her horrifying dreams; and the conversation, in this "domestic circle" (*einheimischer Kreis*) (792), circles around talk of possession by unknown spirits, strange events, and *innerliche Schauer*, "an internal shivering." The telling of these stories itself begins to bring about the uncanny it prepares. Dagobert himself makes the connection between the setting of the story—the storm outside, the sounds within—and the "spirits" it ushers in:

> Die ecthen Sturmwind-, Kamin- und Punschschauer sind nichts anders, als der erste Anfall jenes unbegreiflichen geheimnisvollen Zustandes, der tief in der menschlichen Natur begründet ist, gegen den der Geist sich verge- bens auflehnt, und vor dem man sich wohl hüten muß. Ich meine das Grauen—die Gespensterfurcht. Wir wissen alle, dass das unheimliche Volk der Spukgeister nur des Nachts, vorzüglich gern aber bei bösem Wetter der dunklen Heimat entsteigt und seine irre Wanderung beginnt. (793)

> The real storm winds, the gruesome shivering of the hearth and the punch, are nothing other than the first attacks of that inconceivable secret [*geheim- nisvoll*] condition which is grounded deep within human nature against which the spirit rebels in vain, and from which one must try to protect oneself. I mean the horror—the fear of ghosts. We all know that this un- canny folk of spirit-ghosts only emerge from their homeland at night, and preferably in stormy weather, to begin their mad wanderings. (3:793)

Though the company agrees that Dagobert is teasing, nevertheless he both describes and performs the departure or partitioning of the visible, of what is present—the gurgling of the teapot—which initiates the uncanny, leaving the homeland of its definition for its narrative spacing, its "*irre Wanderung*"—its mad wandering. The attribution of meaning to the inci- dentals of the teapot, for example, resembles the efforts of the narrator of "The Man of the Crowd" to find sense in the wandering of his object. Marguerite, Angelika's French companion, suddenly drops a cup, as if "struck by a magnetic blow," and is filled with horror (*Schauer*) (797). The accumulated anecdotes begin to bother the Obristin, who finally says: "This conversation is getting worse and worse; we are getting lost in things which I cannot bear even to think about. I am asking you right now, Moritz, to tell us something funny and wonderful to put an end finally to these uncanny ghost stories!" ("Immer ärger wird es mit unserm Ge- spräch, wir verlieren uns in Dinge, an die nur zu denken mir unerträglich ist. Ich fordere Sie auf, Moritz, sogleich etwas recht Lustiges, Tolles zu erzählen, damit es nur mit den unheimlichen Spukgeshichten einmal ende" [3:802]). Both beginning and end of the uncanny are elusive.

Moritz begs leave to tell one last story, which will form the last prepara- tion for the entrance of the uncanny guest. He begins a story about a companion in war named Bogislav. Bogislav is haunted by some unknown force; Moritz relates: "often he was overcome suddenly by the thought of something horrible [*Entsetztlisches*] which must have happened to him and

had left the traces of the deepest affliction on his face" (3:803) ("oft über-
mannte ihn plötzlich der Gedanke an irgend etwas Entsetztliches, das ihm
begegnet sein müßte, und das die Spuren des tiefsten Grams auf seinem
Gesicht zurückgelassen hatte" [3:803]). Finally, one night Bogislav reveals
his secret. After killing a rival in a dual in Naples, Bogislav was inexplica-
bly, incomprehensibly rejected by the fiancée for whose sake the murder
was committed. The horrible death-voice of the murdered Count has
haunted him ever since. In the following passage, Bogislav begins his narration, which is interrupted:

> "Durch den stärkesten Kanonendonner, durch das prasselnde Musketen-
> feuer der Bataillone, vernehme ich dicht vor meinen Ohren den gräßlichen
> Jammerton, und alle Wut, alle Verzweiflung des Wahnsinns erwacht in
> meinem Busen!—Eben in dieser Nacht"—Bogislav hielt inne und mich,
> wie ihn, erfaßte das Entsetzen, denn ein lang ausgehaltener herzzerschneid-
> ender Jammerton ließ sich, wie vom Gange herkommend, vernehmen.
> Dann war es, als raffe sich jemand ächzend und stöhnend mühsam vom
> Boden empor, und nahe sich schweren, unsicheren Trittes. Da erhob sich
> Bogislav plötzlich von aller Kraft beseelt vom Lehnstuhl und rief, wilde
> Glut in den Augen, mit donnernder Stimme: "Erscheine mir, Verruchter!
> Wenn du es vermagst—ich nehme es auf mit dir und mit allen Geistern der
> Hölle, die dir zu Gebote stehn—" Nun geschah ein gewaltiger Schlag."—
> In dem Augenblick sprang die Türe des Saals auf mit dröhnendem Geras-
> sel. (805)

> "Through the loudest thundering of cannons, through the crackling fire of
> the battalion's muskets, I hear close to my ears the most horrible moan
> [*Jammerton*], and all the rage, all the despair of madness arises in my
> breast!—Just tonight." Bogislav stopped suddenly, and I, along with him,
> was seized by horror, for just at that moment a long, heartbreaking moan
> could be heard as if coming down the hallway. Then it was as if someone
> were getting up from the floor, moaning and groaning, and approached
> with a heavy and uncertain step. Then suddenly, Bogislav jumped up from
> the chair, animated with tremendous strength, and cried, with a wild gleam
> in his eye and a thundering voice, "Appear, accursed one, if you can! I'm
> ready to fight you and all the hellish spirits at your command!" Now there
> occurred a violent blow—at that moment the doors of the room sprang
> open with a resounding clang. (3:805)

Bogislav's telling is interrupted strangely by an actual tone, "wie vom
gang herkommend," as if coming down the hallway. The uncanny
emerges at the hinge between narrative frames—where the *Jammerton*

Bogislav narrates enters the narrative frame of that telling (recalling previous anecdotes about a strange *Jammerton*). The coincidence of two frames brings about what Freud calls the confusion of the symbol and the symbolized. This uncanny effect takes place when language is seen to produce what it speaks of, epitomized by the ability of the repeated "uncanny" to bring about the effects of the uncanny or the capacity of the uncanny to engender itself. The uncanny comes about as it steps across from the level of the told to that of the telling, acting first as the "heavy, uncertain steps," followed by the *Jammerton*, and then the ghost called upon to appear.

The same type of noncoincidental coincidence of speech and event takes place in the final trajectory of Poe's "Fall of the House of Usher." Similarly, a wild storm rages outside; to calm the ailing Usher, his friend begins to read out loud from a romance called "The Mad Tryst." As passages are read aloud, the narrator hears corresponding sounds: "At the termination of this sentence I started and, for a moment, paused; for it appeared to me (although I at once concluded that my excited fancy had deceived me)—it appeared to me that, from some very remote portion of the mansion, there came, indistinctly to my ears, what might have been, in its exact similarity of character, the echo (but a stifled and dull one certainly) of the very cracking and ripping sound which Sir Launcelot had so particularly described" (243). At the next instance, the sound the narrator hears answers precisely to the image pre-existing in his mind; his reading is exteriorized: "the exact counterpart of what my fancy had already conjured up for the dragon's unnatural shriek as described by the romancer" (244). Finally, Usher describes the premature burial and prophesies: "*I tell you that she now stands without the door!*" As if in the superhuman energy of his utterance there had been found the potency of a spell, the huge antique panels to which the speaker pointed threw slowly back, upon the instant, their ponderous and ebony jaws. It was the work of the rushing gust—but then without those doors there *did* stand the lofty and enshrouded figure of the lady Madeline of Usher" (245). The doubling between text and reality, the move from one narrative level to another, brings the uncanny home. It walks and opens the door.[20] Similarly, in the passage from Hoffmann, Bogislav invokes his ghost; his speech is interrupted by the narrative: "Nun geschah ein gewaltiger Schlag—In dem Augenblick sprang die Türe des Saals auf mit dröhnendem Gerassel" (3: 805) ("Now there occurred a violent blow—at that moment the doors of the room sprang open with a resounding clang"[21]). We expect to find the mystery solved, to see the ghost enter at the doorway; in fact, we are ready to welcome in the uncanny guest. But the text continues, passing first over several lines of blank page: "Sowie Ottmar diese Worte las, sprang auch die Türe des Gartensaals wirklich dröhnend auf und die Freunde erblickten eine dunkle verhüllte Gestalt, die sich langsam mit unhörbaren Geisterschritten nahten. Alle starrten etwas entsetzt hin, jedem stockte der Atem" (3:805–6) ("As Ottmar read these words, the doors to the garden room actually really sprang open with a clang and the friends espied a dark cloaked figure slowing approaching with silent ghostly steps. Everyone stared and gasped with horror"). This interruption, twice crossing over from telling to "reality," seems to show us, or at least them—Bogislav and Moritz, on the one hand, or Moritz and the company in the Colonel's house—the uncanny guest. But the interruption is actually deeper; that is to say, the uncanny figure actually appears in the frame narrative, outside the boundaries of "der Unheimliche Gast" proper. Soon it becomes clear that the arriving figure is in fact Cyprian, the missing member of the Serapion reading group. The uncanny continues here in reverse; for the friend has arrived in the dark garb of a stranger, interrupting the homey circle to which he actually belongs. This interior space, the garden house, is itself "outside." Cyprian explains: "In vollem Unmut renne ich heraus ins Freie und der Zufall will, daß ich, nach der Stadt zuruckkehrend, den Weg einschlage, der bei dem Gartenhause dicht herbeiführt" ("In a rotten mood, I hurried out of doors; coincidence would have it that, turning back towards town, I struck out on a path that led right by the garden house"). Coincidentally, Cyprian is drawn to the garden house by the recognition of a familiar voice—something like the inverse of Lady Madeline's arrival:

> "Es ist mir, als höre ich eine wohlbekannte Stimme, ich gucke durchs Fenster and erblicke meine würdigen Serapions-Brüder und höre meinen Ottmar den unheimlichen Gast vorlesen." "Wie," unterbrach Ottmar den Freund, "wie du kennste schon meine Geschichte?"
>
> "Du vergißt . . . dass Du die Ingredienzen zu dieser Erzahlung von mir selbst empfingest. Ich bin es, der dich mit der Teufelstimme, mit der Luftmusik bekannt mache, der dir sogar die Idee der Erscheinung des unheimlichen Gastes gab, und ich bin begierig, wie du mein Thema ausgeführt hast etc." (806)

> "I seem to be hearing a familiar voice, I peek through the window and see my worthy Serapions-brothers and hear my Ottmar read the uncanny guest aloud." "What!" Ottmar interrupted his friend, "how could you already know my story?"
>
> "You forget that you got the ingredients from this story from me. I am the one who acquainted you with the devil's voice, and the air music—I

even gave you the idea of the appearance of the uncanny guest, and I am eager to hear how you have carried out my theme."

The "treuer Searpions-bruder" appears temporarily as an uncanny guest, unduly unnerving Theodor, one member of the group. The appearance of friend as stranger reverses the relation of familiarity (*heimisch/unheimlich*); likewise, he already knows the story that is about to be read, for he himself is its origin. The "idea" of the uncanny guest arrives from the outside and is thus separated from its appearance. This splitting is in fact constitutive of the uncanny guest; for notice Cyprian says: "Ich bin es . . . der dir sogar die Idee der Erscheinung des unheimlichen Gastes gab" ("I am the one who even gave you the idea of the appearance of the uncanny guest"). The uncanny guest is defined as an appearance of an idea; the idea is not *manifested*—made present—by the guest, but rather comes forth in the process and the motion of his appearance. The idea of the appearance is simply to appear; the space of a ground or interior essence is vacant, held open only by the co-author Cyprian.

In fact, the *appearance* of the uncanny guest is his essence, precisely because the uncanny has no essential core. The uncanny crosses the threshold in the line, "In dem Augenblick sprang die Türe des Saals auf mit dröhnendem Gerassel," (805) ("At that moment the doors of the room sprang open with a resounding clang"), which at least seems to belong to three narrative levels: Bogislav's tale, the homely scene in the Colonel's house, and the reading scene of the Serapions-brothers' garden-house. The collapse of narrative levels, made clear only when interrupted and corrected, enacts the lack of differentiation between reader and critic in Todorov's terms; the text stumbles, interrupts the passage toward signification and points instead only to its own fictive mechanism: "The door suddenly opened." Reading further, after the short conversation with Cyprian in which friend appears as uncanny guest, the scene around the hearth picks up again: "Hinein trat ein Mann von Kopf bis zu Fuß schwarz gekleidet, bleichen Antlitzes, ernsten, festen Blickes" (807) ("In walked a man dressed in black from head to toe, with a pale face and a serious fixed gaze"). The group is struck into silence and can not get rid of the feeling of something uncanny attaching to this figure: "Keiner vermochte, wie gelähmt, ein Wort hervorzubringen" (808) ("As if paralyzed, no one could manage to get a word out"). The uncanny cripples speech as the narrative staggers and stumbles, trips over itself. "Dagobert versuchte sich ins Gespräch zu mischen, das endlich in einzelnen abgebrochenen Reden mühsam fortschlich" ("Dagobert tried to get into the conversation that finally dragged on in small bits of broken-up talk"). Language drags itself around; lost in its own materiality, it cannot get off the floor: "Jeder fühlte seine Brust beengt, jeden drückte wie eine Gewitterschwüle die Gegenwart des Fremden, jedem erstarb das Wort auf den Lippen, wenn er in das tod-bleiche Antlitz des unheimlichen Gastes schaue" (809) ("They all felt a tightening of the chest, the presence of the stranger pressed upon them like the humid pressure of a storm, words died on their lips when they looked into the deathly pale face of the uncanny guest"). The uncanny breaks up language, leaving material remnants, in the presence of the strange, the confusion and exchange between friend and stranger, guest and intruder. Finally, the uncanny of narrative interruption clings to the guest who continues to seem uncanny despite all explanations to the con-trary. The strange Count with a foreign accent is finally identified as a friend of the Colonel's; but he continues to pull with him the conditions of his narrative appearance. As the story progresses, he is welcomed into the center of the family, only finally to be revealed as a magnetizer, an uncanny magician who has secretly taken control of various members of the company.

Thus Count S—I passes from strangeness to familiarity and back again, showing himself finally to be the uncanny force he was at first *mistaken* to be. He thus was what he will become, or is what he is not. He *is* the uncanny guest only because he *appears* to be uncanny, through his narra-tive appearance, yet *is* not. The thematics of the magnetizer, like the prob-lem of premature burial in *The Fall of the House of Usher*, is a decoy that draws attention away from the narrative vortex structuring the uncanny—the mise-en-abîme whose effect persists regardless of later thematic solu-tions or demystifications. The uncanny emerges in the capacity of narrative structure to outlive its thematic recuperation. It emerges in a narrative fold through which the synchronic collapses into the diachronic, historical happening adheres to a result, processes of signification contam-inate any kind of signified. This fold is the fold of reading.

The uncanny comes about in showing its own generation out of the space and time of the materiality of language, in showing the origin of a meaning or a mind in a body that sits or walks. The word "uncanny" generates its signified. We can recognize this aspect of it as the *crocodilic uncanny*, in some senses a subset of the ambulatory uncanny, yet also a larger group; Freud tells us "daß es nämlich oft und leicht unheimlich wirkt, wenn die Grenze zwischen Phantasie und Wirklichkeit verwischt wirkt, wenn etwas real vor uns *hintritt*, was wir bisher für phantastisch gehalten haben wenn ein Symbol die volle leistung und Bedeutung des

Symbolisierten übernimmt und dergleichen mehr" (12:258) ("an uncanny effect is often and easily produced when the distinction between imagination and reality is effaced, as when something that we have hitherto regarded as imaginary appears before us in reality [walks up to us], or when a symbol takes over the full functions of the thing it symbolizes, and so on" [17:244]). The story reads:

> Mitten in der Absperrung des Weltkrieges kam eine Nummer des englischen Magazins 'Strand' in meine Hände, in der ich unter anderen ziemlich überflüßigen Produktionen eine Erzählung las, wie ein junges Paar eine möblierte Wohnung bezieht, I der sich ein seltsam geformter Tisch mit holzgeschnitzten Krokodilen befindet. Gegen Abend pflegt sich dann ein unerträglicher, charakteristischer Gestank in der Wohnung zu verbreiten, man stolpert im Dunkeln über etwas, man glaubt zu sehen, wie etwas Undefinierbares über die Treppe huscht, kurz, man soll erraten, daß infolge der Anwesenheit dieses Tisches gespenstische Krokodilen im Hause spoken. (12:258)

> In the middle of the isolation of war-time a number of the English *Strand Magazine* fell into my hands; and, among other somewhat redundant matter, I read a story about a young married couple who move into a furnished house in which there is a curiously shaped table with carvings of crocodiles on it. Towards evening an intolerable and very specific smell begins to pervade the house; they stumble over something in the dark; they seem to see a vague form gliding over the stairs—in short, we are given to understand that the presence of the table causes ghostly crocodiles to haunt the place, or that the wooden monsters come to life in the dark, or something of the sort. (244–45)

The uncanny effect of this story emerges in its telling, not in its truth. Through the disruptive frame of the world war, the tale *comes into Freud's hands,* as if a fully random event. The emergence of the crocodiles is heralded by a stumbling around in the dark, hitting upon something. When the reader stumbles, the uncanny starts to walk. "Es war eine recht einfältige Geschichte, aber ihre unheimliche Wirkung verspürte man als ganz hervorragend" ("It was a naïve enough story, but the uncanny feeling it produced was quite remarkable"). The uncanny is this imagined connection between signifier and signified, the imagined life of a fictional character, the autonomous movement of a sign, the progression of discourse through its "steps."

The discourse of the uncanny destroys the illusion of a stable subject position, of a final meaning, of a sense separable from language and the body. It points to the finitude and temporality of thinking, as Weber makes clear in "Uncanny Thinking," and "marks the spot where what is (there) and what is not, presence and absence, coming and going, can no longer be clearly distinguished." Weber lets us consider that the uncanny still occupies a peripheral issue for these very reasons: "For it confounds predication, judgment, and lets a certain form of 'constative' discourse reveal itself as always already 'performative'" (21). As Hoffmann writes, "man war darüber einig, daß der Vorwurf des unheimlichen Wesens auf die zurückfalle, die ihm diesen Vorwurf gemacht" ("they were agreed that the charge of the uncanny falls back on the one who makes it") (813).

The doubt and open-ended quality of Freud's essay, as many have pointed out, is not simply a coincidental flaw in Freud's discourse, just as the triple narrative interruption of "The Uncanny Guest" cannot be banned to a narrative frame, but rather also takes part in the uncanny itself. Consider the language of Freud's uncertainty in his well-known concern about the border between psychoanalysis and aesthetics:

> So müssen wir wohl bereit sein anzunehmen, daß für das Auftreten des unheimlichen Gefühls noch andere als die von uns vorangestellten stofflichen Bedingungen maßgebend sind. Man könnte zwar sagen, mit jener ersten Feststellung sei das psychoanalytische Interesse am Problem des Unheimlichen erledigt, der Rest erfordere wahrscheinlich eine ästhetische Untersuchung. Aber damit würden wir dem Zweifel das Tor öffnen, welchen Wert unsere Einsicht in die Herkunft des Unheimlichen vom verdrängten Heimsichen eigentlich beanspruchen darf. (261)

> It is evident therefore, that we must be prepared to admit that there are other elements besides those which we have so far laid down as determining the production of uncanny feelings. We might say that these preliminary results have satisfied *psycho-analytic* interest in the problem of the uncanny, and that what remains probably calls for an *aesthetic* enquiry. But that would be to open the door to doubts about what exactly is the value of our general contention that the uncanny proceeds from something familiar which has been repressed. (247)

Where Freud puts his own thesis fully into question, the ambulatory uncanny responds, about which we cannot say for sure whether it is or is not, but of which it might be (un)safe to say: it walks.

CHAPTER 9

On Risk-Taking in the Psychoanalytic Text: The Reality-Test

Avital Ronell

I stand on light feet now,
Catching breath before I speak
For there are songs in every style,
But to put a new one to the touchstone [*basanôi*]
For testing [*es elegkhon*] is all danger.

PINDAR, *Nemean 8* (19–20)[1]

For once
In visible form the Sphinx
Came on him and all of us
Saw his wisdom and in that test [*basanôi*]
He saved the city.

SOPHOKLES, *Oedipus Rex* (498–510)[2]

Sometimes they have to prove their mettle or demonstrate a hypothesis; at other times, they audition for the part, make a demo, try another way, or determine paternity; there are the endless admissions tests, the existential breathalyzers, the proven and tried version of things, the loyalty tests and medical scanners, Kafka's trials, the sprawl of lab culture, and weapons testing: whether you roll back to the time of the persecution of witches— testing nature, testing the body, pressing forward to push out the truth in the medium of torture and pain—or draw blood in the clinic, it seems as though *everything* has needed to be tested. From the moment Francis Bacon started his experimental wager, torture became linked to the test. The drama of one's love has not been excluded from this scene. Everything was put to the test, torturing the body, flaying the certitudes of knowledge. What is the provenance of this need? What has allowed testing to top out as an essential and widening interest, a nearly unavoidable *drive?* A kind of questioning, a structure of incessant research, perhaps even a modality of being, testing scans the walls of experience, measuring, probing, determining the "what is" of the lived world. At the same time, but more fundamental still, the very structure of testing tends to overtake the certainty that it establishes when obeying the call of open finitude. A new fold in metaphysics, testing—that is, the types and systems of relatedness that fall under this term—asserts another logic of truth, one that subjects itself to incessant questioning while reserving a frame, a trace, a disclosive moment to which it refers.

There is nothing as such *new* about the desire bound up in the test; yet the expansive field of the hegemony of testing poses novel problems and complicates the itinerary of claims we make about the world and its contractions, the shards of immanence and transcendence that it still bears. Our contract with Yahweh, whether piously observed or abominated, involves the multiplication of test sites. Shortly after completing his *Third Critique*, Kant, in response to a public questionnaire, examined the problem of testing the faith of theology students.[3] Can faith be tested or is it not the essence of faith to refuse the test—to go along, precisely on blind faith, without ground or grade? Or again, perhaps the Almighty Himself has proven time and again to be addicted to the exigencies of testing. If God can be said to have a taste for anything, then it may well be in the incontrovertible necessity of the test. No one is not tested by God, at least by the God of the Old Testament, who showed a will to perpetual pursuit, perpetual rupture. Even the Satanic beloved, who got away or was kicked out (depending on whether you are reading the Satanic version of Goethe or God), became a subsidiary testing device for the paradisiacal admissions policy. In German, *Versuch* unites test with temptation—a semantic merger of which Nietzsche makes good use. The devil is the visible mark of a permanent testing apparatus. It is one name for an operation that engages the subject in a radical way. For Nietzsche, our modernity is fatefully determined by what he calls in *The Gay Science* our "experimental disposition."

In *Institution and Interpretation*, Samuel Weber organizes an aspect of his reflections on psychoanalysis around the concept of experimentation. Lacan's laboratory is linked to "the laboratories of experimental science" and is shown to be, in comparison, "as unstable as the margins of a text: not entirely inchoate, to be sure, but also never completely under his control" (xiii). While no scientific lab can be said to be fully under control, the rhetorical ploy is apt. Psychoanalysis belongs to the "epistemic thing" subsumed under the notion of experiment. (Narrow-minded opponents of psychoanalysis turn a blind eye to its experimental cast, opposing it to science precisely where it shares structures of risk-taking, epistemological uncertainty and the community of trial with scientific endeavor.[4]) Weber continues: "It is this instability that distinguishes what Lacan calls 'l'expérience psychanalytique'—a phrase which *also* means psychoanalytical *experiment*—from its scientific homonym. To make one's way under conditions that can never be entirely controlled is a part of what constitutes psychoanalytic truth."[5] One could say that, beginning with Goethe and ranging to observations put forth by Hans-Jörg Rheinberger, the lab is never so stable an entity that it can fully duck the projections of sci-fi or psy-fi—but this is another story that must be dealt with elsewhere.

Part of the culture of experimentation, psychoanalysis proceeds by relentlessly refining the conceptual probity of acts of testing. Paradoxically, the case for testing is all the more rigorous when it appears to be introduced in terms of an irremissible warp or omission.[6] In the prefatory remarks to the *Fragment of a Case of Hysteria* (1905), Freud opens the Dora files by stating some anxiety about the exigencies of testing of which his study appears to fall short: "Certainly it was awkward that I was obliged to publish the results of my inquiries without there being any possibility of other specialists testing and checking them, particularly as those results were of a surprising and by no means gratifying character."[7] Testing consists of two significant levels: the first involves an internal control apparatus; the second postulates a community of verifications and double-checkers. Freud introduces a third area of testing when he formulates the basis for a particularly potent type of psychic probe: the reality-test. None of these controls exclude the possibility of further innovation, for the test site is at each point reconfigured to include "everyone." Everyone has a hand in the Freudian experiment. When he addresses the contested status of his study of dreams, which was seen to lack solidity in terms of verifiability, Freud offers, "There was no validity in the objection that the material upon which I had based my assertions had been withheld and that it was therefore impossible to become convinced of their truth by testing and checking them. For every one can submit his own dreams to analytic examination, and the technique of interpreting dreams may be easily learnt from the instructions and examples which I have given."[8] He goes on to insist that "no one who wishes to shirk" the preparatory labor of investigating thoroughly the problems of dreams—"an indispensable pre-requisite for any comprehension of the mental processes in hysteria and the other psycho-neuroses"—has the "smallest prospect of advancing even a few steps into this region of knowledge."[9] In order to read the case study of hysteria, you will have turned yourself into a scientific laboratory, an apparatus capable of observing unconscious phenomena: you become the observer and observed, the dreamer and its exacting commentator. The community of testing consists of gauging the singularity of each of the innumerable lab partners, the rhetoric of their objects and phenomenology of approach. The cognitive outcome has turned around our relation to speculative knowledge. Weber writes in "The Meaning of the Thallus": "The way to speculation is obscure because it leads away from the known toward the unknown, away from elucidation (*Aufklärung*) and into the murky realm of hypothesis and supposition (*Annahmen*)."[10] The test apparatus installed in the psychoanalytic engine stalls the certainties posited by Freud, rendering his observations vulnerable to recursive probes.

That Freud subjected his work to the unyielding requisites of testing hardly needs to be restated, though the testability of his evaluations has been famously questioned.[11] In an intervention meant to defend psychoanalysis against such persistent charges, Adolf Grünbaum argues for the probative role of tests, reviewing clinical testability and examples of falsifiability in the work of Freud. In order to urge his point, he treats "A Case of Paranoia Running Counter to the Psychoanalytic Theory of the Disease."[12] Another example of falsifiability is furnished by the Lecture "Revision of the Theory of Dreams."[13] Grünbaum demonstrates that "the psychoanalytic aetiology of paranoia is empirically falsifiable (disconfirmable) *and* that Freud explicitly recognized it.[14] Until this instance the psychoanalytic theory of paranoia assumed hypothetically that repressed homosexual love was at the basis of paranoid delusions.[15] For backup, he recounts the following narrative. A woman who was trying to break up her relationship started to mount a campaign against her lover. Freud makes this observation: "The girl seemed to be defending herself against love for a man by directly transforming the lover into a persecutor: there was no sign of the influence of a woman, no trace of a struggle against a homosexual attachment."[16] Freud admits this case into evidence as "a refuting instance of the aetiology he had postulated for that disorder."[17] If the woman was delusional, as it seemed she might be, then the apparent absence of repressed homosexuality "emphatically contradicted" the hypothesis previously put forward by Freud of a homosexual aetiology for paranoia. To underscore the way psychoanalysis rigorously overthrows some of its asserted solutions, Grünbaum discusses the predictive consequence of some of Freud's claims, noting that an apologist for Popper was led to conclude that "the limitation on predictability in psychoanalysis thus avowed by Freud is tantamount to generic nonpredictability and hence to nondisconfirmability."[18] Offering several illustrations of falsifiability and putting a critical probe on neo-Baconian inductivism, Grünbaum resolves that "Popper's refutability criterion is too insensitive to reveal the genuinely egregious epistemic defects that indeed bedevil the clinical psychoanalytic method and the aetiologies based upon it."[19] Judging from the orientation of this statement, we see that it is not so much the case that Grünbaum wishes to defend psychoanalysis outright; rather, he wants to get at its putative "deficit" from another angle, in order to deploy inductivist canons for the validation of causal claims that are said to "have the capability to exhibit these cognitive deficits."[20] Following the course of his argument, one has the sense that Grünbaum takes a sudden U-turn in order to get at Freudian inadequacy in a more "sensitive" and in some ways more pedestrian manner—for instance, he is suddenly interested in such matters as whether Freud really could have known that Paul Lorenz (alias Rat Man) masturbated the day of his saying so, and, on formulating a strict hierarchy of intraclinical testability: "Indeed, it will turn out that the entire testing procedure in the Rat Man case comes out to be probatively *parasitic* on an extraclinical finding."[21] Grünbaum is no doubt bound by the addressees of his argument to stay within the clinical and strictly analytical parameters of his findings. His concerns show the extent to which the fate of psychoanalysis, its day of scientific reckoning, can be seen to hinge on questions of testability. Perhaps if we aim beyond the first rows of addressees and try to reach another audience and auditor, the books might look a bit different, if not more complicated still.

How is the textual experiment set up? So much of what Freud said was set up according to the scruples underlying the controlled experiment. The vocabulary of doubt with which he worked and according to which he established his thought was in many significant ways unprecedented. The case of the obsessional neurotic evolved around the axles of the word *erraten*, to guess, to conjecture. This case tested Freud theoretically and personally—it was his first experience with countertransference; he suffered. On a thematic as well as heuristic level, the analytical work depended for its unfolding on tropes of testing, examinations, failed conjectures, repeated hypothetical positing, and what Weber has exposed as extreme disfiguration (*Entstellung*).[22] The patient's initial evaluation with the analyst took on the contours of a test. One of the most beloved patients of Freud, Lorenz passes the entry examination when telling the doctor that he had run through some of his books. Whereupon Freud agrees to treat him.[23] At the time of his analysis the young man was preparing the equivalent of his bar examinations. Preparations for the exam favored the manifestation of his symptoms.

The analytic session consisted of a series of microtests. At the beginning of every encounter, Freud coached the analysand who, doubling for a disciple, was responsible for repeating and embodying the lesson.[24] It was as if every session terminated in an examination that, as the examining professor indicates at several junctures, the Rat Man passed brilliantly. In fact he was too brilliant, a passing meteor. Freud complains that his cure came about too quickly, the lessons too quickly learned. His examination was done before his time was up. What does it mean to terminate an analysis too quickly? Not in the sense of Dora, who simply bolted (Freud was upset when she bailed: Dora had treated him like a servant, he moaned, giving him two weeks notice). But Lorenz ended too quickly in the sense of having recovered precipitously, passing all the necessary tests too soon, overcoming resistance and other unconscious blocks, leaving the analyst to the solitude of a first countertransference. Freud leaves the case in the mood of mourning a doubly lost object. It is the only case study for which he does not destroy the notes. If the Rat Man passes all the require-ments at warp speed, Freud hangs on to the evidence of an interminable trial. Whether it was too fast or too slow, or both at the same time, the experiment on one level explodes. Its failure was its success. A later foot-note states that the exceptional boy perished in the Great War.

Some years later Freud writes "Mourning and Melancholia." He sets up the probe in the manner of an experiment. Trying to throw some light on the nature of melancholia, he issues a warning against any "overestimation of the value of our conclusions."[25] Moreover, he "from the outset drop[s] all claim to general validity for our conclusions."[26] Upon ending the article he describes a painful wound which calls for an extraordinarily high antica-thexis. Freud abruptly ends the experiment: "—But here once again, it will be well to call a halt and to postpone any further explanation. . . . [We are forced] to break off every enquiry before it is completed—till the outcome of some other enquiry can come to its assistance."[27] Marked as provisional, "Mourning and Melancholia" disrupts itself even as it starts, relying for its grounding only upon the asserted instabilities of hypothetical positing. As a text that cannot as such take hold—it establishes claims for itself as a scien-tific trial without finality—the essay enters its own conditions of mourning. Without staying power it prepares from the start to depart, to leave the scientific observer bereft of an object, abandoned in the end to a state of uncurtained epistemological deficiency.

Unless perhaps—this would be the wager—the figure of understanding that characterizes the scientific observer is turned into that of a melan-cholic reader, holding on precisely to the lost object around which the text is organized. The text, as indicated by its title, elaborates two principal types of mourning. When Freud reverts to the work of mourning he asks: "In what, now, does the work which mourning performs consist? I do not think there is anything far-fetched in presenting it the following way. Reality-testing has shown that the loved object no longer exists, and it proceeds to demand that all libido shall be withdrawn from its attachment to that object. . . . Normally respect for reality gains the day."[28] Two kinds of tests establish our sense of reality. One, *Realitätsprüfung*, regards reality; the other, *Aktualitätsprüfung*, which Freud briefly mentions elsewhere, comes from another paper that was itself lost. In the lost essay Freud presumably has asserted the difference between a test that regards reality and one that regards immediacy (*Aktualität*). Who or what agency puts out the call for such a test? In his "Project" of 1895 Freud demonstrated that the "primary psychical processes" themselves do not require any distinction between an idea and a perception. In the *Traumdeutung* he described how the function of inhibition and delay are crucial in judging whether things are real or not. The first time that Freud used the term reality-test was in 1911, when dismissing the function of attention in "The Principal of Mental Functioning." What is real is not present to the psyche but depends upon exploratory probes that, following significant postponement, bring back the news of what can be constituted as having happened. Primary psychical processes waver between hallucinated and more groundable states. Reality-testing involves work, so it stands to reason that it is recruited into the work force of mourning. In "Group Psychology" Freud attributed the work of reality-testing to the ego-ideal—an attribution revised in a footnote at the beginning of *The Ego and the Id*. Now, for the first time since the "Project," reality-testing was firmly ascribed to the ego. There are further references to reality-testing in "Negation" and the "Mystic Writing Pad" (1925) which fix the ego's habit of sending out periodic exploratory cathexes into the external world. It is as if the ego needed to send out an envoy of surveyors and examiners for the purpose of establishing a reliable measure of its relation to what lies outside its domain. The messengers reassure the ego of its place or indeed create the space for the ego to connect to the coordinates of an outside. In "Negation" Freud traced the course of the development of reality-testing back to the ego's earliest object-relations. Despite Lacan's later objections to the contrary, or his railing on this point, Freud showed increasing interest in ego-psychology. In the end, reality-testing forms the basis of his thought on *Verleugnung* ("disavowal" or "denial"), which had not previously been differentiated from repression and which described the ego's reaction to an intolerable external reality.

In his later writings Freud continued to be preoccupied with reality-testing, particularly in chapter 8 of the posthumous *Outline of Psycho-Analysis*

(1940). "In other words, we gave up hallucinatory satisfaction of our wishes at a very early period and set up a new kind of reality-testing."[29] In these cases, testing involves the renunciation of a closed-off sense of fusional being in which the self assures its own satisfaction. The test results for which the ego calls should, in the best of worlds, confirm and countersign the satisfaction of our wishes, but in fact they put the self at risk. Testing marks a limit, constructing the difference between hallucination and external reality that does not always back up the idea put forth by the self. Without the apparatus of reality-testing the self exists in the mode of a tenuous hypothesis, unconfirmed, at sea. But it is "happy," floating on its own bouncy ground. The self braves reality-testing not only in mourning but also as mourning: test results often imply loss of ground even as the ego gains grounding. It is not clear why the ego would venture out at all on such exploratory probes if it already knows how to build itself an altogether satisfying world without the confirmation of exteriority. But precisely to assure itself that it is not alone it must risk the loss of internal plenitude, its homegrown self-appointed communion. Even in its most hallucinatory condition of satisfaction, the ego senses that something may be missing; it becomes insecure and must start up the machinery of testing.

The process of reality-testing in some ways resembles the development of moral consciousness. Something has to be given up, possibly sublimated, in order for reality to gain the day. Hence reality is to be "respected" ("Normal respect for reality gains the day")—a respect gained after struggle and surrender. Besides being armed with the necessary force to impose its version of what is, reality-testing is equipped to make demands on the ego, obliging it to submit to its law, like a tough-loving superego. In this respect, after having shown that the loved object no longer exists, reality-testing "proceeds to demand that all libido shall be withdrawn from its attachment to that object."[30] Reality-testing is not merely poised as a traffic cop but moves in on the ego like a SWAT team, or the "*non du père*," demanding that ego give it up, release the phantom hostage.

There are times when the ego barricades itself and shoots back, though. It kills the messenger. Freud metaphorizes this occurrence in terms of relating to a faithful servant. In the texts that proliferate around the question of testing, the figure of submission—an allegory of testing—often devolves on a servant, on service, what Kafka fixes as the *Diener*, the one who serves. When the ego cannot accept the test results, it is as if it would "send away its most faithful servant," writes Freud (recalling the sense he conveyed of being sent off by Dora).[31] There occurs a tremendous breakup when the intimate *Diener* is axed. In the "Metapsychology of Dreams"

Freud describes such a breach when introducing the notion of amentia. Amentia occurs when reality-testing is dismantled:

> The *Cs.* Must have at its disposal a motor innervation which determines whether the perc. can be made to disappear or whether it proves resistant. Reality-testing need be nothing more than this contrivance. . . . We know too little . . . We shall place reality-testing among the major *institutions of the ego*, alongside the *censorships* which we have come to recognize between the psychical systems . . . we can learn from pathology the way in which reality-testing may be done away with or put out of action—more clearly in the wishful psychosis of amentia than in that of dreams. Amentia is the reaction to a loss which realty affirms, but which the ego has to deny, since it finds it insupportable. Thereupon the ego breaks off its relation to reality; it withdraws the cathexis from the system of perc.s, *Cs.* With this turning from reality, reality-testing is gotten rid of, the (unrepressed, completely conscious) wishful phantasies are able to press forward into the system of . . . a better reality. Such a withdrawal may be put on a par with the processes of repression.[32]

Testing is linked to exteriority. One ventures out, breaks up a happy if deluded domesticity of self.[33] The test calls for the disruption of blissful certitude. A major egological institution, in league with censorship and repression, reality-testing still raises some questions and scores a number of untallied philosophical points. If reality needs to be tested, what is the status of that which gets established by the ego's probes? In terms of temporality, to the degree that reality-testing depends on inhibition and delay—it is secondary, arriving belatedly on the scene—does the news that it brings imply, as in the case of Kafkaesque bureaucracies, a kind of legitimacy that itself needs to be further refined and tested by the ego? Or is it really news, I mean, when the other ceases to exist—did the ego not experience the other's finitude from the get-go, as an early-bird experience of loss and mourning? Somehow, though, when forgetting descends upon consciousness, and they really rip you apart, testing tells you what it is that is not.

Postscript

Kafka wrote a story, "The Test." One day, the narrator, a jobless derelict, can't hack it anymore; he gets up to leave when he can't answer an intruder's question. As he turns to go, the questioner reaches across the table and pushes him back down. "Stay," he says. "It was just a test. Whoever doesn't answer the questions has passed the test" (*Wer die Fragen nicht beantwortet, hat die Prüfung bestanden*).[34]

Going Along for the Ride: Violence and Gesture—Agamben Reading Benjamin Reading Kafka Reading Cervantes

Samuel Weber

In *State of Exception*,[1] as in many of his other writings, Giorgio Agamben refers to the work of Walter Benjamin at particularly decisive points in his argument. In this book, whose title indicates an indebtedness to Carl Schmitt that Agamben shares with Benjamin, the author elaborates a theory of the "state of exception" as the notion through which a certain Western tradition of "bio-politics" seeks to assimilate the heterogeneity upon which it depends and thereby to treat it as the integrating element of its own "death machine" (145). The "state of exception" thus serves as the pretext of a violence bent on justifying and reproducing a political-legal system that presents itself as the indispensable condition of that "minimal order" (Schmitt) required in order for life to be livable. One particularly emphatic reference to Benjamin by Agamben in this book occurs in chapter 4, "Gigantomachy Around a Void," in which he contrasts Benjamin's "Critique of Violence" with Schmitt's theory of the "state of exception" as that which both defines and legitimates the sovereign as the power that can suspend the reign of positive law—of the Constitution—in order, allegedly, to restore the minimum order required for legality to function. Benjamin, by contrast, in his essay "Critique of Violence," develops a notion of violence as radically distinct from all "law" (*Recht, droit*); this form of violence is defined as "pure means"—which is to say, a "mediality without end" that serves no purpose and therefore has to be "considered independently of the ends it pursues" (105). Agamben, always an incisive and suggestive reader of Benjamin, cites a passage from a letter written in 1919 to Ernst Schoen, which argues for a notion of "purity"—*Reinheit*—that is conditional rather than absolute:

> The purity of a being is *never* unconditional or absolute; it is always subjected to a condition. This condition always differs depending on the being at issue; *never* however does this condition reside *in the being itself*. In other words: the purity of each (finite) being never depends upon it itself [*ist nicht von ihm selbst abhängig*]. The two beings to which we attribute purity above all are nature and children. For nature the external condition is human language.[2]

To be finite, according to Benjamin, is to depend upon something other than itself, upon extraneous conditions. "Purity" thus is not a characteristic of immanence, not a property, but, as Agamben notes, a "relational" category. In the case of violence, he continues, "purity" should be sought not in "violence itself" (*pas dans la violence même*), but "in its relation to something external." Anything that defines its "purity" or identity in terms of its relation to something else is, of course, a "means." But in "Critique of Violence," Benjamin explicitly excludes the traditional and familiar way in which this relation of "means" is defined: namely, as relation to an "end." And Agamben comments:

> Here appears the theme—which shines only for an instant, and yet long enough to illuminate the text in its entirety—of violence as "pure means," which is to say, as the figure of a paradoxical "mediality without end": i.e. a means that, while remaining such, is considered independently of the ends it pursues. (105)

For the Benjamin of "Critique of Violence," it is easy to identify the "end" that must be excluded in order to arrive at a critique of violence—of its conditions of possibility (and perhaps also of impossibility): it is *Recht*: "right" or Law (with a capital L) as that which informs the realm of positive laws (small l) and the reign of legality. But it is far more difficult to describe in positive terms the alternative relationship that would comprise the condition of violence as a means without end, a "pure" means. Agamben takes up Benjamin's suggestion at the end of the previously quoted passage, where he describes the other of nature as being "language"— "For nature the external condition is language." In his 1916 essay on "Language in General and the Language of Man in Particular," Benjamin defines the purity of language as consisting in its ability to communicate nothing other than "a communicability pure and simple," and Agamben extends this to cover that of pure violence as well:

> Just as, in his essay on language, language is pure when it is not an instrument serving the end of communication but rather communicates itself immediately, i.e. communicates a communicability pure and simple; so too violence is pure when it does not find itself in a relation of means to end but rather maintains itself in relation to its very mediality (*avec sa médialité même*). (106)

The "paradoxical figure" that Agamben associates with a "mediality without end" recurs in his paraphrase of Benjamin's notion of "pure language" just quoted, but in a slightly different guise, when he describes the mediality of language as that through which language communicates immediately its own communicability. The German formulation of Benjamin's to which this refers is worth noting: Benjamin writes of the "*Mitteilbarkeit*" of language, which he construes as being "immediate" (*unmittelbar*).[3] To translate *Mitteilbarkeit* into English as "communicability," however, is to efface one of its decisive connotations. A more precise if less idiomatic translation that has on occasion been employed is "impartibility." But there is perhaps an even better possibility in English, one that is both more literal and more idiomatic, although it resists nominalization and thus cannot be used everywhere. This option is "parting with."[4] The mediality of language would thus consist in a movement that separates *from* itself, and yet—here the paradox—in so doing, *relates* (to) itself as *other*. Relating (to) itself as other, it stays "with" that from which it departs. The "purity" of language as medium would thus consist in the immediacy of this "-ability" to stay *with* that from which it parts. As a medium it would be a "means without end" only insofar as the word "without" defines a relation not of simple exclusion or negation, but one of participation "with" the "out"-side of an irreducible and yet constitutive exteriority.[5]

With respect to violence, Agamben formulates the analogical relation to the mediality of language as follows:

> And just as pure language is not another language, does not occupy any place other than that of natural, communicating languages, showing itself in them by exposing them as such, in the same manner pure violence reveals itself only as the *exposing and deposing* of the relation between violence and right. This is what Benjamin suggests immediately following [the passages quoted], by evoking the theme of violence which, as anger, is never a

means but only a manifestation (*Manifestation*). . . . Pure violence *exposes and cuts* the bond between right and violence, and can thus appear not as violence that governs or executes (*schaltende*), but as violence that purely acts and manifests itself (*waltende*). (106)

In this elaboration of Benjamin's notions of "purity" and "mediality" as they operate in his conceptions both of "language" and of "violence," Agamben offers a series of conceptual couples that are as suggestive as they are enigmatic: "exposing and deposing," "exposes and cuts," "executes and acts (or manifests)." From the latter pair, however, it is clear that these concepts only reproduce the paradox of a "mediality without end," or as Benjamin formulates it, of a mediality that would be "immediate," by defining the latter ultimately as a function of the self, as a kind of self-reflexivity: as a "violence that *purely* acts and manifests *itself.*" If, however, the Benjaminian notion of purity is "not substantial but relational" (104), then how can the purity of violence consist in an action that manifests violence "itself" or "as such," apart from every exteriority, everything other than itself. Or is there a kind of manifestation, a kind of act that is defined precisely through such a relation to something other than itself? What, in short, is involved in a violence that is *waltend* but not *schaltend*? Can the two be as clearly separated or distinguished as Agamben, following Benjamin, suggests?[6]

It is from the perspective of such unresolved questions that Agamben turns briefly to Benjamin's reading of Kafka to indicate a possible alternative to the bio-political "death-machine" sustained by a "state of exception" that suspends the rule of law only to totalize it in and as *its other.* Agamben focuses upon two passages in Benjamin's Kafka interpretation. The first is contained in a letter to Scholem, in which Benjamin distinguishes his own reading of Kafka from that of his correspondent: "Your point of departure is the . . . soteriological (*heilsgeschichtlichen*) perspective opened by the trial proceeding; mine is the tiny absurd hope, as well as the creatures who on the one hand are concerned by this hope, but in whom on the other its absurdity is mirrored" (*Briefe* II, 617). The second passage quoted by Agamben is from another letter written by Benjamin to Scholem and concerns the relation of the text to those who study it:

> Whether the text [*die Schrift:* scripture] has been lost by the students, or whether they cannot decipher it, amounts to the same since without its key, the text is not text but life. Life as it is conducted [*geführt*] in the village at the foot of the castle. (*Briefe*, S. 618; cited by Agamben, 107)

Agamben does not cite another remark of Benjamin's in the same letter, which however lends support to his general interpretation and thesis. It concerns the status of the "law" in Kafka's work:

> Kafka's own insistence upon the law I consider to be the dead point (*Totenpunkt*) of his work, by which I mean only that it cannot serve interpretation as a fulcrum from which to set the work into motion.

It is perhaps worth noting that Benjamin's notion of "interpretation" here involves not reproducing the essence or meaning of the work as is, but rather of setting the latter into motion. As such, interpretation seems akin to the relational notion of "purity" previously discussed. Thus, Benjamin's reading of Kafka does not seek to elucidate the religious doctrine that might be implicit in the work, but rather to bring out those aspects which call for change and transformation, for a certain "movement." The category that Benjamin invokes has a Hölderlinian resonance: *Umkehr*, "inversion," reversal or also, turnabout.[7] And he glosses this in a passage that Agamben does not cite: "Kafka's messianic category is '*reversal*' or study" (618). Agamben, who does not dwell here on the notion of reversal, places the motif of "study" at the center of his reading of Benjamin's reading of Kafka:

> To the baring (*mise à nu*) of mythical-juridical violence effectuated by pure violence corresponds, in the essay on Kafka, as a kind of vestige, the enigmatic image of a legality (*d'un droit*) that is no longer practiced but only studied . . . a legality without force or application, like that into whose study the "new lawyer" [the reference is to Kafka's story of that name] plunges in leafing through "our old codes". . . . What could be the sense of a law that were thus to survive its deposing (*sa déposition*)? The difficulty encountered here by Benjamin corresponds to a problem that can be formulated . . . in the following terms: what happens to the law after its messianic fulfillment (*son accomplissement messianique*)? (This is precisely the controversy that opposes Paul to his Jewish contemporaries.) And what happens to the law in a classless society? (This is precisely the debate between Vychinski and Pasukanis). . . . What is important here is that the law—not practiced but studied—is not justice but only the gate that leads to it. What opens a passage toward justice is not the annulling of law, but its deactivation and dereliction (*la désactivation et le désoeuvrement*)—which is to say, another use of it. (109)

In the studies of Kafka's students as Benjamin reads them, Agamben finds the suggestion of an alternative "use" of law, one that would no longer be "contaminated" by application and enforcement and hence would be "liberated from its own value" as use-value: "This liberation is the task of study—or of play," he concludes, inasmuch as such an activity can relate to the world as something "absolutely unappropriable" and therefore incommensurate with any judicial order (109).

From what would such "study" or "play"—and we will shortly try to examine their possible relationship—liberate, however? Agamben's response conflates Schmitt and Derrida, for it points to the *spectrality* of a "law" maintaining itself in and through the state of exception. "Study" and "play" would thus presumably provide a liberating alternative to "the process of an infinite deconstruction, which, by virtue of maintaining law in a spectral life, is no longer capable of finishing up with [or mastering] it (*ne parvient plus à en venir à bout*)" (108). Thus, whereas according to Agamben deconstruction interminably maintains the rule of law in a spectral state of suspended animation, the suspension of the practice of law in its study, or in play, opens the way to a "definitive liberation" (109).

Agamben's powerful and challenging reading of Benjamin on Kafka thus provides him with a glimpse of a positive alternative both to the Schmittian state of exception and to Derridean spectrality. It rests upon an interpretation of Kafka's characters as engaging and suspending not the rule of law as such, but its auto-suspension and spectral reproduction in the state of exception. Since such engagement and suspension are tied, by Agamben, reading Benjamin reading Kafka, to the figures of the "students," let us take a closer look at the role they play in the texts of Benjamin and Kafka.

Benjamin introduces his discussion of them with a brief story. In a Chassidic village one Saturday evening, after the end of the Sabbath, a group of Jews are sitting in a tavern discussing what they would choose if each were granted the fulfillment of a single wish. One opts for money, the next for a son-in-law, yet another for a work-bench and so on. At the end only the village beggar is left and after some hesitation, this is the wish he relates:

> "I wish I was a powerful king ruling in a distant land and lay asleep at night in my palace and from the outermost border [of the country] the enemy attacks and before dawn cavalry reaches my castle without meeting any resistance and I awake in a panic without any time even to get dressed and have to flee with only a shirt to my name and am pursued through mountains and valleys, forests and hills and without rest day and night until I land safe here on the bench in your corner. That's what I would wish."
> The others stare at him clueless. "And what would this wish get you?" "A shirt" was the answer. (II.2, 433)

"This story," Benjamin comments, "leads deep into the household of Kafka's world." And he elaborates with a messianic allusion that can be found frequently in his writings, although here it seems to raise as many questions as it answers: "After all, no one says that the distortions (*die Entstellungen*) that the coming of the Messiah will one day straighten out (*zurechtzurücken*) concern only our space. They also certainly affect our time." In this perspective, the beggar's wish is not to rule forever, to *walten*, but rather more modestly to survive for a while, with a "shirt" on his back—and to his name.[8] Benjamin then goes on to recite a short text from Kafka's collection "The Country Doctor," entitled "The Next Village." In it a grandfather expresses the following concern:

> Life is so astonishingly short. Now in memory it seems so compressed, that for example I can barely comprehend how a young man can decide to ride to the next village without fearing that—not even considering unlucky accidents—even the time of our usual, happily passing life will never be sufficient for such a ride. (433)

It is necessary to recall this sense of urgency in order to situate Benjamin's reading of Kafka's students. For, Benjamin continues, there is a group among Kafka's creatures that "in a very peculiar manner reckons with the brevity of life." This group includes "fools" and "apprentices" (*Narren* and *Gehilfen*), but its true "spokesman and ruler" are the students. Benjamin introduces them through this short dialogue, from Kafka's novel *Der Verschollener*, formerly translated as *Amerika* and more recently as *The Man Who Disappeared*:

> "But when do you sleep?" Karl asked and stared at the student in amazement." Yes, sleep!" said the student. "I'll sleep when I'm finished with my studies." (434)

To study is, among other things, to learn by rote, to remember, and perhaps above all, to repeat. But in listening and observing the student, it becomes clear that there will never be enough time to finish—de *venir à bout*—before it is time to finish. And yet the response to this dilemma is to repeat it. The student responds to Karl's question—"But when do you sleep?"—not by answering it but by repeating its final word in what could almost be an affirmation: "*Ja, schlafen!*" which would perhaps best be rendered in English as "Sleep . . . yes!" But far from being a sign of agreement, the student's affirmative iteration only echoes the question. And what follows—"I'll sleep when I've finished my studies"—puts off the response indefinitely. If, as Benjamin suggests, the students are the *Wortführer*, the spokesmen of that "tribe" (*Sippe*) "that in the most peculiar way reckons with the brevity of life," then this response affirms only that the question has arrived, has been heard, even understood, but nothing more.

Benjamin comments on this passage as follows:

In their studies the students keep watch (*wachen die Studenten*). The hunger artist fasts, the doorkeeper keeps silent and the students keep watch (*wachen*). (434)

The *wachen* of the students is not watchful *waiting* as much as it is watchful waking: that of the insomniac. For there is nothing to wait for; these studies lead to nothing, least of all to fresh knowledge. And yet they are still far from worthless, as Benjamin makes clear:

Perhaps these studies amounted to nothing (*sind ein Nichts gewesen*). But if so, they stand in close proximity to that nothing, which alone makes anything useful (*brauchbar*)—namely, the Tao. (435)

Benjamin's reference here to the dependence of everything *useful—brauchbar*—upon a certain "nothingness"—*Nichts*—recalls Agamben's arguments in *State of Exception*. But when Benjamin elucidates Kafka's Tao by citing a passage from *The Chinese Wall*, it becomes evident that his way leads in a different direction from that envisaged by Agamben. For it goes in the direction not of "play" but rather of a certain kind of *handwork* such as that involved in the following passage from Kafka, cited by Benjamin:

Hammering a table together with such excruciatingly precise skill (*peinlich ordentliche Handwerksmäßigkeit*) that one could not say, "For him such hammering is nothing at all," but rather "For him such hammering is real hammering (*ein wirkliches Hämmern*) and at the same time nothing at all (*auch ein Nichts*)"; with the result that the hammering would become even bolder, more determined, more real and, if you like, more insane. (435)

The specificity of the kind of "use" or practice involved in such "real hammering," which at the same time is "nothing at all," involves a factor that does not seem to play a significant role in Agamben's considerations, although one might expect it to, given its importance in the complex relation of "law" to "life" that is the dominant concern of *State of Exception*. That factor is *repetition*. Thus, the appropriation of "life" by "law" through the state of exception can also be seen as the effort to install and impose a certain repetitiveness upon a singularity that is no less involved in repetition, but in a different way. For the *singular* (as distinct from the *individual*) can only appear—and indeed is only conceivable—as the vestigial or spectral *after-effect of a repetition*, as that which does not efface itself in the reproduction of the identical and yet which by itself is "nothing at all."

It is this dimension of repetition that constitutes the medium of the student's studying, as it is described in Kafka's text.[9] In other words, if, according to Benjamin's remark cited by Agamben, the students no longer possess the "key" to the texts over which they pore, and if this is tantamount to equating those texts with "life," then this transformation of text into life can also be described as the transformation of repetition from a process aimed at reproducing identity to one that allows for the aporetical resurgence of the singular: aporetical, because the singular as such is not identically repeatable, reproducible, but is also not separable from a certain repetition. Such repetition "produces" the unrepeatable in the form of those unexpected, often uncontrolled movements that Benjamin designates as "gestures" (Gebärde, Gestus, II.2, 435). And it is precisely in a certain kind of repetitive "gesture" that Benjamin sees the similarity between the studying of the students and that "hammering" that is both "real" and also "nothing at all":

> It is just such a decisive, fanatical gesture (*Gebärde*) that the students (*die Studierenden*) have in their studies (*bei ihrem Studium*). Nothing could conceivably be more bizarre. The scribes, the students are out of breath. They are always chasing off after something (*Sie jagen nur so dahin*). (435)

It is in such unpredictably spasmodic and interruptive "gestures" that the students, in their own peculiar way—"*auf eigentümlicher Weise*"— "reckon with" a time that is always in danger of running out. The gestures of the students combine the most extreme concentration with the most hectic exertion bordering on loss of control. The student spends most of his time reading, "accompanied by rapid lip-movements," a rapidity that Karl finds again and again in the student:

> He watched silently as the [student] read in his book, turned the pages, now and then looked something up in another book that he grasped with lightning-like rapidity (*mit Blitzesschnelle ergriff*), and often jotted down notes in a notebook, whereby surprisingly he always sank his face deep into the notebook.[10]

"Gesture," which here renders the student faceless, is according to Benjamin the decisive medium of Kafka's writing. Although he does not dwell on this point in his discussion of Benjamin's reading of Kafka in the *State of Exception*, Agamben does deal with the subject briefly but again very suggestively, in his short "Notes on Gesture," published originally in book form in 1978 and translated into English in *Infancy and History*.[11] Although he is not mentioned by name in them, these "Notes" owe much to Walter Benjamin, whose shadow looms large over an argument that looks to cinema for the reintroduction of gestures into the image:

> Cinema leads images back into the realm of gesture. . . . Bringing the element of awakening into this dream is the task of the film-maker. (139)

Strangely and significantly, it is not, however, in the more obvious allusions to Benjamin that the most pertinent part of these notes is contained, at least insofar as the essay on Kafka is concerned. Rather, it is in a concluding quote from Varro, which situates gesture "in the sphere of action," while distinguishing "it clearly from acting (*agere*) and doing (*facere*)":

> A person can make [*facere*] something and not enact [*agere*] it, as a poet makes a play, but does not act it [*agere* in the sense of playing a part]; on the other hand, the actor acts the play but does not make it. So the play is made [*fit*] by the poet, but not acted [*agitur*] by him; it is acted by the actor, but not made by him. Whereas the *imperator* (the magistrate in whom supreme power is invested) of whom the expression *res gerere* is used (to carry something out, in the sense of taking it upon oneself, assuming total responsibility for it), neither makes nor acts, but takes charge, in other words bears the burden of it (*sustinet*).[12]

Varro's distinction between the poet who makes the play, the actor who acts in it, and the *imperator*, who "neither makes nor acts but takes charge" and assumes the burden of carrying out the act, is illuminating with respect to the peculiar status of Kafka's students as read by Benjamin. For it is above all in the *acting of actors on a stage* that Benjamin finds the most telling confirmation of the gestures of the student, both in their suddenness and in their repetitive mixture of reality and nothingness:

> Actors must be quick as lightning in catching their cues. And also in other respects they resemble these assiduous students (*diesen Beflissenen*). For them in fact "hammering [is] real hammering and at the same time nothing at all"—namely, when it is part of their role. They study these roles; only a bad actor would forget any of its words or gestures. (435)

The actor, like the student, is a reader, and above all, a reader whose reading involves memory, attention, speed, and surprise. And the sense or purpose of his acting cannot be separated from its execution, its performance: in that sense it is like that "hammering" that is both "real hammering and at the same time nothing at all," since it accomplishes nothing that can be separated from its own repetition. At the same time, Varro's reference to the *imperator* is no less illuminating, since it highlights, by contrast, what is particularly *"eigentümlich"*—distinctively peculiar—about the students and actors. Neither of the latter "carry through" or "take charge" in the way Varro attributes to the *imperator*. They do not "bear" the same "burden." A remark of Agamben's from the final chapter of the *State of Exception* helps clarify this complex relationship. In that chapter, in a section discussing precisely a passage from the *Res Gestae* of Augustus, Agamben cites the latter's distinction between the *impersonal power* of governing officials (*magistrat*) and the notion of "authority" usually associated with the Emperor, which is held to be inseparable from his person (136). Agamben thus insists on the *"incarnation* of an Auctoritas" in "the physical person" of the sovereign such that the death of that person creates a problem that does not exist with respect to "magistrates." In this he sees a forerunner of the "charismatic" *Führer* or leader of modern fascism, which belongs "to the bio-political tradition of *auctoritas* and not to the juridical tradition of *potestas*" (140). It is this tradition that foresees a convergence of law and life in the "exceptional" figure of the individual sovereign or leader that marks the transformation of "the juridical-political system into a [bio-political] death machine" (145).

It is this convergence that is powerfully disrupted and interrupted by the gestures of students and actors whose studying and acting is both real and nothing at all, which is to say, *leads* to nothing separable from its own repetitive and spectral reenactment. Such repetitive and spectral reenactment subverts the very notion of "act" as "actualization": *acting* is not *action*, and the "actor" is as far removed from the man of action as Kafka's student is from the sage. Or as far removed as are their "gestures" from self-expression.[13] The student's face is hidden by the gesture with which his head sinks into his books. The gestures of actors or students do not express their selves but rather expose and depose those selves irremediably. Which is to say also, for Benjamin at least, *theatrically*. The great "chance" of theater, its sole chance to survive the challenge of the new media, he situated in its *Exponierung des Anwesenden*: which is to say, in its age-old capacity to "expose the present" in the double sense of that word, including both *those present*, the "audience" or *Publikum*—a word Benjamin never cared for—and of the "present" as the notion of a self-contained, immanent temporal moment. Benjamin's notion of gesture entails the interruption and the disruption of all such self-containment, and it does this by staging finitude. In his essay "What is Epic Theater?" Benjamin provides the following account of gesture:

In opposition to the actions and undertakings of people [gesture] has a determinable beginning and a determinable end (*einen fixierbaren Anfang und ein fixierbares Ende*). This strict frame-like closure of each element of a posture (*Haltung*), which nevertheless as a whole is situated within the flow of life, is even one of the dialectical foundations (*Grundpositionen*) of gesture. From this an important conclusion follows: gestures are all the more prevalent where an acting subject (*einen Handelnden)* is interrupted.[14]

Gesture thus interrupts not just the "flow of life" in which it is situated, but also its two most essential constituents: the goal-directed action of a subject, "*eine[s] Handelnden*," and the end-directed movement of a *Handlung*, a plot or story, but also an action: "For epic theater therefore the interruption of the plot—*der Handlung*—is paramount" (521). In thus interrupting the "flow of life" and the flow of intentional activity, gestures expose and deface those that "make" them far less than that they are made, and undone, by them. Such a gesture accompanies the end of the scene in which Karl encounters the student. Karl has asked him for advice as to whether he should leave his current position and gets a surprising response:

> "You advise me, then, to stay with Delamarche?" Karl asked.
>
> "Absolutely," said the student his head sinking already into his books. It seemed as if it were not he who had said those words; as though spoken by a voice that was deeper than that of the student, they resonated long after in Karl's ears. Slowly he went to the curtain, glanced back a last time at the student, who now sat utterly immobile in the light of the lamp, surrounded by profound darkness, and then slipped back into his room. (*Amerika*, 215)

The voice responding to Karl's uncertainty about what to do echoes in his memory as though it had been disembodied, separated from the person ostensibly uttering it; its authority one of disincarnation, and yet in no way detached from the body; it is the voice of a specter rather than of a spirit, its "deeper" tone suggesting a person far older than the presumably still relatively young student. The voice removes itself from the person to whom it is supposed to belong and resounds in memory before fading away into the image of the student sitting motionless in the light of the lamp, surrounded by darkness. This echoing and fading away of the voice—its *Verschallen*—is what defines the "*Verschollener*."

"The gate to justice is study" remarks Benjamin, and the study of the law, when it comes to replace and supplant its practice, Agamben adds, can prepare the way to "liberate" things from their "proper value," rendering them "absolutely unappropriable" (109) and perhaps also absolutely *inappropriate*. Study, for Benjamin no less than for Kafka, is inseparable from *reading*, even and perhaps especially where the text or script or key has been lost: "To read what never was written" was a phrase of Hofmannsthal that Benjamin was fond of quoting. At the end of his essay not just "on" or "about" Kafka, but which is dated and dedicated to the "tenth anniversary of his death,"[15] Benjamin provides an instance of just what such a reading, which repeats that which never was, might entail. In a short piece, he suggests, Kafka may have "found the law of his journey" and succeeded, "at least once" in "bringing its breathtaking speed in line with that epical measured step that he no doubt spent his entire life searching for. He entrusted it to a text (*Niederschrift*) that became his most consummate not merely because it is an interpretation":

> Sancho Panza, who moreover never boasted about it, succeeded over the years, by amassing lots of chivalry and adventure novels for the evening and night hours, in so distracting from him his devil, to whom he subsequently gave the name Don Quixote, that the latter performed (*aufführte*) the craziest deeds, which however for lack of a predetermined object, which should have been Sancho Panza, did no one any harm. Sancho Panza, a free man, perhaps out of a certain sense of responsibility, followed Don Quixote on his crusades with an even temper and gleaned from them great and useful entertainment until his end. (II.2, 438; English: SW 2:816–17)

Benjamin glosses this briefly but conclusively:

> Sober fool and hapless assistant, Sancho Panza sent his rider before him. Bucephalus outlived his. Whether man or horse is no longer so important as long as the burden is lifted from one's back. (438)

Sancho Panza's gesture, which follows rather than leads, has little in common with the imperial *res gestae*, for its "thing" is not action but acting, or rather staging a spectacle and following it out. Or, as Benjamin puts it in the already quoted letter to Scholem (August 11, 1934): "Sancho Panza's existence [*Dasein*] is exemplary [*musterhaft*] because it consists essentially in *rereading his own* [*im Nachlesen des eigenen*], however foolish and quixotic."[16] And if we follow and reread Kafka's short account and Benjamin's even shorter gloss, we may discover that in interpreting (*Auslegung*), rereading, and staging one's own life, a repetition takes place that lifts the burden from the subject who would be sovereign, allows him to divest himself of his rider and simply go along for the ride.

INTRODUCTION

1. Jacques Derrida, "The Future of the Profession or the University Without Condition (Thanks to the 'Humanities,' What Could Take Place Tomorrow)," in *Jacques Derrida and the Humanities: A Critical Reader*, edited by Tom Cohen (Cambridge: Cambridge University Press, 2001), see 32–33.

2. Cited in Alan Cholodenko's postface to *Mass Mediauras: Form, Technics, Media*, edited by Alan Cholodenko (Stanford: Stanford University Press, 1996). See 232.

3. Samuel Weber, *Institution and Interpretation* (Stanford: Stanford University Press, 2001). See xi.

4. See, for example, "The Future of the Humanities: Experimenting" and "The Future Campus: Destiny in a Virtual World," in *Institution and Interpretation* (Stanford: Stanford University Press, 2001). See also the chapters by Susan Bernstein, Gary Hall, and Marc Redfield in this volume.

5. Samuel Weber, *Institution and Interpretation* (Stanford: Stanford University Press, 2001). See 149.

6. Samuel Weber, "Wartime," in *Violence, Identity, and Self-Determination*, edited by Hent de Vries and Samuel Weber (Stanford: Stanford University Press, 1997). See 94.

7. Ibid., 101.

CHAPTER I
"God Bless America!"
Samuel Weber

1. Alexis de Tocqueville, *La démocratie en Amérique*, vol. 1 (Paris: Flammarion, 1981). Page references to this work will be given in parentheses in the body of the text. English translations are my own.

2. Immanuel Kant, *Critique of Judgment*, §15. See my discussion of this passage in *Mass Mediauras: Form, Technics, Media* (Stanford: Stanford University Press, 1996), 19 ff.

3. See 413–17.

4. In passing it may be noted that this is a passage where Tocqueville's text ceases to "resemble itself," at least in one of the current French editions. The Flammarion version of the text, first published in 1981 and prefaced by François Furet, renders the passage quoted above as follows: "J'oppose maintenant les Anglo-Américains *le uns uns aux autres*," instead of "les uns aux autres." By singularizing the plural "les" as "le," the "definite article" loses much of its definition, especially since that which it is supposed to define, the plural collective "uns," is singularly split by being repeated, as though in a stutter. This repetition, in its very senselessness, inscribes a certain alterity in its series even before the "others" are named and addressed as such "aux autres." This involuntary dramatization of what Jean-Luc Nancy in a recent book has called *Être singulier pluriel* (Paris: Editions de Galilée, 1996) recalls not just Freud's theory of parapraxes, but the essay of one of his bitterest critics, Karl Kraus, "Ich glaube an den Druckfehlerteufel" (I believe in the typo-demon). We will return shortly to this problem of "addressing the other." That the word *uns* exists not just in French but also in German, where it no longer designates a plural singular ("ones") but rather the accusative form of the "first person singular" ("us"), can serve as a fortuitous reminder of how the singularly plural medium of language challenges all attempts "to form a more perfect union" of "We, the people." Much of the political theological relation we are trying to explore is already expressed in the German phrase, *Gott mit uns!*, which in turn is the modern political translation of what was to be the name of Jesus: "Immanuel" (Cf. Matthew I:21ff).

5. At the time of writing the present chapter, a particularly striking instance of this is provided by the "preemptive" foreign policy of the current U.S. administration, its wars in Afghanistan, Iraq, and more generally, the "war against terror" it embarked upon following September 11, 2001.

6. Given the structure of writing, it should be noted that this text is being written at the end of August 2003, some six months after the occupation of Iraq by the United States and the United Kingdom. How long a view the planners of this may have had is open to question: but the "febrility" with which it has been put into practice appears more evident with every passing day.

7. It is worth noting that in American English, at least, the word "right" does not correspond to what in French is designated as *Droit* or in German as *Recht*. In political parlance, the word is used only in the "plural," as we see here, to designate "rights" which involve legitimate claims; even where the objects are intangible, such as "life, liberty and the pursuit of happiness," rights always imply, in this usage, property rights. One has a right to them because one is their rightful owner, if only virtually. Government is to "secure" those rights by making such virtuality actual: that is, present. This implicit model for the notion of rights is strengthened by the continual refusal

of American governments to include economic claims other than rights of individuals to own property among the "unalienable rights" to be "secured" by governments. The absence of a word that would distinguish the principle of "law" from its actual implementations—in other words, that would distinguish *loi* from *droit*—is perhaps the condition for endowing an existing text, the U.S. Constitution, with the authority to legitimate law.

8. One indication of the American response to this problem is the lack of restriction on inheritance: whereas in Europe children cannot be disinherited by their parents, in the United States the parent is free to do so. Once again this demonstrates how "rights" are construed in terms of property rights: the owner is free to dispose of his or her wealth as she or he sees fit, independent of any familial obligations.

9. That the traditional American tendency to "isolationism" is perfectly compatible with an imperial, interventionist foreign policy based on an equally deeply rooted messianic political tradition of "Manifest Destiny" is what the current doctrine of "preemptive-preventive" military intervention demonstrates with unmistakable clarity.

10. I prefer this designation to the more familiar and consecrated one of "liberal democracy." The doctrine of "liberty," at least as conceived and practiced in American society, presupposes the notion of an indivisible subject as potential property owner. This quality of subject as proprietor need not be restricted to individual human beings, but can be and has been understood as implying a collective political subject. What is decisive is that this subject be construed not as collective or individual but rather as indivisible, unified and self-contained. Since such qualities are not to be found in living individuals, a religious support is required, although it may and does assume secular forms, as with the cult of "stardom" powerfully purveyed by the audiovisual media. I will return to this shortly.

11. See Giorgio Agamben's "bio-political" interpretation of this complicity in *Homo Sacer: Le pouvoir souverain et la vie nue*, translated by Marilène Raiola. Editions du Seuil: Paris, 1995, 138ff.

12. Cf. John Baer, *The Pledge of Allegiance: A Centennial History, 1892–1992* (Annapolis, Md. Free State Press, 1992). For a short version available on the Internet, see http://history.vineyard.net/pledge.htm.

13. Abraham Lincoln, Gettysburg Address.

14. "La devise de la République est 'Liberté, Égalité, Fraternité.' Son principe est: gouvernement du peuple, par le peuple et pour le peuple." French Constitution, Article II: "De la souveraineté."

15. In its secularized, deinstitutionalized form, such morality can then be adopted by other religions as well, as long as they endorse or accept the principle of a transcendent, indivisible, and self-constitutive subject.

16. Of the seven "assumptions" that MacPherson attributed to possessive individualism, only the last requires revision in this sense. Since MacPherson's classic, first published some forty years ago, may in the meanwhile be unfamiliar to many readers, here are his seven assumptions: "(i) What makes a man human is freedom from dependence on the wills of others. (ii) Freedom from dependence on others means freedom from any relations with others except those relations which the individual enters voluntarily with a view to his own interest. (iii) The individual is essentially the proprietor of his own person and capacities, for which he owes nothing to society. (iv) Although the individual cannot alienate the whole of his property in his own person, he may alienate his capacity to labor. (v) Human society consists of a series of market relations. (vi) Since freedom from the wills of others is what makes a man human, each individual's freedom can rightfully be limited only by such obligations and rules as are necessary to secure the same freedom for others. (vii) Political society is a human contrivance for the protection of the individual's property in his person and goods, and (therefore) for the maintenance of orderly relations of exchange between individuals regarded as proprietors of themselves." C. B. MacPherson, *The Political Theory of Possessive Individualism*. London: Oxford University Press, 1962, 263–64. What Tocqueville, focusing upon American society, demonstrates and what MacPherson apparently did not envisage (Tocqueville is not mentioned in his book, which concentrates upon the period between Hobbes and Locke), is the extent to which a "valid"—or at least, *effective*—"theory of political obligation" required a theological-political foundation in order to withstand the centrifugal forces of "the structure of market society" (MacPherson, 275). What Tocqueville's analysis of American democracy suggests is that the notion of the "human autonomy" embraced by possessive individualism, at least in its American version, was already resolutely Christian in its foundations and only as such could it succeed in maintaining the atomized structure of individual identity as a model for the political collective as a whole.

17. If anything this tendency has been increasing in American political life, as the recent attempt to impeach Bill Clinton demonstrated.

18. It is no accident that the notion of "cult of personality" enjoyed such popularity in the United States: it reflects one of the most powerful tendencies of American society. The difference with its Stalinist variant is of course that in the United States the tempo of ambivalence is far more rapid, and one might say medieval or Boethian: stars rise only to fall, thus providing a spectacular (and Christianized) dialectic of finitude: stars rise and fall, but the spectators survive as a kind of Holy Ghost, assuming that is that they stay put and remain spectators. This reinforces one of the tendencies attributed to American democracy by Tocqueville: its penchant for servitude (I:354).

19. See http://www.atheists.org/public.square/coins.html.

20. How different this response of Poe's anonymous narrator to that of the St. Petersburg barber, Ivan Yakovlevitch, when, upon cutting open his breakfast roll one morning he finds himself confronting a disembodied *nose*. Both tales tell stories of dismemberment, but what in Gogol's *Nose* becomes a point of departure for irony, is associated in Poe's text with anxiety, aggression, and guilt, in a configuration whose significance can hardly be reduced to the narrator's concluding assertion that he has finally attained "a full comprehension of the mystery which had troubled me for so long. It was evident. It was a clear case. Brevet Brigadier General John A. B. C. Smith was the man—the man that was used up." The function of the story, for the narrator at least—and surely for those readers and listeners for whom he (and narrators generally) are only windows onto the world—is to clear up the "mystery" by providing a clear-cut moral, one that provides closure and in this case also a title as well. But in having the title reappear at the story's end, Poe's text underscores that its words cannot simply constitute a summation of the story as a whole, since they remain a part of it. Such participation suggests that the enigma, far from being cleared up through title, is merely cleared away by it, temporarily, to return another day. American history, and in particular, recent American history, can easily be reread in terms of the return of this "trouble" and the responses it provokes, above all that of trying to clear it up by kicking it away. Poe's text can be found at *http://xroads.virginia.edu/~hyper/POE/usedup.html.*

CHAPTER 2

Of Debts, Dreams, and Jokes: or, Weberian Theatricality
Simon Morgan Wortham

Throughout this chapter, I refer to those texts treated by Weber by citing his quotations rather than by making reference to the original source in the main body of my text. For consistency, this is because Weber frequently presents his own translations of texts not originally written in English, or at least occasionally modifies the translation.

1. Samuel Weber, "The Debts of Deconstruction and Other, Related Assumptions," in *Institution and Interpretation*, expanded edition (Stanford, Calif.: Stanford University Press, 2001), 102–31, see 108. All further references to Weber's essay are given in the body of the text.

2. In this part of his essay, Weber refers to Jacques Derrida, *La Carte postale* (Paris: Flammarion, 1980), 362.

3. The reference here is to *La Carte postale*, 353.

4. Ibid., 415.

5. Weber quotes from Nietzsche's *On the Genealogy of Morals* (New York: Random House, 1967), 88–89. However, he does note that the translation by W. Kaufmann and R. J. Hollingdale is "occasionally modified."

6. Samuel Weber, *The Legend of Freud*, expanded edition (Stanford, Calif.: Stanford University Press, 2000). See 56. All further references will be given in the body of the text.

7. Weber here refers to Sigmund Freud, *Standard Edition of the Complete Psychological Works*, edited and translated by James Strachey (London: Hogarth Press, 1958). See 5:506–7.

8. Samuel Weber, "The Divaricator: Remarks on Freud's *Witz*." *Glyph*, 1 (1977): 1–27. All further references will be given in the body of the text.

9. See Freud, *Standard Edition* 8:121.

10. Ibid., 139.

11. Ibid., 128.

12. The "economics" and "economy" of the joke receive a great deal of attention in *The Legend of Freud* and in Weber's earlier articles on laughter, joking, and psychoanalysis. Much more could be said on this topic, via careful and detailed reading of Weber's own analyses here. In particular, Weber explores and questions Freud's assertion that it is a "principle of economy" which unifies the different facets of the *Witz*, constituting its fundamental character. According to Freud, the pleasure derived from relieving psychical expenditure, not least in respect of the lifting of inhibitions and thus of the energy expenditure required to maintain them, aligns the *Witz* with a certain tendency to compress or save. However, the economy suggested by one kind of reduction would appear to be more than balanced by the expenditure of intellectual effort entailed by the joke-technique itself. Freud's own—unanswered—question, of who then saves and who gains, once more raises the matter of unbalanceable accounts and unredeemed debts (as well as that of the conflictual force-field constituting the subject of the joke). In the sections of *The Legend of Freud* devoted to the psychoanalytic treatment of jokes, Weber also explores the inevitable shortcomings, in the Freudian text, of an "economic" description of laughter; and in "Laughing in the Meanwhile" we find a preliminary attempt to relate laughter to a thinking of the gift. Finally, in regard to this issue of the "economy" or "exchange" of the joke, it is also worth noting the following remark by Weber in the section of *The Legend of Freud* called "The Shaggy Dog": "The contract that binds the parties engaged in the joke . . . diverges from that of liberal, bourgeois jurisprudence: the contracting parties agree to a process of exchange without being certain that they will be able to accomplish the obligations they incur" (149). This quote is perhaps especially significant when considering Weber's recounting of the joke apparently told him by Jacques Derrida. The "parties engaged in the joke" here might be the Pole and the Jew, Derrida and Weber . . . among others.

13. Might it be possible that the Pole in fact *doubly* dupes the Jew, artfully dispossessing him of his secret so as to extract a surplus or profit in terms of the benefit ultimately derived from the proceeds of the *Aufsitzer*, while at the same time merely feigning annoyance or irritation so as to pander to the Jew's narcissistic self-assurance that, ultimately, he remains in control of the *Aufsitzer*? In this case, a semblance or ruse of meaning, purpose, rationality (the Jew's apparent "masterfulness") might be being promoted and exploited (via the Pole) only in order to lift, more fundamentally, the obstructions or inhibitions standing in the way of the *Aufsitzer*'s proceeds or its play. Yet even if the Jew is deluded or divided against himself, the very same goings-on will doubtless apply, in turn, to the Pole . . . of whom no one (not even himself) can ever be sure if he "fools" or is "fooled" by the Jew.

14. Samuel Weber, "The Unraveling of Form." In *Mass Mediauras: Form, Technics, Media*, edited by Alan Cholodenko (Stanford, Calif.: Stanford University Press, 1996) 9–35. See 23. All further references will be given in the body of the text.

15. Samuel Weber, "Goings On: Discussion with Rex Butler," in *Mass Mediauras*, 209–30. See 229–30.

16. Samuel Weber, "Catching Up with the Past: Discussion with the Weber Reading Group," in *Mass Mediauras*, 168–208, see 179.

17. Samuel Weber, "Taking Place: Toward a Theater of Dislocation," in *Opera Through Other Eyes*, edited by D. J. Levin (Stanford, Calif.: Stanford University Press, 1994), 107–46. Further references will be given in the body of the text.

18. Here Weber refers to Theodor Adorno's essay "Opera," in *Introduction to the Sociology of Music*, translated by E. B. Ashton (New York: Seabury, 1976), 71–84, esp. 81–82. He notes, however, that the passage quoted contains modifications to the translation of this text.

19. See *Opera Through Other Eyes*, 252–3.

20. Samuel Weber, "The Blindness of the Seeing Eye," in *Institution and Interpretation*, expanded edition, 73–84. Further references will be given in the body of the text.

21. Weber here refers to Freud, *Standard Edition*, 5:506–7.

22. Weber here refers to ibid., 5:514.

23. Weber here refers to ibid., 5:530.

24. Samuel Weber, "The Future of the Humanities: Experimenting," in *Institution and Interpretation*, 236–52, see 251.

25. Jacques Derrida, "Mochlos: Or, The Conflict of the Faculties," in *Logomachia: The Conflict of the Faculties*, edited by Richard Rand (Lincoln: University of Nebraska Press, 1992), 1–34, see 28–31.

26. Jacques Derrida, "The Principle of Reason: The University in the Eyes of Its Pupils." *Diacritics* 13, 3 (1983): 3–20, see 10.

CHAPTER 3

Technica Speciosa: Some Notes on the Ambivalence
of Technics in Kant and Weber

Peter Fenves

This essay grows out of reflections on the first seminar I attended in graduate school, which was taught by Samuel Weber and concentrated on the *Critique of Judgment*. Near the beginning of the seminar, commenting on the opening sections of both the original and the published version of the introduction to the third *Critique*, Weber said that Kant distinguished "technical" from "practical"—a remark that perplexed me then, as it still does now.

1. Kant's "Erste Einleitung in die 'Kritik der Urteilskraft' " is contained in volume 20 of his *Gesammelte Schriften* (Berlin: de Gruyter, 1900–   ). All further references to Kant are in parentheses to this edition; translations are my own.

2. Samuel Weber, *Mass Mediauras: Form, Technics, Media* (Stanford, Calif.: Stanford University Press, 1996), 51.

3. See, in particular, Heidegger, *Kant und das Problem der Metaphysik*, 4th ed. (Frankfurt am Main: Klostermann, 1973), 161–62.

4. Heidegger, *Kant und das Problem der Metaphysik*, 208: "Was hat sich aber im Geschehen der Kantischen Grundlegung eigentlich ergeben. Nicht daß die transzendentale Einbildungskraft der gelegte Grund ist, nicht, daß diese Grundlegung eine Frage nach dem Wesen der menschlichen Vernunft wird, sondern, daß Kant bei der Enthüllung der Subjectivität des Subjekts vor dem von ihm selbst gelegte Grund zürückweicht." This paragraph makes it altogether clear that *Kant and the Problem of Metaphysics* is at bottom a *biography*— the writing of a life that shrinks from the abyssal ground it itself lays down.

5. See ibid., 162.

6. See Kant's letter to Jacob Sigismund Beck, December 4, 1792 (letter 549). For a full account of the textual history of the First Introduction, see Norbert Hinske's remarks in Immanuel Kant, *Erste Einleitung in die Kritik der Urteilskraft: Faksimile und Transkriptionen*, edited by Norbert Hinske, Wolfgang Müller-Lauter, and Michael Theunissen (Stuttgart–Bad Constatt: Fromann-Holzboog, 1965), esp. iii–xii.

7. As Kant writes to Beck, "it [the introduction] appears to me still to contain much that contributes to a more complete insight into the concept of the purposiveness of nature" (11:396).

8. Heidegger, *Kant und das Problem der Metaphysik*, 158–59.

9. In Kant's *Anthropology from a Pragmatic Point of View*, Kant briefly reprises the language of the original introduction to the third *Critique*: "Gestalten der Dinge (Anschauungen), so fern sie nur zu Mitteln der Vorstellung

durch Begriffe dienen, sind Symbole, und das Erkenntnis durch dieselbe heißt symbolisch oder figürlich (speciosa)" (7:191).

10. Samuel Weber, "Ambivalence," in *Institution and Interpretation*, expanded version (Stanford, Calif.: Stanford University Press, 2001), 138.

11. Ibid., 150.

12. Ibid., 142.

13. Ibid., 151; quoting from Kant, *Critique of Judgment*, translated by J. H. Bernard (New York: Hafner Press, 1951), 160; § 49.

14. Ibid., 151.

15. Weber, *Mass Mediauras*, 29.

16. Ibid., 30.

17. Ibid., 210.

18. Ibid., 99.

19. Ibid., 101.

20. Ibid., 107.

CHAPTER 4

Surfing Technics: Direction and Dispersion in the Age of Information
R. L. Rutsky

1. As Weber has noted in an interview, "To interpret deconstruction as instituting or aggravating a cleavage between practice and theory is to misinterpret it in an unnecessarily unproductive manner." See "Catching Up with the Past," in *Mass Mediauras: Form, Technics, Media* (Stanford, Calif.: Stanford University Press, 1996), 198.

2. Weber notes, "It is clear that anything like a theoretical discourse that seeks to confront this ambivalent coming-to-pass of singularity is going to have to be extremely suspicious of any notion of 'application'. . . . Application is very difficult to construe outside of a logic of subsumption." See "Goings-On," in *Mass Mediauras*, 211.

3. Samuel Weber, "Upsetting the Setup: Remarks on Heidegger's 'Questing After Technics,'" in *Mass Mediauras*, 55–75. Further references will be given in the body of the text.

4. Norbert Wiener, *The Human Use of Human Beings: Cybernetics and Society*, 2nd ed. (New York: Avon Books, 1954), 23.

5. Claude E. Shannon and Warren Weaver, *The Mathematical Theory of Communication* (Urbana: University of Illinois Press, 1949). Further references will be given in the body of the text.

6. Samuel Weber, "Objectivity and Its Others," in *Mass Mediauras*. See 53.

7. Samuel Weber, "Television: Set and Screen," in *Mass Mediauras*, 116. Further references will be given in the body of the text.

8. Weber, "Objectivity and Its Others," 53.

9. Samuel Weber, "Theater, Technics, and Writing," *1–800* (Fall 1989): 16.

10. In the case of this quotation, the critic is Fredric Jameson, "The Cultural Logic of Late Capitalism," in *Postmodernism, or, The Cultural Logic of Late Capitalism* (Durham, N.C.: Duke University Press, 1991), 54.

11. Samuel Weber, "Capitalizing History: Notes on The Political Unconscious." *Diacritics* 13. 2 (Summer 1983): 25.

12. Weber, Samuel. "Mass Mediauras, or: Art, Aura and Media in the Work of Walter Benjamin," in *Mass Mediauras*. See 78.

13. Gilles Deleuze, *Negotiations*, translated by Martin Joughin (New York: Columbia University Press, 1995). See 121.

14. Samuel Weber, "Catching Up With the Past," 195.

CHAPTER 5

IT, Again: How to Build an Ethical Virtual Institution
Gary Hall

1. Samuel Weber, "The Future of the Humanities: Experimenting," *Culture Machine* 2 (2000), http://culturemachine.tees.ac.uk/Cmach/Backissues/j002/Articles/art_webe.htm.

2. Weber provides another account of his use of the concept of "experimenting" in his reflections on Kierkegaard:

> I am thinking here . . . of the kind of experimenting practised by Kierkegaard, for instance in his study of *Repetition*, which bears the subtitle: *A Venture in Experimenting Psychology*. . . . Kierkegaard invokes this notion [of a different kind of experiment] as a necessary corollary of a temporality of repetition that excludes all immanence and cognitive control, in which reflexivity does not come full circle to produce a concept of itself, but instead doubles up into a language that can no longer be assigned to a single, authoritative speaker or to a reliable, truthful voice. . . . For Kierkegaard, experimenting has to do with the way concepts emerge and operate in a singular situation: "I wanted to let the concept come into existence in the individuality and the situation," he writes. The situation he here describes could be described as a virtual situation; it is that of a text whose import only is accessible to a reading that moves it elsewhere; and it is that of a theatre, in which the spectacle moves the spectator somewhere else (Samuel Weber, "The Future Campus: Destiny in a Virtual World." *Hydra* [1999], http://www.hydra.umn.edu/weber/text1.html).

3. Samuel Weber, *Institution and Interpretation* (Minneapolis: University of Minnesota Press, 1987), xv. Further page references are given in parenthesis in the body of the text.

4. Samuel Weber, *Institution and Interpretation*, expanded edition (Stanford: Stanford University Press, 2001).

5. Weber, in fact, establishes a link in *Institution and Interpretation* between such professionalization and the "institutions and practices which marked the development of the humanities disciplines in general, and those of literary studies in particular" (27) as the "process of isolating, as constitutive of the establishment of professions and of disciplines, requires itself an isolated, relatively self-contained social space in which to operate. Historically, this space was provided by the university" (31).

6. The DSpace archive (http://www.flinders.edu.au/dspace), established at Flinders University in Australia, has focused on the humanities, but CSeARCH is the only one I am aware of (at the time of writing) to focus on cultural studies and cultural theory. For definitions of open access, see the 2001 Budapest Open Access Initiative (http://www.soros.org/openaccess); the 2003 Bethseda Statement on Open Access Publishing (http://www.earlham.edu/~peters/fos/bethesda.htm#summary); and Peter Suber's Open Access blog (http://www.earlham.edu/~peters/fos/fosblog.html).

7. Joseph Stiglitz, "Remarks at the Department for Trade and Industry and Center for Economic Policy Research." *The World Bank Group*, London, January 27, 1999.

8. Another example of an open access archive is the CogPrints archive (http://cogprints.soton.ac.uk/) that has been established for cognitive psychology by Stevan Harnad at the University of Southampton, to mention just one of the best-known. However, this is really only the tip of the iceberg as far as the electronic publication of academic material is concerned. Many universities now provide opportunities for their staff to both publish their papers electronically via local repositories, and to access other stores held by universities participating in the Open Society Institute (OSI) and the Scholarly Publishing and Academic Resources Coalition (SPARC) international initiative (http://www.arl.org/sparc), a project designed to reduce the cost of published research work, bypassing commercial publishers of increasingly expensive journals, whether printed or electronic. SHERPA (Securing a Hybrid Environment for Research Preservation and Access) has also set up institutional archives of open access research papers with, in August 2006, thirty-seven British universities being listed at its site (http://www.sherpa.ac.uk/repositories). According to a JISC Open Access briefing paper of April 2005 (a version of which is available at http://www.jisc.ac.uk/publications), "by the beginning of 2005, there were almost 40 Open Access archives in the UK." A list of open access archives is available on the http://www.eprints.org/ site. There is also a Directory of Open Access Journals (DOAJ) in Lund in Sweden, available at http://www.opendoar.org/. In November 2006 this contained more than 2,400 journals. In October 2006 OpenDOAR also produced a quality assured list of 798 repositories.

9. Bill Readings, *The University in Ruins* (Cambridge, Mass.: Harvard University Press, 1996) 118; Robert Young, "The Idea of a Chrestomatic University," in *Logomachia: The Conflict of the Faculties*, edited by Richard Rand (Lincoln: University of Nebraska Press, 1992), 112; Diane Elam, "Why Read?" *Culture Machine* 2 (2000), http://culturemachine.tees.ac.uk/Cmach/Backissues/j002/Articles/artelam.htm.

10. I explore some of the "limits" cultural studies has imposed on its own interrogation of the idea of politics in *Culture in Bits: The Monstrous Future of Theory* (New York: Continuum, 2002).

11. For more on the issue of authority and legitimacy in digital publishing see my article "Digitise This," *The Review of Education, Pedagogy, and Cultural Studies* 26.1 (January–March 2004).

12. Steven Harnad, "For Whom the Gate Tolls? How and Why to Free the Refereed Research Literature Online Through Author/Institution Self-Archiving, Now." (2001), http://www.ecs.soton.ac.uk/~harnad/Tp/resolution.htm. The references to Harnad that follow are all to this text.

13. Jacques Derrida, *Adieu: To Emmanuel Levinas* (Stanford, Calif.: Stanford University Press, 1999); *Of Hospitality* (Stanford, Calif.: Stanford University Press, 2000), 147.

14. For more on the "golden" and "green" roads to open access, see Jean-Claude Guédon, "The 'Green' and the 'Gold' Roads to Open Access: The Case for Mixing and Matching," *Serials Review*, 30.4 (2004).

15. See Lev Manovich, "Database as a Symbolic Form" (1998), http://www.manovich.net/docs/database.rtf; revised and reprinted in his *The Language of New Media* (Cambridge, Mass.: MIT Press, 2001). For more on codework, see Katherine Hayles, "Deeper into the Machine: The Future of Electronic Literature." *Culture Machine* 5 (2003), http://culturemachine.tees.ac.uk/Cmach/Backissues/j005/Articles/Hayles/NHayles.htm

16. Andy Miah, "(e)text: Error . . . 404 Not Found! Or The Disappearance of History," *Culture Machine* 5 (2003), http://culturemachine.tees.ac.uk/Cmach/Backissues/j005/Articles/AMiah.htm.

17. Jean-Claude Guédon (with the collaboration of Guylaine Beaudry for the section on SGML), "Meta-Surfaces or Ends and Means to grow a viable electronic scholarly journal," *Surfaces* (1996), http://pum12.pum.umontreal.ca/revues/surfaces/meta-surfaces.html#AII.

18. Jacques Derrida, "Remarks on Deconstruction and Pragmatism," in *Deconstruction and Pragmatism*, edited by Chantal Mouffe (London: Routledge, 1996), 86.

19. Ibid., 84.

20. Bernard Stiegler, "The Discrete Image," in Jacques Derrida and Bernard Stiegler, *Echographies of Television: Filmed Interviews* (London: Polity, 2002).

21. Geoffrey Bennington, "Postal Politics and the Institution of the Nation," in *Nation and Narration*, edited by Homi K. Bhabha (London and New York: Routledge, 1990), 132.

22. Derrida, "Remarks on Deconstruction," 84.

23. Adrian Johns, *The Nature of the Book: Print and Knowledge in the Making* (Chicago: University of Chicago Press, 1998), 31–32.

24. Jacques Derrida, "Signature Event Context," in *Margins of Philosophy* (London: Harvester Wheatsheaf, 1982), 315, 318.

25. Samuel Weber, "It," *Glyph*, 4 (1978). Further page references are given in parenthesis in the body of the text.

26. Weber, "The Future of the Humanities."

27. This is the logic that links repetition to alterity and that distinguishes iterability from mere repetition (Derrida, "Signature Event Context").

28. See Weber, "The Future Campus." Indeed, lest my shift to the topic of cognition in this "node" seem a little strange, it is worth noting that, for Weber, "insofar as the institutional role of the humanities is inseparable from the university, it must also be considered in relation to an element it has often tended, deliberately or not, to exclude from its discourse: *cognition*." (Weber, *Institution and Interpretation*, 135.)

29. Weber, *Institution and Interpretation*, xvi, xix.

30. Weber, "It," 7.

31. Weber, "The Future Campus."

32. Weber, *Institution and Interpretation*, 27.

33. Ibid., 27, 30.

34. Weber, "The Future of the Humanities."

35. Weber, *Institution and Interpretation*, 11.

36. Weber, "The Future of the Humanities."

37. Weber, *Institution and Interpretation*, 149.

CHAPTER 6

Ambivalence: Media, Technics, Gender

Marc Redfield

1. Jacques Derrida, "Above All, No Journalists!" in *Religion and Media*, edited by Hent de Vries and Samuel Weber, translated by Samuel Weber (Stanford, Calif.: Stanford University Press, 2001), 58. Derrida adds:

> There are of course phenomena of mediatization in all religions, but there is a trait that is absolutely singular in the power and structure of Christian mediatization, in what I have proposed calling 'globalatinization'. . . . If you go to the United States (the reference to America here is fundamental) and if you watch religious programs on television, you will of course remark that there are also Jewish, Moslem, and other programs. . . . However, the non-Christian programs consist in filming a speech, pedagogy, or discussions, but never events.

During a Christian mass, by contrast, the thing itself, the event takes place in front of the camera: communion, the coming of real presence, the Eucharist in a certain sense, even the miracle (miracles are produced on American television)—the thing actually takes place 'live' *as* a religious event, *as* a sacred event. (ibid.)

For a fine summary of and contribution to recent work on media and religion, see Hent de Vries, "In Media Res," in *Religion and Media*, 3–42.

2. Building on Benedict Anderson's great insight into the role of media in the origin of nationalism, I discuss the mutual entanglements of nationalism, technics, and aesthetics in my *Politics of Aesthetics: Nationalism, Gender, Romanticism* (Stanford, Calif.: Stanford University Press, 2003). For Anderson's classic argument, see Benedict Anderson, *Imagined Communities: Reflections on the Origin and Spread of Nationalism* (London: Verso, 1991 [1983]).

3. Samuel Weber, *Mass Mediauras: Form, Media, Technics* (Stanford, Calif.: Stanford University Press, 1996), 123. Subsequent references to this work will be given parenthetically in the body of the text.

4. Samuel Weber, "Wartime," in *Violence, Identity, and Self-Determination*, edited by Hent de Vries and Samuel Weber (Stanford, Calif.: Stanford University Press, 1997), 94. Subsequent references to this work will be given parenthetically in the body of the text.

5. See above all Weber's essay "Ambivalence: The Humanities and the Study of Literature," in *Institution and Interpretation*, expanded edition. (Stanford, Calif.: Stanford University Press, 2001).

6. For the classic texts under discussion, see Martin Heidegger, "Die Zeit des Weltbildes," in *Holzwege* (Frankfurt am Main: Klostermann, 1963), translated by William Lovitt as "The Age of the World Picture," in *The Question Concerning Technology and Other Essays* (New York: Harper and Row, 1977); Walter Benjamin, "Das Kunstwerk im Zeitalter seiner technischen Reproduzierbarkeit," in *Gesammelte Schriften*, I/2, edited by Rolf Tiedemann and Hermann Schweppenhäuser (Frankfurt am Main: Suhrkamp, 1980), translated by Harry Zohn as "The Work of Art in the Age of Mechanical Reproduction," in *Illuminations* (New York: Schocken Books, 1968).

7. See Walter Benjamin, "Über einige Motive bei Baudelaire," *Gesammelte Schriften* I/2, translated as "On Some Motifs in Baudelaire" in *Illuminations*.

8. In Elissa Marder's usefully precise translation: "The deafening street around me was screaming. / Long, slim, in deep mourning, majestic grief, / A woman passed, raising with a delicate hand, / The trim and hem of the flounces of her gown; // Graceful and noble, with her statue's leg. / And I drank, frozen like a madman, / In her eye, livid sky where the storm breeds, / The softness that fascinates and the pleasure that kills. // A flash . . . then night!—O fleeting beauty / Whose look made me suddenly be reborn / Shall

I not see you again but in eternity? // Elsewhere, far from here! Too late! Never, perhaps! / I know not where you flee, you don't know where I go, / You, whom I would have loved, you who knew it was so." As given in Elissa Marder, *Dead Time: Temporal Disorders in the Wake of Modernity (Baudelaire and Flaubert)* (Stanford, Calif.: Stanford University Press, 2001).

9. On fetishism and *Schein*, see my *Phantom Formations: Aesthetic Ideology and the Bildungsroman* (Ithaca, N.Y.: Cornell University Press, 1996), 171–200.

10. Samuel Weber, "Religion, Repetition, Media," in *Religion and Media*, 43–55 (here 51). Subsequent references to this work will be given parenthetically in the body of the text, by page number.

11. Soren Kierkegaard, *Repetition*, translated by Howard V. Hong and Edna H. Hong (Princeton, N.J.: Princeton University Press, 1983), 166–67.

12. Samuel Weber, *Unwrapping Balzac: A Reading of La Peau de Chagrin* (Toronto: University of Toronto Press, 1979). Subsequent references to this work will be given parenthetically in the body of the text. I presume that *Unwrapping Balzac* is Weber's earliest written text, since it is based on the dissertation he defended at Cornell in 1971. Because this text bears close superficial resemblances to Roland Barthes's *S/Z* (1970) but contains no reference to it, Weber appends an illuminating if necessarily rather structurally awkward "Postface" to the book: "When *S/Z* first appeared in 1970, *Unwrapping Balzac* had already been written" (163). Perhaps the present endnote, dedicated as it is to the recollection of awkward contingencies, is the proper place to say that to my regret I have not been able to obtain and examine Weber's original German versions of *Rückkehr zu Freud* (1978) and *Freud-Legende* (1979), and have had to work from the revised and translated versions, as given below.

13. Samuel Weber, *Return to Freud: Jacques Lacan's Dislocation of Psychoanalysis* (Cambridge: Cambridge University Press, 1991), 4. (Subsequent references to this work will be given parenthetically in the body of the text.) Thus, for instance, Weber's discussion of Lacan's famous splitting and restaging of the Saussurian signifier as the signifier "Hommes–Dames" over the signified as two identical doors pays almost no attention to the fact that the signifier has imposed a law of gender: see *Return to Freud*, 41–45.

14. Samuel Weber, *The Legend of Freud* (Minneapolis: University of Minnesota Press, 1982), 82. Subsequent references to this work will be given parenthetically in the body of the text.

15. I give here a translation based on the Greek text of the *Symposium* edited by Sir Kenneth Dover (Cambridge: Cambridge University Press, 1980); subsequent references to Plato's *Symposium* are to this edition, and are given by Stephanus number.

16. Marshall McLuhan, *The Mechanical Bride* (New York: Vanguard Press, 1951). It may be noted more generally that McLuhan's work formulates a

remarkable number of the themes that circulate in contemporary discussions of media and postmodernity. Long before Benedict Anderson, McLuhan was championing the idea that the printing press and above all the newspaper created the possibility of nationalism. He was one of the early influential writers on the paramount role of information in the new economy; and his writing on language as a general technology and alphabetic script as a particular version of this technology still well repays reading, burdened though it is with unexamined tropes related to what I shall discuss in a moment as the figure of prosthesis ("Language extends and amplifies man, but it also divides his faculties" [*Understanding Media: The Extensions of Man* (New York: Signet Classics, 1964), 83]). The connection between media and religion also surfaces frequently in his work, though it is never subjected to much analysis ("Today computers hold out the promise of a means of instant translation of any code or language into any other code or language. The computer, in short, promises by technology a Pentecostal condition of universal understanding and unity" [*Understanding Media*, 84]). McLuhan, in short, deserves to be read attentively, both because he has shrewd things to say and because he needs, precisely, to be *read*: he both registers and evades (particularly by way of his famous trope of the "global village") the fragmenting power of mediation. I note below his tendency to imagine a unified body prior to technology; and this naturalizing tendency possibly links up to the ethnocentrism and racism that occasionally surface in his writing (e.g.: "The German defeat had thrust them back from visual obsession into brooding upon the resonating Africa within. The tribal past has never ceased to be a reality for the German psyche" [*Understanding Media*, 262]).

17. McLuhan, *Understanding Media*, 55.

18. And though such technicity cannot be reduced to the closed loops of cybernetics, McLuhan's frequent references to Wiener and the construction of "mechanical brains" may also be read as a symptom of this instability.

19. One finds similar rhetorical yokings of femininity with popular culture, media, and the like throughout the archives of modernity. Since I have been citing Weber's work on Balzac in previous pages, let me recall a sentence he quotes from Balzac's *Monographie de la presse parisienne* (Paris: Pauvert, 1965; written in 1842): "La presse, comme la femme, est admirable et sublime quand elle avance un mensonge, elle vous lâche pas qu'elle ne vous ait forcé d'y croire; et elle déploie les plus grands qualités dans cette lutte où le public, aussi bête qu'un mari, succombe toujours" (210–11, as cited in Weber, *Unwrapping Balzac*, 53). The example should serve to suggest that the demonizing feminization of media technology is not a pathology restricted to postwar American consumer culture. For a powerful study of the figure of woman in relation to modern technics and the writing of Baudelaire and Flaubert, see Marder, *Dead*

Time. For a study linking femininity with commodity consumption, see, among others, Rita Felski, *The Gender of Modernity* (Cambridge, Mass.: Harvard University Press, 1995).

20. Throughout McLuhan's writing, technology is represented as a "blow" suffered, a blow that amputates and anaesthetizes (*Understanding Media*, 71, passim).

21. Mark Seltzer, *Bodies and Machines* (New York: Routledge, 1992), 28–29, my italics. Seltzer's delineation of naturalism maps nicely onto a range of texts in the American tradition from the early to the late twentieth century; and from this perspective, a text well worth reading in conjunction with *The Mechanical Bride* would be Thomas Pynchon's *V* (New York: Harper and Row [Perennial Library], 1990 [1961]). Pynchon, incidentally, probably knew McLuhan's book (he certainly knew McLuhan's later work on media by the time he wrote *The Crying of Lot 49* (New York: Harper and Row [Perennial Library], 1986 [1966]); for an argument that he had probably read *The Mechanical Bride* by the late 1950s, see David Seed, *The Fictional Labyrinths of Thomas Pynchon* (Iowa City: University of Iowa Press, 1988). Direct influence, however, in the end has little to do with the remarkably similar bouquet of themes and anxieties these texts exhibit; one is surely better off thinking of a "logic of naturalism" informing their production. Pynchon's novel, as is well known, turns around the slant-appearances of a mysterious, possibly fictional woman known as "V.," who grows more and more inanimate—more burdened with prostheses; more of a literal "mechanical bride"—as the narrative evolves. The resonances between McLuhan's and Pynchon's texts are far richer than any brief summary can suggest. There is a common range of reference—McLuhan, like the narrator of *V.*, will refer frequently to the famous interpretation of the dynamo as "the twentieth-century equivalent of the twelfth-century 'cult of the Virgin'" in *The Education of Henry Adams* (*Mechanical Bride*, 96). And both texts are fascinated by a certain reduction-to-zero figured by the fetishistic zeroing-in of the "V" itself, which some time ago I tried to analyze as a persistent motif in Pynchon's fiction. See Marc Redfield, "Pynchon's Postmodern Sublime," *PMLA* 104 (1989): 152–62. Compare McLuhan: "What would be found as one stripped away these layers, each marked with the pattern of sex, technology, and death? Exactly nothing" (*Mechanical Bride*, 13). These "abstract and zero-degree white zones," Seltzer suggests, in the course of an analysis of Jack London's fiction, capture "the unnaturalness of Nature in naturalism" (167), which in turn leads to the "replacement of the mother by the machine" in naturalist fantasizing (168). The entropic, zero degree behind the eroticizing veil is one of the many legacies of the naturalist tradition that both McLuhan and Pynchon inherit, invest in, and squander.

It may also be noted that a proliferation of "V"s always threatens to broach the borders of Pynchon's text, and that in the present context one might point to the valley, the "cône renversé" to which Raphael de Valentin retreats in *La peau de chagrin* (see Weber's discussion, *Unwrapping Balzac*, 139–44). "The 'inverted cone' configures the imaginary form—an inverted triangle—of Raphael's translation of the pact inscribed in the skin, as well as reflecting the 'V' and 'val' contained in his name, 'Valentin'" (143). On the play of the signifier in *V.*, see, in addition to my own article cited above, Alec McHoul and David Wills, *Writing Pynchon: Strategies in Fictional Analysis* (Urbana: University of Illinois Press, 1990).

22. Jacques Derrida, "Faith and Knowledge: The Two Sources of 'Religion' at the Limits of Reason Alone," translated by Samuel Weber, in *Religion*, edited by Jacques Derrida and Gianni Vattimo (Stanford, Calif.: Stanford University Press, 1998), 1–78.

CHAPTER 7

Modernism and the Medium: On Greenberg and Weber

Andrew McNamara

1. Immanuel Kant, *Critique of Judgment*, translated by Werner S. Pluhar (Indianapolis: Hackett, 1987), § 49, 182.

2. Thomas Crow, *The Rise of the Sixties: American and European Art in the Era of Dissent* (New York: Abrams, 1996), 60.

3. Samuel Weber, "The Future of the University: The Cutting Edge," in *Ideas of the University*, edited by Terry Smith (Sydney: Power Publications, 1996), 65.

4. Samuel Weber, "Upsetting the Setup: Remarks on Heidegger's 'Questing After Technics,'" in *Mass Mediauras: Form, Technics, Media*, edited by Alan Cholodenko (Sydney: Power Publications, 1996), 73.

5. In fact, Barrett ultimately views Pollock's *Blue Poles* as the cultural "metonym for the narratives of Whitlamism in general"; indeed, for Barrett the work is the marker of the decline of both the Whitlam government and of Pollock's creative powers. See Lindsay Barrett, *The Prime Minister's Christmas Card: Blue Poles and Cultural Politics in the Whitlam Era* (Sydney: Power Publications, 2001), 238.

6. Mark Rothko, quoted by Serge Guilbaut, "The New Adventures of the Avant-Garde in America," in *Pollock and After: The Critical Debate*, edited by Francis Frascina (London: Harper and Row, 1985), 161; cited in Barrett, *The Prime Minister's Christmas Card*, 85.

7. Barrett references congressional debates of the time, notably Republican George Dondero's speech "Modern Art Shackled to Communism," but he quotes Guilbaut to reinforce his ultimate point: "the values represented in the

pictorial work were especially cherished during the Cold War (the notion of individualism and risk being essential to the artist to achieve complete freedom of expression). . . . Risk . . . was what distinguished a free society from a totalitarian one." Cited by Barrett, *The Prime Minister's Christmas Card*, 86.

8. Clement Greenberg, "Towards a Newer Laocoon" (1940), in *Collected Essays and Criticism*, edited by John O'Brian (Chicago: University of Chicago Press, 1986), 1:32.

9. Clement Greenberg, "Avant-Garde and Kitsch" (1939), in *Collected Essays and Criticism*, 1:6.

10. Many decades later, Lyotard returned to the theme of kitsch in order to dissociate the "postmodern" from "eclecticism"—"the degree zero of contemporary general culture" (76)—and to align it instead with "part of the modern" (79). To quote Lyotard: "By becoming kitsch, art panders to the confusion which reigns in the 'taste' of the patrons. Artists, gallery owners, critics, and public wallow together in the 'anything goes,' and the epoch is one of slackening." This directly echoes Greenberg's comments about "motionless Alexandrianism." "But this realism of the 'anything goes,'" Lyotard continues, "is in fact that of money; in the absence of aesthetic criteria, it remains possible and useful to assess the value of works of art according to the profits they yield. Such realism accommodates all tendencies, just as capital accommodates all 'needs,' providing that the tendencies and needs have purchasing power. As for taste, there is no need to be delicate when one speculates or entertains oneself" (76); Jean-François Lyotard, "Answering the Question: What is Postmodernism?" In *The Postmodern Condition: A Report on Knowledge*, translated by Régis Durand (Minneapolis: University of Minnesota Press, 1984).

11. Laurence A. Rickels and Samuel Weber, "Theory on TV: 'After-Thoughts,'" in *Religion and Media*, edited by Hent deVries and Samuel Weber (Stanford, Calif.: Stanford University Press, 2001).

12. Greenberg, "Avant-Garde and Kitsch," 12, 14, 16.

13. Avant-gardism, Greenberg argues, amounts to "a progressive surrender to the resistance of its medium," and, in painting, a radical espousal of "the flat picture plane" over "realistic perspective space;" Greenberg, "Towards a Newer Laocoon," *Collected Essays and Criticism*, 1:34.

14. Greenberg, "Avant-Garde and Kitsch," 8–9.

15. Rosalind Krauss, *"A Voyage on the North Sea": Art in the Age of the Post-Medium Condition* (New York: Thames and Hudson, 2000), 6–7. With the advent of a practice like that of the Belgian artist Marcel Broodthaers, specificity assumes a new role. Krauss asserts that installation scatters into a "multiplicity of sites—each of them now termed 'specific,'" except that now, twenty-five years later, "the international spread of the mixed-media installation has

become ubiquitous"; 15, 20. A medium is better understood as "self–differ-ing," "aggregative" ("a matter of interlocking supports" and layered conven-tions") (44), or "as a layering of conventions never simply collapsed into the physicality of their support" (53).

16. Rosalind E. Krauss, "Grids," in *The Originality of the Avant-Garde and Other Modernist Myths* (Cambridge, Mass.: MIT Press, 1987), 9.

17. Thierry De Duve, "The Readymade and the Tube of Paint," *Artforum* (May 1986): 111.

18. Rickels and Weber, "Theory on TV: 'After-Thoughts,'" in *Religion and Media*, 98–99.

19. Samuel Weber, "Television: Set and Screen," in *Mass Mediauras: Form, Technics, Media*, edited by Alan Cholodenko (Sydney: Power Publications, 1996), 120.

20. The notion of a "screen" works in three different ways as far as televi-sion is concerned, Weber argues: one, "a screen which allows distant vision to be watched"; two, which screens "in the sense of selecting or filtering" what is watched; and, third, a screen "between the viewer and the viewed" (ibid., 123).

21. Thierry De Duve, *Clement Greenberg Between the Lines* (Paris: Éditions Dis Voir, 1996), 45–46, 53. It is interesting, but also telling, for the intrigu-ingly convoluted strategy it necessitates, that Lyotard adopts similar argumen-tation in explicating and defending the "postmodern." After endorsing de Duve's proposition that the "modern aesthetic question" is "what is art" (or "what can be said to be art"), rather than "what is beautiful," Lyotard then goes on to dismiss as "kitsch" the idea that the postmodern amounts to an "anything goes" style of relativism. Kitsch therefore can be multiple and het-erogeneous; what is crucial in all instances outlined here is that it fulfils itself in a subsuming and consuming identification. See Jean-François Lyotard, "Answering the Question: What Is Postmodernism?" in *The Postmodern Con-dition: A Report on Knowledge*, translated by Régis Durand (Minnesota: Univer-sity of Minnesota Press, 1984), 75–76.

22. De Duve writes that by falling back upon the expression "stand for," Clark "refers to representation in the sole sense of replacement, of deputa-tion," and this postulate leads directly to the issue of "legitimacy." But if it is true that the avant-garde poses one lack for another, de Duve continues, "Clark cannot keep his concept of representation-that-doesn't-dare-speak-its-name from taking on its traditional sense of image and figuration" and this flies in the face of modernism's very challenge: "if there is one thing that has been aggressively denied, attacked, destroyed, and flattened by modernism in all the arts, it is representation" (ibid, 56–57). De Duve goes on to declare that he sides with Clark in regard to the formulation of "the question of

address in its collective dimension"; it is just that for him the "notion of *convention*" is pivotal rather than representation and its "entire *episteme*" (ibid. 61).

23. Stephen Melville focuses on this point, too, but somewhat differently: "The crux for de Duve is that what Greenberg puts as the 'opacity' or 'resistance' of the medium is construable as a division in the work's destination—its address toward the past, its reception in the future." Melville, "Kant After Greenberg," *Journal of Aesthetics and Art Criticism*, 56:1 (Winter 1998): 70.

24. One could extend this to say that the term *postmodernism* as it was used in the visual arts was also thoroughly determined by Greenberg's definition of modernism.

25. Weber, "The Future of the University: The Cutting Edge," in *Ideas of the University*, 65.

26. Greenberg, "Towards a Newer Laocoon," 34. Melville, like de Duve, reads this as a key point in considering Greenberg's work ("Kant After Greenberg," 67).

27. Greenberg, "Towards a Newer Laocoon," 32.

28. Many years later, in his 1960 essay, "Modernist Painting," Greenberg develops this argument further by shifting his claims from a question of (medium) distinctiveness to the securing of a greater historical overview. Uncovering the immediately sensuous reveals the precedence of past masters for the first time from a unique perspective: Modernism in dispensing with the indispensable allows a viewer to appreciate that "though the past did appreciate these masters justly, it often gave wrong or irrelevant reasons for doing so." See Greenberg, "Modernist Painting" (1960), in *Collected Essays and Criticism*, 4:92. In an interview contained in de Duve's book, Greenberg notes that his rhetoric in this essay "left something to be desired," though his chief concern is to counter arguments that he strove to "legislate" taste; cited in de Duve, *Clement Greenberg Between the Lines*, 150.

29. Greenberg, "Avant-Garde and Kitsch," 15.

30. De Duve, *Greenberg Between the Lines*, 86.

31. Greenberg, "Modernist Painting," *Collected Essays*, 4:90. It is intriguing to compare this version of Kant with that cited by Thomas Crow at the outset concerning "an expressive communication" and a "contemplative spectator" because these readings of Kant coexist to produce a rather incongruous explanation of modern art.

32. De Duve, *Greenberg Between the Lines*, 14.

33. Innovation for innovation's sake can also be like "kitsch" (which, as we can see, becomes an enormously expansive category)—that is, formulaic and mechanical. This is the prime lesson of the 1960s, with its rapid succession of "isms." "Today everybody innovates. Deliberately, methodically. And the innovations are deliberately and methodically made startling. Only it turns out

not to be true that all startling art is necessarily innovative or new art. This is what the '60s have finally revealed." Greenberg, "Avant-Garde Attitudes: New Art in the Sixties," (1969), *Collected Essays and Criticism*, 4:300. "Kitsch" then—as the name for all that is formulaic and mechanical—prevails everywhere—in theory and in practice; for a fascinating study of the anxieties provoked by the perceived pervasiveness of the "mechanical," see Catherine Liu, *Copying Machines: Taking Notes for the Automaton* (Minneapolis: University of Minnesota Press, 2000).

34. The rhetoric of virility and emasculation is provided by Greenberg's biographer, Florence Rubenfeld, concerning the post-Sixties situation: "the energy powering the glory days of American postwar art ran out. . . . Postsixties art is less virile and more conceptual" (304). One ponders whether this waning is attributed to art and the artists or to the dissipation of Greenberg himself because, coincidentally, this is the period Rubenfeld refers to as Greenberg's "years of debauchery" (305). See Florence Rubenfeld, *Clement Greenberg: A Life* (University of Minnesota Press: Minneapolis, 1997). For another study of Greenberg, more of an intellectual biography, see Sheila Christofides, "The Intransigent Critic: reconsidering the reasons for Clement Greenberg's formalist stance from the early 1930s to the early 1970s" (Ph.D. diss., College of Fine Arts, University of New South Wales, 2004).

35. Krauss, *"A Voyage on the North Sea,"* 46.

36. For an account that both examines installation as a more viable practice and considers it in relation to Samuel Weber's work, see Catherine Liu, "Cornering the Set-Up," in *Kunsthalle Basel/Liz Larner*, ed. Peter Pakesch, Madeline Schuppli, and Gabrielle Léwy (Basel: Schwabe, 1997).

37. For example, in 1946 Greenberg asserted, "the School of Paris remains . . . the creative fountainhead of modern art." See Rubenfeld, *Clement Greenberg: A Life*, 95. In 1948, he was more explicit, arguing that "Matisse's hot color" and "Picasso's calligraphy" constituted the two major pinnacles of modernist visual art; they were only then being challenged by the expansive canvases issuing from Greenwich Village that outstripped the parameters of easel painting. Clement Greenberg, "The Situation at the Moment" (1948), in *Collected Essays and Criticism*, edited by John O'Brian (Chicago: University of Chicago Press, 1986), 2:215.

38. Kant, *Critique of Judgment*, trans. Pluhar, § 31, 143–44.

39. Samuel Weber, "Ambivalence: The Humanities and the Study of Literature," in *Institution and Interpretation* (Minneapolis: University of Minnesota Press, 1987), 141.

40. Greenberg's essay, "Modernist Painting," presents the clearest evidence of him outlining a determinate history of art (from the Renaissance to date), though it was written against a background in which his own account

seemed to be unraveling. De Duve's incisive criticism of his postulation of the "fairly constant distinction" also mitigates Greenberg's assertions that he never proscribed.

41. Samuel Weber, "The Foundering of Aesthetics: Thoughts on the Current State of Comparative Literature," in *The Comparative Perspective on Literature: Approaches to Theory and Practice*, edited by Clayton Koelb and Susan Noakes (Ithaca, N.Y.: Cornell University Press, 1998), 65.

42. Thierry De Duve, "The Readymade and the Tube of Paint," *Artforum*, May 1986, 121.

43. Weber, "The Foundering of Aesthetics," 69.

44. "The ego becomes more and more unassuming and modest, and the object more and more sublime and precious, until at last it gets possession of the entire self-love of the ego." Sigmund Freud, "Group Psychology and the Analysis of the Ego," in *The Penguin Freud Library*, translated by James Strachey (New York: Penguin, 1991), 2:142–43.

45. Immanuel Kant, *Critique of Judgment*, translated by Werner S. Pluhar (Indianapolis: Hackett, 1987), § 60, 231.

46. Weber, "Ambivalence: The Humanities and the Study of Literature," 143–44. Following references to this text occur in brackets.

47. Weber notes that the term for sociability, *Geselligkeit*, is substituted after the first edition for *Glückseligkeit*, "happiness" or "bliss" (ibid., 144). In addition, I believe this emphasis upon arresting meaning, while ambivalent, points to an emphasis that is not commonly associated with deconstruction— see, for example, de Duve's characterization of it cited above.

48. Samuel Weber, "Once and for All," *Grey Room* 20 (Summer 2005): 110.

49. Rickels and Weber, "Theory on TV," *Religion and Media*, 111.

50. Weber credits this attention to singularity to Jacques Derrida: "One of the most compelling, difficult and challenging legacies left by the writings of Jacques Derrida consists in the obligation of respecting the singularity of the situation in which one finds oneself." "Once and for All," *Grey Room*, 106. It is not my intention here to spark a debate about attribution, except to point out that it is Weber's rigorous attention to such a conception of singularity and both its challenges to and sources within traditional aesthetic inquiry that distinguish his contribution. For an extended analysis of singularity and the medium, see Weber, *Theatricality as Medium* (New York: Fordham University Press, 2004).

51. Hélène Cixous, *Readings: The Poetics of Blanchot, Joyce, Kafka, Kliest, Lispector, and Tsvetayeva*, translated by Verena Andermatt Conley (Minneapolis: University of Minnesota Press, 1991), 93.

52. Weber, "The Future of the University: The Cutting Edge," 46.

53. Weber, "Mass Mediauras, or: Art, Aura and Media in the Work of Walter Benjamin," in *Mass Mediauras*, 97.

CHAPTER 8
It Walks: The Ambulatory Uncanny
Susan Bernstein

1. This phrase refers to Weber's text "Criticism Underway: Walter Benjamin's *Romantic Concept of Criticism*," in which he focuses on Benjamin's understanding of criticism not as "self-identical critical reflection, but [in] a practice of reading." In *Romantic Revolutions: Criticism and Theory*, edited by Kenneth R. Johnston et al. (Bloomington and Indianapolis: Indiana University Press, 1990), 315.

2. Samuel Weber, "The Sideshow, or: Remarks on a Canny Moment," *MLN* 88 (1973): 1102–33, reprinted in *The Legend of Freud* (Stanford, Calif.: Stanford University Press, 2000).

3. Weber notes specifically Hélène Cixous, "Fiction and Its Fantoms: A Reading of Freud's *Das Unheimliche*," *New Literary History* 7 (Spring 1976): 525–48.

4. Landmark texts include Neil Hertz, "Freud and the Sandman," in *The End of the Line: Essays in Psychoanalysis and the Sublime* (New York: Columbia University Press, 1985), 97–121; Sarah Kofman, *Freud and Fiction*, translated by Sarah Wykes (Cambridge: Polity Press, 1991); and Jacques Derrida, *Disseminations*, translated by Barbara Johnson (London: Athlone, 1981).

5. Anthony Vidler's *The Architectural Uncanny: Essays in the Modern Unhomely* (Cambridge, Mass.: MIT Press, 1994) is an allusive survey of the uncanny as a phenomenon of modern alienation. Aptly analyzing a wide range of texts, he focuses on a specifically modern dialectic alienation between inside and outside underscored by the role of architecture. See also Mark Wigley, *The Architecture of Deconstruction: Derrida's Haunt* (Cambridge, Mass.: MIT Press, 1993). Wigley follows Heidegger in arguing that "the process of alienation is understood to be an ancient one that is only becoming manifest with modernity" (98). Nicholas Royle's recent *The Uncanny* (Manchester: Manchester University Press, 2003) provides encyclopedic coverage of the topic, including many astute analyses and a thorough bibliography. The devotion of a book-length study to the uncanny, however, cannot help but position it as a theme and an object. Yet the uncanny undermines the identity of any member of a comparison and thus leads to ultimately illegible distortions and disaggregations. For example, Avital Ronell writes: "This . . . is your habitation in the world, this your *unheimlich* familiarity prior to any opposition of the 'subject' and 'object,' or 'self' and 'other.'" *The Telephone Book* (Lincoln: University of Nebraska Press, 1989), 69. Maria Tatar has contributed to the discussion of Hoffmann and the uncanny in "E. T. A. Hoffmann's 'Der Sandmann':

Reflections and Romantic Irony," *MLN* 95 (1980), 585–608. The latter also provides an excellent summary of prior secondary literature; see also Tatar's "The Houses of Fiction: Toward a Definition of the Uncanny," *Comparative Literature* 33.2 (Spring 1981): 167–82. Another useful source is the introductory essay in *Ghosts: Deconstruction, Psychoanalysis, History*, ed. Peter Buse and Andrew Stott (London: Macmillan, 1999). This gives a good overview of the importance of the destabilizing effect of the uncanny in the three fields it names, and is published along with a wide variety of more specialized essays.

6. Sigmund Freud, "Das Unheimliche," *Gesammelte Werke* (Frankfurt am Main: Fischer Taschenbuchverlag, 1999), 12:235; *Standard Edition of the Complete Psychological Works*, ed. James Strachey (London: Hogarth Press), 17:224.

7. Martin Heidegger, *Wegmarken* (Frankfurt am Main: Vittorio Klostermann, 1978), 404.

8. Martin Heidegger, *Pathmarks*, edited by William McNeill (Cambridge: Cambridge University Press, 1998), 310.

9. Friedrich Wilhelm Josef von Schelling, *Sämmtliche Werke* 2:2, 649 (1857).

10. Weber uses the word "chiaroscuro" to talk about the movements of concealing/revealing pertinent to Heidegger. The moment of "Mystery" indicated here is reminiscent of Shelley's poem, "Lift not the painted veil"—a veil that, like the poetic narrative that presents it, conceals the nothing that it does not reveal.

11. In both "Zur Seinsfrage" and "Einführung in die Metaphysik," the terms *aufbrechen* and *Aufbruch* describe the "irrupting" or breaking open of Being. Both Grimm and Wahrig point to the use of this word to describe the opening up of a wound that begins to bleed anew. It also means "to leave," with military connotations: to break camp, to mobilize, to get going. Weber mentions the military overtones of *Musterung*, "the marshaling of forces, conscription, constraint and conflict" (210), and of Heidegger's term *ausrücken*, "to move out, as an army would do," but also "to back out" (26–27).

The primary meaning of *aufbrechen* is given as "to break open," as of a box, castle or door; and additionally, to break open the earth in plowing; or the breaking out, the opening, of plant buds. It is also no coincidence that Heidegger, like Schelling, associates the uncanny with the mystery of the beginning, a beginning that cannot itself "appear" or become manifest. In "Einführung in die Metaphysik" he writes: "Der Anfang ist das Unheimlichste und Gewaltigste. Was nachkommt, ist nicht Entwicklung, sondern Verflachung als bloße Verbreitung, ist Nichtinnehaltenkönnens des Anfangs, ist Verharmlosung und Übertreibung des Anfangs zur Mißgestalt des Großen. . . . Die Unerklärbarkeit dieses Anfangs ist kein Mangel und kein Versagen unserer Erkenntnis der Geschichte. Im Verstehen des Geheimnischarakters dieses Anfangs liegt vielmehr die Echtheit und Größe des geschichtlichen Erkennens. Wissen von einer Ur-geschichte ist nicht Aufstöbern des Primitiven und Sammeln von Knochen. Es ist weder halbe noch ganze Naturwissenschaft, sondern, wenn es überhaupt etwas ist, Mythologie" (119).

12. Freud, "Das Unheimliche," 12:249.

13. Edgar Allan Poe, *Complete Tales and Poems* (New York: Vintage, 1975), 475. Poe does not correct the gender of the pronoun, thus presaging the collapse of the story and "the man." In this edition, the *a* is without an umlaut as well.

14. In terms of what Derrida first called "logocentrism," presence asserts the priority of meaning over the history of its coming to be. Meaning shines forth in presence and is present to the subject; writing is instrumentalized and located at the exterior of meaning. At least, this is how it "should" be. One could interpret the history of western metaphysics as one long attempt to enforce this hierarchical model. Already in Plato, as is well known, the quarrel between philosophy and literature displays the threat of the letter; the display of its autonomy and its contribution to the production of meaning is noxious and dangerous and must be put down. Derrida's critique of logocentrism as the interpretation of the meaning of meaning (as well as Being) as presence (and writing as absence) and Heidegger's critique of the model of adequation converge in the uncanny.

15. Tzvetan Todorov, *The Fantastic: A Structural Approach to a Literary Genre*, trans. Richard Howard (Ithaca, N.Y.: Cornell University Press, 1975), 3. While it is easy to make a straw man of Todorov, his procedure here is representative of many types of literary criticism.

16. Tzvetan Todorov, *Introduction à la Littérature Fantastique* (Paris: Editions du Seuil, 1970), 30.

17. In "Freud and the Sandman," Neil Hertz points out, "The feeling of the uncanny would seem to be generated by being reminded of the repetition compulsion, not by being reminded of whatever it is that is repeated. The becoming aware of the process is felt as eerie, not the becoming aware of some particular item" (101). In this sense, the origin of the uncanny is always receding, since it occurs as a recollection that is part of the structure of repetition. Hertz draws attention to Freud's sense of figurative language as what "gives color" to impulses and thus allows them to appear. His essay proposes a

> compound analogy . . . between that-which-is-repeated, coloring matter, and figurative language. All three, I suggested, could be thought of as means of representing processes and energies that might otherwise go unnoticed. But this model seems unsatisfactory and wishful in at least two ways. First, it depends upon the notion of a real preexistent force (call it sheer repetition, the death instinct, or whatever) that is merely rendered more discernable by that-which-is-repeated, or by the lurid colors of the erotic, or by some helpful figure of speech. . . . But we know that the relation between figurative language and

what it figures cannot be adequately grasped in metaphors of vision; and we might well doubt that the forces of repetition can be isolated—even ideally—from that-which-is-repeated. (120–21)

The relationship I am suggested between the uncanny and repetition is rather one of synonymity; the uncanny appears through repetition and vice versa. Philippe Lacoue-Labarthe analyzes the uncanny in terms of the appearance of repetition "itself," that is, of what cannot simply "appear" but is only recognized later. The uncanny is here fundamentally related to rhythm and its action to "la césure du sujet." See *Le Sujet de la Philosophie* (Paris: Aubier-Flammarion, 1979), 283–85.

18. Quoted in Tatar, "E. T. A. Hoffmann's 'Der Sandmann,'" 585.

19. This is why the uncanny plays an important role in Harold Bloom's *Anxiety of Influence*. Royle sees Bloom as central to the discourse of the uncanny in *The Uncanny*. Lacoue-Labarthe brilliantly coarticulates the problems of figuration, mimesis, the desire for originality and the uncanny, drawing on René Girard's notion of mimetic desire, in "Typographie." In *Mimesis desarticulations* (Paris: Aubier-Flammarion, 1975), esp. 224–48.

20. The prominence of walking in the uncanny could be described as a collapse of the figurative into the literal. On the other hand, it could also be read the other way around, as if material or literal elements are doubled by figurative or animated counterparts. Adam Bresnick argues for the latter in focusing on the problem of animation in "The Sandman" in his essay "Prosopoetic Compulsion: Reading the Uncanny in Freud and Hoffmann," *Germanic Review* 71.2 (1996): 114–32. Investigating "the reality of aesthetic experience," Bresnick speaks of a reader where I would note only a shift of diegetic level; likewise what temporarily occupies the position of referent or "reality" simply belongs to another opening discursive frame. The uncanny seems to me to be generated through the passage through and across frames; thus literal and figurative senses can only be pinpointed at relative positions. Bresnick sees the moment of animation as a narcissistic overinvestment—the prosopoetic compulsion. He tends to pathologize psychologically what I would identify rather with a feature of reading in general.

21. Translations of "Der Unheimliche Gast" are mine.

CHAPTER 9
On Risk-Taking in the Psychoanalytic Text:
The Reality-Test
Avital Ronell

1. Pindar, *Victory Songs*, trans. Frank J. Nisetich (Baltimore: Johns Hopkins University Press, 1980), 218. On the Pindaric tradition and the significance of this poem, see William Fitzgerald, *Agonistic Poetry: The Pindaric Mode in*

Pindar, Horace, Hölderlin and the English Ode (Berkeley: University of California Press, 1987), 55 ff.

2. Cited in Page du Bois, *Torture and Truth* (New York: Routledge, 1991), 16.

3. Immanuel Kant, "On the miscarriage of all philosophical trials in theodicy," in *Religion and Rational Theology*, translated and edited by Allen W. Wood and George Di Giovanni (Cambridge: Cambridge University Press, 1996), 24–37; "Über das Mißlingen aller philosophischen Versuche in der Theodizee," in Immanuel Kant, *Werkausgabe XI: Schriften zur Anthropologie, Geschichtsphilosophie, Politik und Pädagogik I* (Frankfurt: Suhrkamp, 1981), 105–24, which begins by affirming tests within tests when stating that "the human being is justified, as rational, in testing all claims, all doctrines which impose respect upon him, before he submits himself to them, so that this respect may be sincere and not feigned" (24).

4. See, in this regard, Weber's discussion of professional phobias in "The Limits of Professionalism," in *Institution and Interpretation* (Minneapolis: University of Minnesota Press, 1987), 30 ff.

5. Ibid.

6. See Weber's *Return to Freud: Jacques Lacan's Dislocation of Psychoanalysis*, translated by Michael Levine (Cambridge: Cambridge University Press), 1991.

7. Sigmund Freud, *Standard Edition of the Complete Works of Sigmund Freud* (London: Hogarth Press and the Institute of Psycho-Analysis, 1953–1974), 7:7.

8. Ibid., 10. Consider also Weber's discussion of the Freudian "Denksystem" in *Freud Legende* (Freiburg: Walter Verlag, 1979).

9. Ibid.

10. See Weber's *The Legend of Freud* (Minneapolis: University of Minnesota Press, 1982), 71.

11. For Karl Popper, Freud is a pseudoscientist to the extent that nothing can disprove his claims. See note 33.

12. Freud, *Standard Edition*, 22:7–30.

13. Ibid., 14:265–66.

14. Adolf Grünbaum, "Retrospective Versus Prospective Testing of Aetiological Hypotheses in Freudian Theory," in *Testing Scientific Theories*, edited by John Earman (Minneapolis: University of Minnesota Press, 1983), 323.

15. Freud, Standard Edition, 14:265–66.

16. Ibid., 265.

17. Grünbaum, "Retrospective Versus Prospective Testing," 321.

18. Ibid., 325.

19. Ibid.

20. Ibid.

21. Ibid., 341.

22. See Weber's *Legend of Freud*, xvii.

23. The heuristic and probative dimension of Freud's work, with special attention to the Rat Man case, is discussed by Adolf Grünbaum in "Retrospective Versus Prospective Testing," 315–49; and by Paul E. Meehl, "Subjectivity in Psychoanalytic Inference: The Nagging Persistence of Wilhelm Fliess's Achensee Question," ibid., 349–411. Grünbaum writes: "The strategy involved in the Rat Man case is essentially the same as a strategy very frequently used in testing physical theories." Glymour himself had pointed out that the major argument of this case is similar to the one underlying Book III of Newton's *Principia*.

24. I analyze these sessions more closely in "The Sujet Suppositaire," in *Finitude's Score: Essays Toward the End of the Millennium* (Lincoln: University of Nebraska Press, 1994), 105–29.

25. Freud, *Standard Edition*, 14:243.

26. Ibid.

27. Ibid., 258.

28. Ibid., 244.

29. Ibid., 23:198.

30. Freud, "Mourning and Melancholia," in *Standard Edition*, 14:244.

31. Ibid., 254.

32. Ibid., 233.

33. That Freud submitted his work to relentless testing hardly needs to be restated, though the testability of his observations has of course been famously contested. For Popper, Freud is a pseudoscientist to the extent that nothing can disprove his claims; even resistance is said to prove the hypothesis, if not the thesis, he puts forward. This tendency of psychoanalysis to find its own truth, to "recognize" itself as Derrida later says, pointing to the prearranged and proper place of the phallus in Lacan, poses significant problems for those who assert a science free of its pregivenness or science without compromising presuppositions. Yet Grünbaum makes a reasonable argument for the probative role of tests, clinical testability, and examples of falsifiability in the work of Freud. One such example is "A Case of Paranoia Running Counter to the Psychoanalytic Theory of the Disease" (*Standard Edition*, 22:7–30); another example is furnished by the Lecture "Revision of the Theory of Dreams" (ibid., 14:265–66). Grünbaum shows that "the psychoanalytic aetiology of paranoia is empirically falsifiable (disconfirmable) *and* that Freud explicitly recognized it" (Grünbaum, "Retrospective Versus Prospective Testing," 323).

34. Franz Kafka, "Die Prüfung," in *Kritische Kafka-Ausgabe: Nachgelassene Schriften und Fragmente II* (Frankfurt/Main: S. Fischer Verlag, 1992), 329; "The Test," in *Description of a Struggle* (New York: Schocken Books, 1958), 209.

CHAPTER 10

Going Along for the Ride: Violence and Gesture—Agamben Reading
Benjamin Reading Kafka Reading Cervantes
Samuel Weber

1. Giorgio Agamben, *État d'Exception*, trans. Joël Gayraud (Paris: Editions du Seuil, 2003). Further references will be given in the body of the text. Translations into English are mine.

2. Walter Benjamin, *Briefe*, 1:206 (except for the first two words, my italics—SW); Agamben, *État d'Exception*, 104.

3. "Das Mediale, das ist die Unmittelbarkeit aller geistigen Mitteilung, ist das Grundproblem der Sprachtheorie, und wenn man diese Unmittelbarkeit magisch nennen will, so ist das Urproblem der Sprache ihre Magie" ("The medial, which is [to say] the immediacy of all spiritual imparting, is the fundamental problem of the theory of language, and if this immediacy is called magic, then the originary problem of language is its magic," my translation—SW). GS II.1, 142.

4. Parting with, imparting, setting apart, the part and partition are recurrent themes in Weber's own work, notably in *Institution and Interpretation* and *Mass Mediauras* (Eds.).

5. Cf. Jacques Derrida, "Le sans de la coupure pure," in *La vérité en peinture* (Paris: Flammarion, 1978), 95–135.

6. This question is already posed by Benjamin's transformation of the common German idiom, which pairs *"schalten und walten"* in order to suggest unrestricted control or domination. By condemning and rejecting a "mythical" violence that either posits law or sustains and administers (*verwaltet*) it, in the name of a "divine" violence that is neither *schaltend* nor *verwaltend* but rather *waltend*, Benjamin places a heavy burden on this linguistic-semantic distinction, which can also be seen to hang on the presence or absence of the prefix *ver-*: *verwaltend* vs. *waltend*. The only other determination provided by Benjamin at the end of his highly enigmatic "Critique of Violence" is, however, not without a certain pertinence for the questions raised by Agamben. For Benjamin does not end his distinction of *schaltend* and *waltend* before noting that the latter, by virtue of its being "purely immediate" (*als reine unmittelbare*), is "never the means of divine execution" (*heiliger Vollstreckung*), but is rather "insignia and seal" (*Insignium und Siegel*). These two words may provide a precious hint as to the distinction Benjamin is introducing between *schalten* and *walten*. Both words involve a certain relation of force. *Schalten*, "switching" or "shifting," presupposes a network of exchanges and circulation and is used today, for instance, to designate an "integrated circuit board" (*Schaltbrett*). It suggests a change of direction or of "gears"; both of these meanings

preserve what seems to have been in its earliest significance, that of "setting or keeping in movement" (as in "shoving" or "pushing" a boat with poles. Cf. Duden's *Herkunftswörterbuch*, S. 620). *Walten*, on the other hand, which is far less frequently used in current German, derives from words meaning "to be strong, to dominate" and suggests a more direct manifestation of strength, but one which is still, to use Agamben's terms, more "relational" than "substantial." Whereas *schalten* suggests a change in direction, however, *walten* connotes the overcoming of resistances and a certain imposing of *sameness*. What happens when this imposition is construed as "insignia and seal" is a question to which we will return later in this essay. But even at this point it is impossible to ignore how Benjamin's choice of terms echoes the celebrated formula of Nietzsche: "To *impress* the character of being upon becoming—that is the highest will to power" ("Dem Werden den Charakter des Seins *aufzuprägen*—das ist die höchste Wille zur Macht." *Werke III*, Schlechta, S. 895).

7. Hölderlin develops his notion of the "patriotic reversal" (*vaterländische Umkehr*) in his comments to Sophocles' *Antigone*, noting that "patriotic reversal is the reversal of all forms and modes of representation." In his seminar on Hölderlin's poem, the *Ister* (1942), Heidegger translates *Umkehr* as "catastrophe," noting that in the second chorus of *Antigone*, "man is one single catastrophe" but adding that far from being simply a calamity, this may also constitute his most profound possibility.

8. Although this is probably not the place to go into it, it should at least be noted that the beggar's wish—and the Jewish joke that it punctuates—operates a convergence between Nietzsche's thought of the Eternal Return and Benjamin's ambivalent relation to the Messianic. In what way the affirmation of the Eternal Return might "straighten" or "iron out"—*zurechtrücken*—the distortions and displacements (*Entstellungen*) of time, is a question that will have to be addressed elsewhere.

9. Already the revised title, *Der Verschollener*, in contrast to its English translation as *The Man Who Disappeared*, suggests a certain repetition: someone who is "*verschollen*" has not been "*heard* from *again*," someone whose (acoustical) trace has been lost. The German word connotes the acoustical fading away of a *Schellen* or *Schall*, a *re*-sonance that has become inaudible.

10. Franz Kafka, *Die Romane* (Frankfurt am Main: S. Fischer Verlag), 1965, 215.

11. Giorgio Agamben, *Infancy and History*, translated by Liz Heron. New York: Verso, 1993, 135–40.

12. Varro, *De Lingua Latina*, VI, 77, in Agamben, *Infancy and History*, 139–40. In the English translation, these "Notes" are either truncated or were expanded subsequently by Agamben. The "Notes sur le Geste" that is published in the French edition of *Moyens sans fins* (Paris, 1995, 59–71) contain a

commentary on the Varro citation that goes very much in the direction I elaborate in this paper. In it Agamben defines the gesture as that which "exhibits a mediality, renders visible a means as such" and relates it to theatrical practices such as "dance" and "mimicry." In an argument that is manifestly indebted to Benjamin—without however referring to Benjamin's own theory of gesture, for instance in the essay on Kafka—Agamben defines the gesture with respect to language as that which exposes the mediality of language: "The gesture in this sense is communication of a communicability. Properly speaking it has nothing to say because what it shows is the being-in-language of man as pure mediality" (70). The "purity" of language as medium Agamben then relates to the "gag" as that which "gags" the mouth, preventing it from speaking, and relates this to "the improvisation of the actor who thereby seeks to compensate for a lapse of memory (*pallier un trou de mémoire*) or the impossibility to speak." Although Agamben thus brings out the *theatricality* of the gesture, as this last example demonstrates, he still thinks of it, in part at least, as the result of a conscious intention of a subject—that of the *actor* seeking to "palliate" for a "hole in memory"—rather than as that which, as we will see in a moment, defaces and undoes the very notion of "man," at least in the case of Kafka's "student."

13. The political consummation of the ideal of "self-expression" Benjamin saw in fascism: "Fascism seeks to organize the newly emerging proletarian masses without touching the property-relations that they strive to abolish. It sees its salvation (*Heil*) in helping the masses express themselves" (afterword to "The Work of Art in the Age of its Technical Reproducibility," GS I.2, 506).

14. Benjamin, GS II.2, 521.

15. Or more literally, "On the tenth recurrence of his death-day" ("Zur 10. Wiederkehr seines Todestages"), GS II.2, 409.

16. *Briefe*, 2:618, my italics.

SELECTED WORKS IN ENGLISH
BY SAMUEL WEBER

"The Madrepore." *MLN* 87 (1972): 915–61.

"The Sideshow, Or: Remarks on a Canny Moment." *MLN* 88 (1973): 1102–33.

"The Responsibility of the Critic: A Response." *MLN* 91 (1976): 814–16.

"Saussure and the Apparition of Language: The Critical Perspective." *MLN* 91 (1976): 913–38.

"The Divaricator: Remarks on Freud's *Witz*." *Glyph* 1 (1977): 1–27.

"It." *Glyph* 4 (1978): 1–31.

Unwrapping Balzac. A Reading of La Peau de Chagrin. Toronto: University of Toronto Press, 1979.

"Closure and Exclusion." *Diacritics* 10.2 (1980): 35–46.

"Translating the Untranslatable." Introduction to Theodor Adorno, *Prisms*, translated by Samuel M. Weber and Shierry Weber. Cambridge: MIT Press, 1981.

The Legend of Freud. Minneapolis: University of Minnesota Press, 1982.

"The Limits of Professionalism." *Oxford Literary Review.* 5.1–2 (1982): 59–74.

"A Stroke of Luck." *Enclitic* 6.2 (1982): 29–31.

"The Critics' Choice." In *Reading, Writing, Revolution*, edited by Francis Barker et al., 147–58. Colchester: University of Essex, 1982.

"Capitalising History: The Political Unconscious." *Diacritics* 13.2 (1983): 14–28.

"Reading and Writing—*chez* Derrida." *Tijdschrift Voor Filosofie* 45.1 (1983): 41–62.

"The Debts of Deconstruction and Other, Related Assumptions." In *Taking Chances: Derrida, Psychoanalysis, and Literature*, edited by Joseph H. Smith and William Kerrigan, 33–65. Baltimore: Johns Hopkins University Press, 1984.

"Taking Place: Toward a Theater of Dislocation." *Enclitic* 8.1–2 (1984): 124–43. Republished in *Opera Through Other Eyes*, edited by David J. Levin, 107–46. Stanford, Calif.: Stanford University Press, 1993.

"How Not to Stop Worrying." *Critical Exchange* 15 (1984): 17–25.

"The Debt of Criticism: Notes on Stanley Fish's *Is There a Text in This Class?*" *Critical Exchange* 15 (1984): 17–26.

"The Intersection: Marxism and the Philosophy of Language." *Diacritics* 15.4 (1985): 94–110.

"Literature—Just Making It." Afterword to Jean–Francois Lyotard and Jean–Loup Thebaud, *Just Gaming*, translated by Wlad Godzich, 101–20. Minneapolis: University of Minnesota Press, 1985.

"Ambivalence: The Humanities and the Study of Literature." *Diacritics* 15.2 (1985): 11–25.

"Introduction." *Glyph* 1 (New Series) (1986): ix–xii.

"Caught in the Act of Reading." *Glyph* 1 (New Series) (1986): 181–214.

"Laughing in the Meanwhile." *MLN* 102 (1987): 691–706.

Institution and Interpretation. Minneapolis: University of Minnesota Press, 1987.

"The Foundering of Comparative Literature." In *Aspects of Comparative Literature*, edited by Clayton Koelb and Susan Noakes, 57–72. Ithaca, N.Y.: Cornell University Press, 1998.

"Introduction." In D. P. Schreber, *Memoirs of My Nervous Illness*, vii–liv. Cambridge, Mass.: Harvard University Press, 1988.

"The Monument Disfigured." In *Responses: Paul de Man's Wartime Journalism*, edited by Werner Hamacher et al., 404–25. Lincoln: University of Nebraska Press, 1989.

"Theater, Technics, Writing." *1–800* (Fall 1989): 15–19.

"Upsetting the Setup: Remarks on Heidegger's Questing After Technics." *MLN* 104 (1989): 976–91.

"The Vaulted Eye: Remarks on Knowledge and Professionalism." *Yale French Studies* 77 (1990): 44–60.

"On the Balcony: The Theater of Technics." In *Bild–Sprache: Texte zwischen Dichten und Denken*, edited by L. Lambrechts and J. Nowe, 283–97. Louvain, Belgium: Louvain University Press, 1990.

"Criticism Underway: Walter Benjamin's *Romantic Concept of Criticism*." In *Romantic Revolutions: Criticism and Theory*, edited by Kenneth R. Johnston et al., 302–19. Bloomington: Indiana University Press, 1990.

"Genealogy of Modernity: History, Myth, and Allegory in Benjamin's *Origin of the German Mourning Play*." *MLN* 106 (1991): 465–500.

"Deconstruction Before the Name." *Cardozo Law Review* 13.4 (1991): 1181–90.

"The Media and the War." *Alphabet City* (Summer 1991): 22–26. Republished in *Emergences* 3–4 (1992): 16–26.

Return to Freud: Jacques Lacan's Dislocation of Psychoanalysis, revised and expanded edition of the German original, translated by Michael Levine. Cambridge: Cambridge University Press, 1991.

"In the Name of the Law." In *Deconstruction and the Possibility of Justice*, edited by Drucilla Cornell et al., 232–57. New York: Routledge, 1992.

"Taking Exception to Decision: Walter Benjamin and Carl Schmitt." *Diacritics* 22.3–4 (1992): 5–18. Republished in *Enlightenments: Encounters between Critical Theory and Contemporary French Thought*, edited by Harry Kunneman and Hent de Vries, 141–61. Kampen, Netherlands: Pharos, 1993.

"Breaching the Gap: On Lacan's *Ethics of Psychoanalysis*." In *Politics, Theory, and Contemporary Culture*, edited by Mark Poster, 131–58. New York: Columbia University Press, 1993.

"Objectivity Otherwise." In *Objectivity and its Other*, edited by W. Natter et al., 33–50. New York: Guilford Press, 1995.

"Upping the Ante: Deconstruction as Parodic Practice." In *Deconstruction Is/In America: A New Sense of the Political*, edited by Anselm Haverkamp, 60–75. New York: New York University Press, 1995.

"The Future of the University: The Cutting Edge." In *Ideas of the University*, edited by Terry Smith, 43–75. Sydney, Australia: Research Institute for the Humanities and Social Sciences, 1996.

Mass Mediauras: Form, Technics, Media. Stanford, Calif.: Stanford University Press, 1996.

"Reading—'to the end of the world.'" *MLN* 111 (1996): 819–34.

"Double Take: Acting and Writing in Genet's *L'étrange mot d'. . .*" *Yale French Studies* 91 (1997): 28–48.

Violence, Identity, and Self-Determination, edited by Hent de Vries and Samuel Weber. Stanford, Calif.: Stanford University Press, 1997.

"Benjamin's Writing Style." In *Encyclopedia of Aesthetics*, edited by Michael Kelly, 1:261–64. New York: Oxford University Press, 1998.

"Nomos in *The Magic Flute*." *Angelaki* 3.2 (1998): 61–68.

"Family Scenes: Some Preliminary Remarks on Domesticity and Theatricality." *South Atlantic Quarterly* 98.3 (1999): 22–28.

The Legend of Freud, expanded edition. Stanford, Calif.: Stanford University Press, 2000.

"Benjamin's Excitable Gestures." *Hybridity* 1.1 (2000): 55–76.

"Psychoanalysis and Theatricality." *Parallax* 6.3 (2000): 29–48.

"The Virtuality of Medium." *Sites* 4.2 (2000): 297–319.

Religion and Media, edited by Hent de Vries and Samuel Weber. Stanford, Calif.: Stanford University Press, 2001.

Institution and Interpretation, expanded edition. Stanford, Calif.: Stanford University Press, 2001.

"Replacing the Body: An Approach to the Question of Digital Democracy." In *Public Space and Democracy*, edited by Marcel Henaff and Tracy Strong, 172–88. Minneapolis: University of Minnesota Press, 2001.

"Globality, Organization, Class." *Diacritics* 31.3 (2001): 15–29.

"War, Terrorism, and Spectacle: On Towers and Caves." *South Atlantic Quarterly* 101.3 (2002): 449–458.

"Responding: A Discussion with Samuel Weber." *South Atlantic Quarterly* 101.3 (2002): 695–724.

"'Streets, Squares, Theaters': A City on the Move—Walter Benjamin's Paris." *boundary* 2 30.1 (2003): 17–30.

Theatricality as Medium. New York: Fordham University Press, 2004.

"Targets of Opportunity: Networks, Netwar, and Narratives." *Grey Room* 15 (2004): 6–27.

Targets of Opportunity: On The Militarization of Thinking. New York: Fordham University Press, 2005.

"Once and For All." *Grey Room* 20 (2005): 105–16.

SUSAN BERNSTEIN is associate professor of comparative literature and German studies at Brown University. Bernstein received her doctorate from Johns Hopkins University, B.A. from Yale, and M.A. from the University of California, Berkeley. She also studied at the Freie Universität Berlin and the Ecole Normale Supérieure in Paris. She has published articles on Nietzsche, Kant, Heine, Shelley, and others. Her book *Virtuosity of the Nineteenth Century: Performing Music and Language in Heine, Liszt and Baudelaire* was published in 1998.

PETER FENVES is Joan and Sarepta Harrison Professor of Literature and Professor of German and Jewish Studies at Northwestern University. He is the author of *A Peculiar Fate: Metaphysics and World-History in Kant* (1991), *"Chatter": Language and History in Kierkegaard* (1993), *Arresting Language: From Leibniz to Benjamin* (2001), and *Late Kant: Towards Another Law of the Earth* (2003). He is also the editor of *Raising the Tone of Philosophy: Late Essays by Kant, Transformative Critique by Derrida* (1993), coeditor of *"The Spirit of Poesy": Essays on Jewish and German Literature and Philosophy in Honor of Géza von Molnár* (2000), and translator of Werner Hamacher's *Premises: Literature and Philosophy from Kant to Celan* (1996). Recently he wrote a new introduction to Max Brod's novel *Tycho Brahe's Path to God* (2006).

GARY HALL is senior lecturer in media and studies at Middlesex University. His books include *Culture in Bits: The Monstrous Future of Theory* (2002) and, with Clare Birchall, *New Cultural Studies: Adventures in Theory* (2006). He is founding coeditor of the online journal *Culture Machine* (www.culturemachine.net), series editor of Berg's *Culture Machine* book series, and director of the cultural studies open access archive CSeARCH (www.culturemachine.net/csearch). His work has appeared in numerous journals, including *Angelaki, Parallax, The Review of Education, Pedagogy and Cultural Studies, The South Atlantic Quarterly*, and *The Oxford Literary Review*. He is currently completing a monograph entitled *Digitise This!*

ANDREW McNAMARA teaches art history and theory at Queensland University of Technology (QUT), Brisbane. His most recent publication is *Modernism and Australia: Documents on Art, Design, and Architecture, 1917–1967*, with Ann Stephen and Philip Goad.

MARC REDFIELD is professor of English and holds the John D. and Lillian Maguire Distinguished Chair in the Humanities at Claremont Graduate University. His publications include *Phantom Formations: Aesthetic Ideology and the Bildungsroman* (1996) and *The Politics of Aesthetics: Nationalism, Gender, Romanticism* (2003). He coedited *High Anxieties: Cultural Studies in Addiction* (2002) and edited *Legacies of Paul de Man* (2007). He is completing a book on the romantic origins of the notion of a "war on terror."

AVITAL RONELL is professor of German, English, and comparative literature at New York University, where she taught an annual course with Jacques Derrida every fall. She is also director of the Trauma and Violence Transdisciplinary Project at NYU, and holds the Jacques Derrida Chair in Philosophy and Media Studies at the European Graduate School. She is a regular contributor to *Artforum*. Her latest books are *The Test Drive* (2005) and *American Philo: Discussions with Anne Dufourmentelle* (2006).

R. L. RUTSKY teaches in the Department of Cinema at San Francisco State University. He is the author of *High Techne: Art and Technology from the Machine Aesthetic to the Posthuman* (1999) and coeditor *of Information in an Age of Consumption, Strategies for Theory: From Marx to Madonna* (2005), and *Film Analysis: A Norton Reader* (2005). He has also published work on new technologies, film and media theory, and cultural studies in many collections and journals.

SAMUEL WEBER is Avalon Foundation Professor of Humanities at Northwestern University, director of Northwestern's Paris Program in Critical Theory, and codirector of its program in comparative literary studies. He is the author of numerous books, including *The Legend of Freud* (1982/2000), *Institution and Interpretation* (1987/2001), *Return to Freud: Jacques Lacan's Dislocation of Psychoanalysis* (1991), *Mass Mediauras: Form, Technics, Media* (1996), *Theatricality as Medium* (2004), and *Targets of Opportunity* (2005). He is currently completing work on a new book, entitled *Benjamin's -abilities*.

SIMON MORGAN WORTHAM is reader in literary studies at the University of Portsmouth. His books include *Rethinking the University: Leverage and*

Deconstruction (1999), *Samuel Weber: Acts of Reading* (2003), and *Counter-Institutions: Jacques Derrida and the Question of the University* (2006). He has written numerous essays for journals such as *Diacritics, New Literary History, Cultural Critique, Textual Practice, New Formations,* and *Parallax,* and is currently writing a book on the work of Giorgio Agamben.

Index